The Management of College and University Archives

William J. Maher

The Society of American Archivists
and
The Scarecrow Press, Inc.
Metuchen, N.J. & London
1992

British Library Cataloguing-in-Publication data available

Library of Congress Cataloging-in-Publication Data

Maher, William J.
    The management of college and university archives /
William J. Maher.
        p.   cm.
    Includes bibliographical references and index.
    ISBN 0-8108-2568-6 (alk. paper)
    1. Universities and colleges—Archives—Administration.
2. Universities and colleges—United States—Archives—
Administration. I. Title.
CD3065.M34 1992
025.1'977—dc20   92-11667

Contents

List of Illustrations

Preface

William Maher's *The Management of College and University Archives* represents the culmination of over two decades of discussion among academic archivists in the United States about the need for such a volume. In many respects that need, despite the significant professional archival advances that have occurred in the interim, remains as urgent today as it was two decades ago. Indeed, this volume embraces those significant advances particularly as they relate to archival practices in repositories at institutions of higher learning. To be sure, archival practice at academic institutions is richer and more mature than it was when the need for this volume was first articulated by academic archivists; yet nowhere, until the appearance of this volume, was this practice systematically codified and made available in a readily accessible publication. The appearance of this book marks the most significant advance made to date in the continuing development of archival practice in academic repositories.

The emergence of large numbers of archival repositories at colleges and universities in the United States is a relatively new phenomenon dating only from the 1950s. A qualitative expansion in both the number and enrollments of institutions of higher learning came in response to the demand for college-educated workers, a demand precipitated by the post-World War II economic boom. This led to a qualitative increase in the number of academic archives.

Augmenting this post-war structural basis for the growth of academic archival repositories was the fact that numerous American colleges and universities were celebrating their centennials during the mid-twentieth cen-

tury. Centennial celebrations frequently included the
preparation of institutional histories, which in turn required the setting up of an archives to collect the records
upon which the histories could be based.

Archival practice at these newly minted academic repositories was largely pragmatic, drawing in part upon
practices employed in public records repositories and in
part upon methods used in manuscripts repositories,
which were in turn heavily influenced by library science
methodology. By the 1960s, a somewhat common archival
practice had emerged in many academic repositories, a
practice developed and honed by such pioneer academic
archivists as Jesse Boell at the University of Wisconsin
and Clifford Shipton at Harvard, and later by Maynard
Brichford at the University of Illinois.

This practice was passed on to younger archivists, who
learned "in the trenches" and, as they themselves became
head archivists at other colleges and universities, implemented it in their own repositories. Until publication in
the mid-1970s of the Society of American Archivists Basic
Manual Series, most academic archivists still acquired
their archival training as apprentices who learned their
trade on the job.

It was in this context, then, that the need was first
articulated for a basic manual that could codify archival
practice in an academic archives. The notion that a manual for college and university archives might be useful was
sporadically raised during the late 1960s and early 1970s
at meetings of the Society of American Archivists' College
and University Archives Committee, the predecessor of
the present SAA College and University Archives Section.

In 1974, Nicholas C. Burckel, then of the University of
Wisconsin-Parkside, prepared a draft for such a manual,
the core of which was published in articles in *College and
Research Libraries* and *The Midwestern Archivist.* Next
came the 1979 publication of *College and University Archives: Selected Readings,* which drew together the two
Burckel articles along with fifteen other journal contributions. These articles were selected by a subcommittee of
the College and University Archives Committee, chaired

by Charles B. Elston of Marquette University, as the most salient contributions to the literature.

The most significant step forward in the process of codifying and generalizing archival practice in academic archives came with the publication of the "Guidelines for College and University Archives" in the Spring 1980 issue of the *American Archivist*. These "Guidelines" had been drafted in 1978 by another subcommittee of the College and University Archives Committee chaired by Jon K. Reynolds of Georgetown University and approved by the Council of the Society of American Archivists. The "Guidelines," which drew heavily upon the earlier "Core Mission and Minimum Standards for University Archives" that had been prepared by the University of Wisconsin System Archives Council provided a description of a complete academic archival facility that was within the means of most institutions of higher learning. The subcommittee hoped "that the 'Guidelines' would provide the framework for discussion of a general statement of minimum standards for college and university archives."

Although minimum standards for college and university archives were never developed, the 1980s proved to be a particularly fruitful decade for discussion of archival practice in academic archives. The College and University Archives Committee was transformed, as part of an extensive reorganization of the Society of American Archivists' structure, into the present College and University Archives Section. Through the concerted efforts of the Section's leadership in the early 1980s, the long-discussed notion of a manual for academic archives finally began to be realized. In 1982, as the Section's chair, I asked William Maher, then the Section's Vice-Chair, to reexamine the need for and identify the prospective content of such a manual. Maher prepared a preliminary report, which he, after becoming Section Chair, assigned to a Section committee, chaired by J. Frank Cook of the University of Wisconsin-Madison, for further development. Cook's committee issued a report in 1984 that reaffirmed the need for a manual, outlined its prospective content, and established a process to see it through to publication. At the time, Cook remarked that "We impatiently await the time when we can read the manual instead of reading reports about it." In 1985, the SAA Publications Management Board asked William Maher to author the manual, which, to our good fortune, turned out to be the substantive volume that these remarks preface. Much as Kenneth Duckett's 1975 book, *Modern Manuscripts: A Practical Manual for Their Management, Care, and Use,* helped to codify and synthesize practice for general and cultural (i.e., manuscripts) repositories, so will *The Management of College and University Archives* do likewise for academic archives.

With this volume, William Maher has provided a wealth of information for novice and veteran academic archivists alike, as well as for academic administrators, librarians, and indeed anyone interested in archival practice in repositories at an academic institution. He has contributed significantly to the continuing maturation of the archival profession by offering a clear theoretical framework and sound practical advice for archival practice at academic institutions. The manual that was, for two decades, just a recurring dream of academic archivists, follows these remarks.

Patrick M. Quinn
Northwestern University

Acknowledgments

No book requiring more than five years to research and write can be complete without recognizing the assistance and many contributions of colleagues, friends, and family.

J. Frank Cook (University of Wisconsin-Madison) and the 1983-84 Manual Committee of the Society of American Archivists' College and University Archives Section provided a solid grounding for this work through the clear articulation of the need, audiences, and prospective content of this book. Edmund Berkeley, Jr. (University of Virginia) and Wilma Slaight (Wellesley College), on behalf of the SAA Editorial Board, were patient readers who were able to see beyond the roughness of the early drafts and who offered many valuable comments to improve and shape the text. Susan Grigg (Smith College), Chair of the Editorial Board, oversaw the review of the text, guided it through the editorial process, and provided a very useful close reading of the text. Special thanks are due to David Biesel of Scarecrow Press for his great patience, skill, and sensitivity in translating the manuscript into an attractive and readable book.

Greatly appreciated were the clarifying comments on specialized issues provided by a number of colleagues: Timothy L. Ericson (University of Wisconsin-Milwaukee), Toby Murray (Tulsa University), Helen W. Samuels (Massachusetts Institute of Technology), Lee Stout (Pennsylvania State University), Nancy K. Turner (Ball State University), and Mary Jo Pugh.

The financial support of the Library Research and Publication Committee of the University of Illinois at Urbana-Champaign (UIUC) covered the bibliographic work of graduate assistant Kathleen Peterson and typing assistance. UIUC students Rochelle Ruhmann and Sally Marion did the word-processing for most of the text, and they deserve special commendation for their ability to decipher an often messy scrawl, uncover gaps and grammatical flaws in the text, and patiently enter multiple revisions of the text.

Without the encouragement and guidance of two leading university archivists, Maynard Brichford and Patrick Quinn, this book could not have been completed. Maynard's accomplishments during his nearly 30 years of academic archival work as well as his penetrating comments and critiques, have served as a framework for the present text. It is the clarity of Maynard's vision of academic archives that has provided a goal that I hope this book will enable other archivists to achieve.

Patrick Quinn (Northwestern University) deserves special commendation for his many years of dedication to seeing that the college and university archives manual project be undertaken. Without his persistence, the project would not have been initiated, and without his guilt-inflicting reminders, I may not have completed this much-delayed work. Patrick's work at Northwestern has provided an inspiration for the kind of academic archives this text attempts to outline. Furthermore, on short notice, he read the entire manuscript and offered both a detailed critique and suggestions to resolve several important questions.

Finally, one cannot complete a project of these dimensions without the patience and support of one's family. One, then two growing daughters forfeited far more of their father's playtime than I would have wished as the book grew at such a painful pace. My wife, Terry, not only has shown extraordinary patience, but also a sensitivity to the substance of academic archives that has been of great assistance in shaping this book. As a professional writer and editor, Terry has made an even greater contribution to this work by completing a detailed edit of the entire manuscript. For little more compensation than an occasionally gruff "thank you," she resolved confusing

ulum handbooks outlining the nature of specific curricula, and degree requirements.

8. Faculty, staff, student, and alumni directories showing name, title, departmental affiliation, address.

9. Newspapers, newsletters, and other publicity issuances from students and official campus offices and student and faculty organizations.

10. All other publications issued by administrative, teaching, research, and student bodies, even if these are also available in the campus library. These can range from scholarly journals and official reports to departmental newsletters and student organization announcements and broadsides produced at the local copy shop.

This list emphasizes publications and documents produced in multiple copies as core holdings because they provide a solid base of information for much archival work and answer a significant number of reference questions.

An equally fundamental part of the archives' holdings will be administrative or office records, which provide fuller documentation and explanation of what appears in the summary records. The most common forms of office records are manuscript and typescript copies of incoming and outgoing correspondence, file and field notes, internal reports, statistical tables, and supporting publications. The scope and format of such office records is nearly unlimited and also includes microforms (e.g., student grade records), machine-readable data files (e.g., budgetary and financial information), photographs, architectural drawings, and sound and video recordings (e.g., proceedings of faculty senate meetings). The names of the files containing this information and the way the information is maintained by campus offices are limitless. Thus, the archivist should pay more attention to what is being or needs to be documented than to the presence or absence of specific types of files.[3] Some of the common files that are likely candidates for archival retention are subject files, project files, case files (in limited amounts), and summary financial records.

references, discovered unclarities, and stood vigilant against logical inconsistencies. Her patience, guidance, and thoughtfulness have been truly heroic.

William J. Maher
University of Illinois
at Urbana-Champaign

Introduction

This book introduces the basic elements required for an archival program to meet the documentary needs of a college or university. It is intended for both archivists and their administrative superiors who wish to obtain a thorough understanding of archival work and its importance to their institution. Beginning academic archivists, experienced academic archivists, archivists outside of academe, and related professionals all should benefit from *The Management of College and University Archives*. For the first group, the book will be a starting point for daily archival practice and long-term program planning. For experienced academic archivists, the book can be a foundation for conceptualizing and articulating the cohesive nature of academic archival work, despite the diversity induced by institutional circumstances. For public records archivists, business archivists, manuscript curators, and related professionals, the book explains how the important area of academic archives draws from archival theory and practice and adapts these to the unique circumstances of higher education. For everyone, the book will demonstrate the importance of academic archives as a field with a distinctive mission and approach.

Satisfying all of these interests is an ambitious goal, but it does not preclude accomplishing the basic purpose of providing direction for archival work. The book's organization emphasizes a practical sequence through which this can be achieved. The starting point is a statement of the mission of academic archives and a delineation of the fundamental elements of archives in colleges and universities. These include such essentials as establishment of the archives, administrative location, personnel, and basic service goals. Then, to link the academic archivist's work to the standard practice of the profession, a key part of the book explains the basic archival functions, such as appraisal, arrangement, and preservation. Given the extensive archival literature on these subjects and the continuing advances in such technical areas, the section's emphasis is more on fitting archival techniques together and on specific applications appropriate to higher education than on a definitive treatment of each specialized area.

Attention then turns to special records problems, special administrative problems, and special opportunities found in colleges and universities. These topics range from how to handle dissertations and theses to how to work with the historical consciousness of the higher-education community. Because the archives must be more than an assemblage of holdings and techniques, the book closes with a review of major programmatic activities, such as records management and manuscripts collecting, which are essential to strong programs.

AUDIENCE AND PURPOSE

As a guide to work in an area as technique-oriented as archives, *The Management of College and University Archives* is driven by practical considerations. Thus, for the beginning archivist or the new archival program, the book will provide a systematic description of what the archives should contain and accomplish, and it will offer basic direction on how to perform each key aspect of archival work. A more important goal for this audience, however, is to explain how each element can be adapted so that an overall balance can be maintained.

This book also is intended for experienced archivists and those in older academic archives who may have far less need for its technical directions but who may find in it the first full articulation of academic archives as a distinctive field. They may take issue with some of the procedures and techniques and the way that these have been brought together, but agreement on all of these issues is not expected. Rather, it is hoped that by assembling the elements of academic archives into a single text, *The Management of College and University Archives* can serve as a platform from which further research and theoretical investigations of academic archives can proceed. For those who take exception to parts of the book, it can serve as a stimulus for them to propose a different view of academic archives.

In addition to these practical and broad theoretical purposes, *The Management of College and University Archives* is intended to help both new and old archivists in their dealings with administrators by making archival practices more intelligible to resource allocators. It is hoped that the book will thereby help to provide legitimacy for archivists' claims to a distinctive methodology and practice. While few administrators will need to read the technical sections closely, the book demonstrates that archivists are not gadflies arbitrarily resisting control, but specialists who seek a recognition of their authoritative knowledge and their need for autonomy to accomplish the mission of their profession.

ARCHIVAL LITERATURE

Despite this insistence on the distinctiveness of academic archival practice, it is not so unique as to be unrelated to the rest of archival practice. In fact, academic archival practice is deeply indebted to the theory and practices developed in European governmental archives in the nineteenth and early twentieth centuries, and refined in American federal and state archives in the middle decades of this century. Although the application of these theories and practices within higher education gives academic archives their unique character, the general archival literature provides the best way to understand the full implications of relevant practice. Because this book can only describe archival practice in the most general terms and because its purpose is not to explain all the subtleties of each archival function, those needing more detail should set aside this book temporarily in favor of the many texts and articles that address the problem at hand. Appropriate bibliographic references are provided for practical guidance, but a comprehensive bibliographic introduction to archival theory and practice is beyond the scope of this volume.[1]

TERMINOLOGY

To assist in the standardization of academic archival practice and to aid the writing of this text, certain terminological conventions have been followed. Beyond the terms specifically defined in this book, the Society of American Archivists (SAA) glossary explains the meaning and common usage of many archival terms.[2] Archival terms also can be understood by referring to the relevant section of this book and to works cited in its footnotes. Some institutionally based terms, however, bear explanation here:

- "Colleges and universities" refers to all institutions of postsecondary education, ranging from two-year colleges offering associate degrees to large research universities and professional schools offering doctorates and professional degrees.
- "Academic archives" is a shorthand term for the institutional records programs of colleges and universities. By adopting this term for the archives of institutions of higher education, the author does not wish to diminish the importance of archival programs for secondary education or other educationally focused institutions, such as educational associations. Indeed, their archivists may find much of value, but the emphasis here must be on the most common kinds of educational

institutions with archives—colleges and universities.

- "Parent institution" or "institution" refers to the overarching corporate body or organization that the archives documents (e.g., the University of North Carolina, Carleton College, Georgetown University).

- "Parent department" or "administrative superior" refers to the organizational unit to which the archives is subordinated for purposes of budgeting and reporting. These units might include the campus library, an academic or administrative vice-chancellor, or a public relations department.

- "Departments," "units," and "offices" are used rather loosely to refer to the many organizational units into which the institution is divided to accomplish its mission, including academic departments, student service offices, and administrative bureaus.

- "Colleges," when used separately from the term "universities," refers to the larger administrative groupings of faculties within a university. These are sometimes called "faculties," "schools," or "divisions" within two- and four-year colleges. The term is used here to refer to organizational bodies such as a college of arts and sciences, engineering, law, medicine, or fine arts.

Finally, it is essential that the reader start with an understanding of the fundamental and pervasive terms "archives" and "manuscripts," since the distinction between the two is pivotal to many of this book's recommendations and to one's success as an archivist.

- "Archives" are the noncurrent records[3] of an organization or institution retained for their continuing value in providing 1) evidence of the existence, functions, and operations of the organization or institution that generated them, or 2) other information on activities or persons affected by the organization. "Archives" also refers to the agency responsible for selecting, preserving, and making available noncurrent records with long-term value and to the building or part of the building housing them.

- "Manuscripts" are documents (in any format) accumulated, collected, and/or generated by a private individual(s) and subsequently donated to or acquired by a repository to ensure their retention and public accessibility. "Manuscripts" include personal papers with organic unity, artificial subject collections of documents acquired from diverse sources, and individual documents acquired and retained by a repository for their potential research use.

These distinctions can blur quickly in practice, especially in an academic setting. College and university archivists will find that their repositories must include both archives and manuscripts if they are to ensure minimal documentation of the parent institution. However, daily management will be facilitated greatly if archivists keep these distinctions clearly in mind as archetypes, particularly when dealing with questions of appraisal, arrangement, description, and service to users.[4]

OVERVIEW OF ACADEMIC ARCHIVES

Given archives' close ties to the field of history, it would seem appropriate to begin this book with a historical overview of the development of college and university archives. Indeed, the earlier history of one's own college or university archives can be intriguing and important work for the current archivist. However, it will not provide a very fertile ground for understanding modern archival practice because it generally reveals a long-term focus on local needs and services rather than on broader professional issues. Another way to obtain a sense of the development of the field of college and university archives would be to survey the development of academic archival programs in the United States, as Ernst Posner did for state archives.[5] Not only would this be beyond the scope of the current study, but it would also lack the depth that Posner found in the far more developed area of state archives, many of which could trace their roots at least to the early decades of the twentieth century. Admittedly a few colleges and universities (e.g., Harvard University and Northwestern University) took steps before the 1940s to provide for their historical records. Nevertheless, most programs were managed from antiquarian, library, or genealogical perspectives, rather than from a belief in the importance of institutional history and in the multiple service roles now held by most academic archives.

In the decades following World War II, however, academic archives began to develop a distinctive perspective and methodology. This development was driven by three factors. First, in the two decades after the establishment of the National Archives (1934) and the Society of American Archivists (1936), the many advances in government archivists' practices for handling modern records laid a basis for the development of modern archives outside of governmental institutions. These national events combined with the important practical and theoretical work of American state archivists, such as Margaret Cross Norton, to professionalize and systematize archival work. Without these developments, the transformation of academic manuscripts programs from "collegiana" collections to archives would have been highly unlikely.[6]

Second, there was a tremendous expansion in the size and diversity of American higher education from 1945 through the early 1970s. Although this was partially a result of population changes, it also reflected a substantial broadening of colleges and universities as they sought to extend higher education to social and economic classes not traditionally part of academe. The archival effect of this expansion was twofold. As existing institutions grew larger and new institutions were established, the need for archives became more urgent. At the same time, the inter-

nal history of these institutions became relevant to a far
broader segment of society than it had been four or five
decades earlier.

Third, in the midst of rapid growth in enrollments and
the higher education economic boom of the 1950s and
1960s, many major institutions also approached key anniversaries. These centennial and sesquicentennial celebrations provided an immediate need and a source of funds
for improving control over the institution's documents,
especially to permit writing an institutional history. Establishing an archives thus could be a symbolic and practical expression of the institution's concern for its past
while it faced rapid growth and change.

With the resultant creation or consolidation of academic archival programs, the development of academic
archives as a specialized field became possible in the
1970s. A conceptual framework for academic archives now
began to emerge because a substantial body of records
from higher education had been brought under archival
control, a solid foundation in modern archival theory and
technique was readily available, and a critical mass of
archivists at colleges and universities were increasingly
aware of their common needs and interests.

As important as these shared traditions are, the tremendous diversity in American colleges and universities
should not be overlooked when one tries to understand the
nature of their archives. In fact, the variety of programs
makes it difficult to define common ground or to consider
academic archives as a distinct entity. Given how closely
archival practice is tied to the administration of an institution, it should not be surprising that the character of the
parent institution can lead to great diversity among academic archives. Particularly significant institutional variables are the differences between private versus public
universities, small (less than 1,000 students) versus large
(10,000 or more students), old (established from the sev-
enteenth through the early nineteenth centuries) versus
young (established since 1945), and general versus denominational or disciplinary (e.g., seminaries, sectarian colleges, or engineering and fine arts schools).

A significant effect of this diversity is to raise the question of whether there can ever be a single model for academic archival programs, no matter how flexibly drawn. *The Management of College and University Archives,* however, starts from the premise that an outline of the goals and activities of academic archives is necessary because there is a common base on which academic archivists can build. This base is composed of common goals of colleges and universities (to communicate and advance knowledge); common incidental effects of these institutions (the socialization and acculturation of youth); common functioning in an environment where archival survival and growth must be articulated in terms of educational and knowledge-based goals; and common benefit to be gained from the theory and practice developed by the archival profession.[7]

PURPOSE, HOLDINGS, AND CONSTITUENCIES

Before specific goals and methodologies for program operation can be outlined, there must be an understanding of the purposes, holdings, and constituencies common to all college and university archives. This understanding can be achieved best by answering three simple questions: What should an academic archives do? What should an archives contain? Whom should an archives serve?

What Should an Academic Archives Do?

Often, the answer to this question is a list of all the technical archival functions developed to ensure that historical documents survive and can be made usable. However, more fundamental is that an archives should fulfill several institutional information needs. It is especially important that the archives provides the institution with a memory and a method to verify, refute, or modify the recollections of its members and the outside community about its past. The archives thus enables the institution to rethink itself by preserving the record of its failings as well as its accomplishments. In this sense, the archives can be as much the institution's conscience as its memory. The archives also provides the most effective means of understanding and managing the institution's information resources. Because the archives works with the total documentary record of the institution, it is in a particularly strong position to understand how administrative efficiency can be improved. In addition, the archives provides tools for the institution to use in justifying itself to the public based on the record of its ability to fulfill its goals. Through archival support of teaching and research, the institution is aided in accomplishing its basic mission of communicating and expanding knowledge. Finally, the archives supplies ways for the institution to reach out to the community by using its documentary resources to meet the information and cultural preservation needs of the community.

What Should an Archives Contain?

The specific holdings of each archives may vary, but some holdings are so basic that they should be considered universal. At a minimum, the archives should contain a complete set of all publications of the institution, carefully selected series of organizational and operational documents, and personal papers of selected members of the institution to reflect their careers, contributions, and perspectives on the institution. There can be no blanket criteria for the archival retention of specific types of records—that will depend on how the individual archives balances professional guidelines, institutional resources, and the needs of local constituencies.

The academic archives often will hold records, papers, and other documents from individuals and organizations with little or no direct connection to the institution. These manuscript and regional history collections have become a critical responsibility, allowing academic archives to contribute substantially to the preservation and accessibility of the documentary heritage of society beyond academe.

Whom Should an Archives Serve?

Too often, descriptions of archives focus heavily on their holdings and the specialized techniques needed to manage them. Although holdings and techniques are important, the most fundamental element of academic archives should be an emphasis on service. That is, the archives gathers records and manuscripts and applies specialized techniques solely to ensure that important information is available for the archives' many publics. This book, therefore, is based on the principle that each university archives should identify and cultivate its own constituencies from the following broad categories: the administrative staff of the parent institution, faculty and students, alumni, and national as well as local communities of researchers. To understand how these constituencies relate to the archives' basic purposes, it is useful to enumerate the fundamental kinds of service that archives should render:

1. Administrative service, especially concerning the retrieval of facts and documents to assist in current work, and sometimes concerning development of efficient records systems.
2. Reference and research service, including more complex analyses and interpretations of documents.
3. Instructional service, including teaching students and neophyte users the basics of research methodology and the techniques of using archival documents.
4. Outreach service via support of the institution's public relations activities, especially through exhibits, publications, and responses to media requests for information.

Possibly the most important service rendered by the archives is the selection and preservation of the strategic body of documents necessary for the survival of the institution and the maintenance of its identity. The daily work of appraisal, acquisition, arrangement, and description is thus an overarching service that is critical to the health of the institution and its community. Some might argue that this service is so broad that it has little operational meaning, but it should not be dismissed lightly. This service role implies that a major justification for an academic archives will come from the unpredictable uses of the archives by unforeseeable groups of users. In the late twentieth century, this abstract reference to hypothetical future users of the record of the past may be greeted with skepticism by institutions that increasingly focus on immediate, practical functions to justify themselves. Archivists should counter such skepticism with examples of current practical uses of archival records and services, but they should not lose sight of the broader and more important cultural justification of archives as providers of heritage and preservers of memory.

HOW TO USE THIS BOOK

One of the most challenging aspects of writing this book has been determining what specific directions to give to academic archivists. Basic archival theory and techniques certainly have been well explained throughout the literature, and it can provide ready and authoritative answers to many problems found in academic archives. This book does not aspire to supplant these other works; rather, the emphasis is on how all archival components can be brought together in a single program to serve the needs of higher education. To explain the nature of archival programs, it starts with a description of the core elements of each area of archival work. Since it reflects the convictions of a seasoned observer of archival programs, it also comments on areas of archival practice that are open for debate. Finally, it attempts to guide archivists in deciding how far to go in implementing each specific archival activity.

The difficulty in outlining this full range of archival practice is that there are many variables in the colleges and universities served by archives. These include the age and size of the institution, its status (government-supported versus private) or affiliation (e.g., denominational), its geographic location (especially urban versus small town), and its proximity to other institutions. Furthermore, the administrative location or reporting line of the archives (e.g., to the library, an academic department, or the central administration) can have a significant effect on how archival practice must be adjusted to the institution's expectations.

A critical variable that has often been overlooked is the age of the archival program itself. Archives, like other institutional units, undergo a maturing process during which needs and opportunities evolve. The archivist, therefore, should vary agendas and approaches depending on the program's age. For example, a new archives may need to be far more vigorous in its accessions and may have less time for rigorous appraisal. The adolescent program may need to focus on improving and restructuring reference procedures to facilitate access. The middle-aged program may turn its attention to records management or processing backlogs. The mature archives may need to analyze and reappraise its holdings and initiate programs for outreach and publicity to new constituencies. The effects of aging can be accented when there have been a few archivists of long tenure directing the program. While this adds continuity, it can also mean that practices may not be reexamined so frequently as required for good management.[8]

Any one of these characteristics can induce enough variations that some might question the applicability and validity of this book's recommendations. That is why it is necessary to remember that dogmatic insistence on the methodology described in manuals and textbooks can restrict an archival program so severely that it will become unresponsive to local needs. Conversely, if the archivist insists on local variations in practice without reconciling these to commonly accepted archival goals, the result will be to dilute severely the long-term effectiveness and growth of a professional program. The answer to this dilemma lies in flexibly applying externally developed standards and procedures. Archives that ignore the concepts and approaches outlined in this and other archival texts will risk becoming less a program and more an institutional oddity. However, some very good programs may choose to forego some of the practices recommended here after due consideration of their underlying principles and purposes in relation to local constraints and opportunities. Those programs that can master this "balancing act" will show the highest degree of professionalism and institutional service, regardless of the abundance or scarcity of their resources.

Notes

1. An excellent starting point for the academic archivist's reading is *College and University Archives: Selected Readings* (Chicago: Society of American Archivists, 1979). It provides insight into distinctive problems and opportunities faced by college and university archives, as well as practical guidance on many issues.

2. "Basic Glossary for Archivists, Manuscripts Curators, and Records Managers," *American Archivist* 37 (1974): 415-33, the glossary current during the research and writing of this book, has since been superseded and greatly expanded by Lewis Bellardo and Lynn Lady Bellardo, *A Glossary for Archivists, Manuscript Curators, and Records Managers* (Chicago: Society of American Archivists, 1991).

3. "Records" are all documents, regardless of physical form, produced or received by any agency, officer, or employee of an institution or organization in the transaction of its business. For a more detailed definition of college and university "records," refer to the section on "Records Management."

4. Despite the insistence on the distinction between archives and manuscripts, this book will use the term *archivist* generically to describe the person responsible for either archives or manuscripts. For a discussion of the kinds of manuscript collections most important for academic archives, refer to the chapter on "Manuscripts Programs." For a perspective that deempha-

Fundamentals of
Academic Archives

Many who pick up this book may be tempted to skip immediately to sections answering their specific technical questions, such as how to create an arrangement scheme for their college's archives. This approach is certainly legitimate, but a focus on technique may miss very important points concerning exactly what college and university archives are, or should be. If one examines the practice at many of the archival programs in America's more than 3,340 colleges and universities, one might conclude that an academic archives is merely a historical records program that happens to be situated on a college or university campus and that documentation of the institution of higher education occupies only a small part of its attention and resources. This impression of a lack of focus, however, is insufficient justification for not defining what a college or university archives should be. This section on the fundamentals of an academic archives outlines the basic program elements that must be in place if a historical records program is to aspire to the name of academic archives.

DEFINITION

A college or university archives is a program consisting of policy, personnel, holdings, and facilities structured to preserve and make accessible the documentary heritage of an institution of higher education. The documents are

selected and handled in a systematic way based on archival theory and technique. The basic goal of the archives is
to aid the institution in its survival and growth, especially
by making sure that the institution's roots in the past are
not severed. At the same time, the academic archives
contributes to the institution's educational mission by
enriching the lives of the campus community. The archives
should support teaching and learning and assist scholars
and the general public in using documents to understand
and explain the past.

This definition attempts to draw all college and university archives into a coherent body, each member striving to translate basic archival theory into a program that
meets the needs of its own institution and serves as a
model for all other academic archives, but the real world
of academic archives is not nearly so simple. Instead, one
finds such tremendous variations that one may legiti-
mately question whether there could ever be a single
model, or even a handful of models, of what an academic
archives should be. Some observers might argue that this
condition is merely the result of a chronic lack of standards
and that commonality could, and should, be achieved
through greater adherence to standards established by
professional bodies. While there is some validity in this
argument, it fails to recognize that standards and guidelines for academic archival practice have been available in
recent decades and that some of the variations in practice
result from the creative responses of individual archivists
adapting high professional standards to their own institution, often with severely inadequate resources.[1]

Much good work has been done within these constraints—much that represents the highest achievements
of American archivists. These broad variations, even
though essential, do not provide a satisfactory basis for
describing what the academic archives should aspire to be.
This book, therefore, begins with an outline of the basic
elements that must be in place before a historical records
program at a college or university can truly be considered
an academic archives. These fundamentals are mission

and establishment, administrative location, holdings, personnel, space and facilities, and service goals.

MISSION AND ESTABLISHMENT

Logically, the first step in establishing a systematic academic archival program is to define the archives' mission and authority, but the history of academic archives shows that they often evolve from isolated efforts to assemble their institution's records and papers to meet the research interests of a few faculty, administrators, librarians, or alumni. In many cases, these efforts were intermittent and often quite at odds with what is now seen as acceptable professional practice. The fact that most programs have begun and will continue to emerge in this fashion should not deter us from examining the logical steps one would follow to create an archives. Thus, while this outline may not describe the historical evolution of any particular archives, it provides the theoretical framework for creating an academic archives and a point of reference for those wishing to assess whether existing programs incorporate the fundamentals of a professional archives.

The first and most fundamental element of an academic archives is a clear statement of its purpose. This statement of mission will need to vary to meet the character of each institution, but there are common elements, which are well stated in the *Guidelines for College & University Archives:*

- To appraise, collect, organize, describe, make available, and preserve records of historical, legal, fiscal, and/or administrative value to their institution.
- To provide adequate facilities for the retention and preservation of such records.
- To provide information services that will assist the operation of the institution.

- To serve as a resource and laboratory to stimulate and nourish creative teaching and learning.
- To serve research and scholarship by making available and encouraging the use of its collections by members of the institution and the community at large.
- To promote knowledge and understanding of the origins, aims, programs, and goals of its institution, and of the development of these aims, goals, and programs.
- To facilitate efficient records management.

The development of a mission statement incorporating these elements, tailored to one's institution, is an important basis for future action and can be seen as one of the first signs that an archival program is being developed, as opposed to just a gathering of documents or a "collegiana" collection. If an existing repository does not have such a mission statement, drafting one should receive the primary attention of the archivist.

The next step in establishing an archives is to draft and secure institutional approval of a document to authorize the archives' existence and confer the authority necessary to accomplish its mission. This document should be brief—one to two pages—and include the following elements:

1. Statement of the program's mission.

2. Definition of college/university records. This should provide that all documents created or used in the course of institutional business are institutional records and are the property of the institution.

3. Designation of the archives as the unit responsible for the disposition of all institutional records with long-term administrative or research value.

4. Statement of the communities that the archives is to serve, who may use it, and general access conditions. This statement should be phrased to permit the broadest access possible and avoid inferences that the archives exist primarily

to serve a single group of users, such as campus administrators, alumni, scholars, or media personnel.

5. Authorization of the archivist as the person to conduct all activity necessary to accomplish the program's mission according to the standards of archival practice.

6. Delineation of the core elements of the archives program, especially regarding the responsibility to collect, preserve, and provide access, as well as delineation of other elements which may be delegated to a given program (e.g., records management, faculty papers, regional manuscripts, or oral history).

7. Explanation of the reporting line or administrative location of the archives.

The importance of such an authorizing document cannot be overemphasized. Regardless of the vagaries of institutional budgets and the changes in archival and campus administrative personnel, such a document can provide continuity, direction, and protection for the archives. Its standards may seem too high in difficult times, and its scope may seem too narrow in expansive times, but it will always provide a rationale for the program to ensure stability and protection of basic archival goals.

Once such a statement is prepared, the archivist should secure its approval by the highest officials of the institution, preferably the chancellor or president as well as the governing board of trustees or regents. To secure these approvals, however, a great deal of care will be necessary. The document must be phrased in terms of general documentary principles, and its rationale should be linked clearly to the institution's basic mission and the main reasons for having an archives. Its approval should follow the institution's requirements for authorizing statements as outlined in statutes, procedure manuals, or general operating rules. Care is also necessary in securing approval lest the archivist's actions be seen as threatening to the current loci of campus power, whether they be legitimate bodies or fiefdoms claimed by the existing academic nobility.

Drafting and securing approval of an authorizing document can require a period of years, depending on how many institutional hurdles must be overcome. While it is of critical importance, much archival work can and should proceed in the meantime. During this period, it can be particularly useful for the archives to operate with an oversight or advisory committee, which can lend the archival operations greater authority. The committee can also provide access to information about the institution's operations that is often quite difficult for the new archivist to secure. Within the limits of institutional rules on committees, an advisory committee might be composed of representatives from some of the following units: president, chancellor-central administration; faculty senate; library; academic departments, especially history, architecture, historic preservation, English, or political science; admissions and records office; student affairs; administrative services, such as personnel or accounting; and students. In many cases, a single individual may represent more than one interest.

The committee will function best if it consists of six to ten individuals and meets no more than four to six times annually. The governance and operation of the committee will be highly variable, depending on the institution and the personalities of its members, but its primary roles should be to advise the archivist and marshal support for key policies and major program initiatives. The presence of such a committee will be most critical to the beginning archival program or to the newly arrived archivist at an institution, but it will also be useful to the mature program under the direction of an archivist with long tenure.

ADMINISTRATIVE LOCATION

One of the most basic elements of archival program management is to resolve the question of where the archives should be placed in the hierarchy of the college or university. This location will have great influence on the authority, visibility, and perception of the archivist. There are a variety of options for the administrative location, including library, academic department (especially history), alumni office, public relations, development, and central administration, such as president, chancellor, or secretary of the board of overseers. Placement has been a popular topic of discussion for academic archivists, but a thorough examination of the relative merits of each location would require more time and space than can be allocated here.[2] More importantly, too much attention to the issue of location can obscure the fact that no single location is best for all purposes because the mission of an academic archives cuts across the programmatic, technical, and disciplinary interests of all the possible parent departments. Too often, archivists' attention to the question of location is driven by dissatisfaction with limits imposed by the current parent department and the hope that some other parent would provide better support.

An alternative approach is to start with the recognition that no department can be a fully suitable parent and that archival work is an independent profession requiring autonomy to accomplish its mission. If this perspective is adopted, there is far greater chance that the current parent can be made to understand why and when the archives must go to other campus units for direction, authority, and resources. If administrative superiors can accept and support the archivist in these endeavors, then the archives' current home is clearly the best. If not, then efforts to move elsewhere may be appropriate. In all cases, however, both the archives and the parent department should recognize that a modest amount of tension is inevitable in their relationship. After all, a great deal of divergence is inherent in the archives' core mission and services, since the archives must support administration, research, teaching, preservation, public awareness, and promotion of understanding of the past. Therefore, regardless of administrative location, the archivist is responsible for ensuring that the nature of the program's parent does not lead to an overemphasis on any single area (e.g., administrative service, scholarly research, or public relations), lest the integration and diversity fundamental to an archives are lost.

One particularly effective way to ensure that the archival program does not become out of balance is to develop strong relationships with a number of allied programs on campus. These programs may include any offices focused on institutional information, such as the central administrative and research computer centers and public information office. Other allied units are those academic departments focused on historical research and teaching, and programs for the public display of artifacts of historical value. Perhaps the most obvious allied units are the comprehensive information providers—libraries. Each of these programs shares some of the goals of the campus archives; for example, both the archives and the library provide information for classroom and research purposes, and both the archives and the alumni or publicity offices collect and distribute large quantities of information about the accomplishments of former students and faculty.

Clearly, effective operation of the archives and all related campus units requires close cooperation even though their size, goals, and methodologies may be quite divergent. While local variations in college and university structure are too great for specific suggestions on how to maintain good relationships, there are important principles that should guide action on each campus. In all dealings with such allied units, the archives must respect the legitimacy of the mission, operations, and methodologies of these units. Equally important, campus administrators need to recognize the legitimacy of the archives' claim to a distinct mission that cannot be subsumed under that of any other campus unit. It is critical that the archives be granted sufficient autonomy and status so that it can operate as a peer of these allied programs. In the common arrangement of the archives being organizationally part of the library, it is essential that all parties grant the legitimacy of the archives' claim to a campus-wide program, as well as authority in all areas needed to accomplish its core mission. Thus, even if the archives' personnel and budget are administered through the library or alumni office, the archivist must have direct access to campus offices and wide-ranging authority in any issue regarding the documentation of the parent institution.

HOLDINGS

Few would dispute that the essence of an academic archives is the holdings of records and manuscripts documenting a college or university. Indeed, while it can often be difficult to secure understanding of such other fundamentals as policy, staff, and space, only rarely will the archivist need to explain the importance of retaining documents. Nevertheless, there are sufficient variations in what kinds of records are actually held by academic archives that this issue merits consideration as one reviews the fundamentals for the existence of an archival program.

Certainly the type (public or private), size, age, and importance of the college or university will have a great effect on the kind and extent of documentation available. However, the following types of records are so basic that their preservation and accessibility should be the core of all academic archives.

1. The founding charter, statute, or legislative documents creating the institution, as well as subsequent legislation or authorizing documents substantially affecting the mission of the institution.

2. Agendas, minutes, and supporting documents for meetings of the governing board of control (e.g., trustees or regents).

3. Agendas, minutes, and supporting documents for meetings of faculty, faculty-student, and student governing bodies, such as senates and university councils.

4. Correspondence and office records of chief executives, deans, and policy makers. Published and unpublished annual reports of chief executives, and academic and administrative officers.

5. Student academic records.

6. Summary budgets and financial reports.

7. Publications covering basic institutional mission, especially course catalogs, timetables or schedules of classes, curric-

The variations in content and importance of files from office to office are so great that uniform guidelines on retaining or destroying a given type of file are inadvisable even within the confines of one institution, let alone across the broad array of American colleges and universities. For example, even within a single college, it would be inadvisable to routinely destroy or retain the subject or personnel files of academic departments without first examining the files, assessing the importance of each department, and determining how well its files document its archivally important functions. As a general rule, however, subject files and general correspondence files illustrating the development of policy and the occurrence of nonroutine incidents should be retained for all major campus units. In many cases, project files, special events files, and major construction and capital development files should also be retained. Certain kinds of case files, at carefully selected levels of the institution, should be retained. These might include files on academic personnel, alumni careers, student discipline, and registration of student organizations.

Overall, the archivist needs to adjust retention decisions when moving from level to level within the institution. The logical assumption that more records should be retained for key central offices than for departments needs to be regarded cautiously, but it can provide a useful guideline. Archivists will have to apply their own appraisal criteria to each group of records they encounter, and general rules, beyond the criteria discussed in the section on appraisal, are unlikely to be of broad application.

In addition to publications and office records, academic archives should make a major effort to acquire personal papers from faculty and administrators. These papers are essential because the nature of colleges and universities is such that individuals play a preeminent role in shaping the direction of the institution. These institutions also have large concentrations of highly professionalized employees. Increasingly, during the twentieth century, faculty and significant numbers of salaried staff have considered themselves professionals first and employees second. This tendency to place one's loyalties outside the institution in one's disciplinary community has had a significant impact on the shape of colleges and universities, and it is closely related to the fact that in colleges and universities, one's authority depends less on position than on academic and scholarly credentials. In a government or business, on the other hand, authority is, in the classic bureaucratic sense, vested in the office rather than the person. While many aspects of higher education are highly bureaucratic, the underlying emphasis on the authority of the person rather than the position has substantial impact on the nature and quality of documents. It affects not only how academics work, but how they maintain records of their institutional and disciplinary work. Unlike a governmental or other more bureaucratic setting, where great attention is paid to creating and maintaining files to document a depersonalized handling of the organization's business, the files of academic administrators and faculty are far more likely to blur the lines between institutional business, individual research, and professional growth. This mixing of institutional, professional, and scholarly activities is a conscious one and is a part of the essence of American higher education. Thus, college and university files can be both more interesting and less ordered than those found in government. Recognizing how much these characteristics pertain to one's own institution and to each body of records one encounters is essential to the success of the academic archivist.

Many academic archives also hold the papers of former students to document their student days, subsequent careers, or both. Beyond coverage of student life, these papers generally are not essential to documenting the parent institution and may be only secondary to the archives' core mission. However, collecting papers relating to distinguished careers of alumni has become an important part of many academic archival programs. These collections furnish important research documentation, fuel institutional pride, and can be linked to memorials and monetary bequests.

PERSONNEL

While no archives can exist without a body of institutional records, the records repository cannot be called an archival program until appropriate staff are allocated to its management. The amount and type of personnel must vary with the size of institution and archival program, but the following comments describe a minimum level upon which institutions can build as their records and programs grow.

For a repository to be an archives, it should have a full-time, permanent staff member with responsibility and authority to accomplish all actions necessary to meet the goals of the archival program. Even though rank is often based on the size of a program's staff and archivists typically have only a few staff to supervise, their broad responsibilities call for them to hold a rank comparable to that of other directors of campus-wide programs such as libraries and public relations offices. Furthermore, archivists should have the same employment status as other non-teaching professionals. Archivists are often grouped with librarians, and this can be appropriate for personnel classification. However, because of the academic archivist's campus-wide responsibilities, he or she should have a higher rank than a line-reference, subject, or branch librarian and have authority comparable to that of the library's director or assistant director.

Perhaps more important than rank is the need to start personnel planning with the recognition that archival work is a distinct profession. Position descriptions and educational requirements should mandate that the director of the program be a professional with archival training and experience.[4] The program director's primary professional community should be archivists rather than historians or librarians, although this is not a justification for archivists to isolate themselves from these communities. Indeed, archives are enriched by close ties to allied professions, especially history, librarianship, and records management.

In many programs, the archivist may have responsibilities that fall outside core archival work. These might include handling rare books or other special collections, managing a campus micrographics program, teaching history courses, or writing library friends' publications. Assigning these activities to the archivist may be a fact of life at many institutions, but it is far from the ideal way to staff an archives. In practice, if some smaller colleges require only a modest amount of archival work, then non-archival tasks could be added to the archivist's duties, but only if the alternative is no archival program at all.

Beyond a professional archivist, the academic archives will need a paraprofessional or nonacademic staff person as a reference and clerical assistant. Ideally, there should be at least one full-time support staff person devoted to the archives to assist in operations and handle reference service. Such support staff is essential if the archivist is to have time to attend to the comprehensive development of the archives. It is also needed to provide operational staffing when the archivist is out of the office for records inventories, meetings on campus records issues, and professional service. Too often, archives have had to subsist with no more than access to a common pool of clerical and reference help. This arrangement can work when a young archives is part of a larger unit, such as a special collections department, but it will become increasingly inadequate as the archival program grows.

Academic archives usually include varying levels of student assistance, including undergraduates on scholarships, work-study, or hourly wages, and graduate assistants. Student help, in the range of one-half to two full-time equivalent staff, can be of enormous assistance to the archives. Student staffing also represents a key way to keep the program vital and to introduce new talent to the archival profession.

Staffing of a professional archivist, a nonprofessional assistant, and student help is the minimum needed in an academic archives. As a program grows, staff at each level should be added. There are no clear guidelines on how large one's holdings should be before adding a second, third, or fourth professional; determining the proper staffing level is difficult because most academic archivists would argue that their archives are understaffed, as many are. As a general guideline, at least three full-time employees (FTE) in addition to one FTE of student help, will be needed by the time a repository reaches 2,000 to 5,000 cubic feet of holdings, or current annual additions of 200 cubic feet, or an annual use rate of 1,000 inquiries. Should the archives also include extensive pre-1900 records or valuable literary manuscripts and books, the number of staff could be substantially higher.

SPACE AND FACILITIES

Given that the space and facilities available to academic archives range from corners and closets to state-of-the-art archival buildings, this section can only suggest the basic functional requirements of archives. The space for an academic archives can be divided into three components—storage, staff, and public. Archives require sufficient storage or stack space to house current processed and unprocessed holdings and accommodate influxes of records transfers and manuscript acquisitions. Overcrowding is one of the most chronic problems of archives because of the growth of modern records, the high costs of reformatting on microfilm, and institutional unwillingness to assign a high priority for records storage in light of other pressing space demands for classrooms and offices. Thus, the archivist must plan constantly for securing and retaining adequate storage space. This may include the option of constructing or leasing a low-cost remote storage facility, but the archives should resist attempts to place its holdings in areas without adequate security and environmental controls.

The archives will also require space for staff and public functions. While most archival office and clerical functions do not differ from other academic offices, archives will also need a modest amount of space for processing collections. Another key part of archives will be public areas for reference and exhibits—often combined. Many search rooms, or the adjoining anterooms and hallways, can accommodate exhibit cases to display documents from the archives. For reference areas, archives can often function quite effectively with an area of 400 to 600 square feet supplied with a few reference tables, staff desks, filing cabinets, and bookcases.

Whenever possible, storage, staff, and public space should be dedicated solely to the use of archives. Too often, sharing a reference room or stack area leads to inefficient reference service, conflict with other occupants, and reduced security. If space must be shared, it should only be with units of a similar function and with the same administrative superiors.

Depending on the breadth of the program, archives require access to a number of specialized facilities and services, especially archival supplies, office equipment, and photocopy machines for use by researchers and staff. Facilities or services for duplication of photographic and audiovisual material will often be needed to meet research and administrative needs. Equipment and supplies for modest in-house conservation, such as cleaning, minor repair, and encapsulation, should be available for routine archival processing. Access to specialized services such as fumigation, deacidification, and document restoration may be required depending on the nature of the records and the time available to conduct these activities. Other services should be made available as the program expands.

SERVICE GOALS

In defining the essential elements of an archival program, attention has been focused on tangibles, such as staff, space, and policies. Equally important is defining a set of communities to whom the archives can offer its services. On a campus, the classic archival constituencies are administrative officers, faculty, students, alumni, and the general public. To this list one might add the broad constituency of the archival profession in that each academic archives represents a crucible in which advances in archival science can be made. Some of these constituencies will already have been identified and may even be demanding services when the archives opens its doors; others will need to be developed. It is the archivist's responsibility to foster all these constituencies. Addressing the distinct interests of each group makes the archives' role both interesting and challenging. For example, the archives should strive to meet faculty and student needs for information to help them in governance or in monitoring the institution's administration; it should also supply basic research resources for their work in transmitting and expanding knowledge. Likewise, the archives should serve an administrative constituency by appraising current files for disposal or retention and by retrieving files when needed to help develop new policies.

The vibrant archival program will strive to meet the needs of all these constituencies and avoid becoming overly focused on the interests of any particular group. A program too closely tied to a single constituency risks losing its identity as an integrative and multi-disciplinary force, and can come perilously close to becoming an extension or subordinate of the agency it is trying to serve. Thus, the archivist's function is akin to that of a juggler—several balls must be kept aloft at once, none can receive as much attention as the juggler would like, and none can be allowed to crash against the interests of the other. Being at the center of this activity is the essence of the professional nature of archival work.

Notes

1. The *Guidelines for College and University Archives* (Chicago: Society of American Archivists, 1979), while not technically standards, provides a solid basis for performance goals for academic archives. Furthermore, the expansion of the archival literature in the 1970s and 1980s has provided a framework for the coordination of archival practice.

2. For a discussion of administrative location, refer to Burckel, "Establishing a College Archives: Possibilities and Priorities," *College and Research Libraries* 36 (1975): 384-92, reprinted in *College and University Archives: Selected Readings* (Chicago: Society of American Archivists, 1979), 38-46.

3. This is the approach recommended by Helen Samuels in her recent Mellon-funded project to study the documentation of higher education. Refer to her report, *Varsity Letters: Documenting Modern Colleges and Universities* (Chicago: Society of American Archivists, forthcoming), for a detailed explanation of the process.

4. While the employment criteria and credentials of archivists are changing, employers need to recognize that there is no single educational sequence for archivists. Rather, a mixture of backgrounds, predominantly in history and librarianship, has prevailed. Library administrators considering whether to require the Masters of Library Science as a minimum employment credential should note that archivists fall under the "other professional training" rubric of the American Library Association's *Library Education and Personnel Utilization* policy statement.

Archival Theory, Procedures, and Techniques

INTRODUCTION

Practices at college and university archives may need to vary considerably from institution to institution, but an underlying unity can be achieved through reference to the archival theories, procedures, and techniques that have evolved over the past two centuries. These will be much the same as for business, religious, or governmental archives. Indeed, it is this sharing of a common body of archival science that places the director of each college or university archives in a broader community and elevates academic archival work from an occupation to a profession.

The basic elements of archival theory and practice are well covered in a few general texts on archives—each with its own strengths and weaknesses. The academic archivist should have a number of these available for ready reference.[1] Elaboration on key aspects of archival practice can be found in items that should be part of the archives' own reference library, including the SAA's Basic Manual Series and its more recent archival fundamentals series.[2] The publications of the American Association for State and Local History provide additional guidance on many technical areas of archival practice. Finally, a regular review of the four North American archival journals—the *American Archivist, Archivaria, Midwestern Archivist,* and *Provenance*—will enable the academic archivist to remain abreast of the continuing evolution of archival theory and practice.

Given the strength of this literature, it is neither necessary nor desirable for the college and university archivist to develop a distinct body of theory and practice. Instead this book will consider these issues in an abbreviated form only. The focus will be on identifying the fundamental elements of each domain or key area of archival practice, noting sources for additional information, and citing applications of the archival theory appropriate to an academic setting. The purpose is to identify those archival principles that the archivist needs to master, and address only those detailed aspects of archival theory and techniques that need clarification to help the academic archivist in daily work. Equally important will be a focus on how best to manage these activities and on the administrative controls that enable the archivist to balance each technical area with the others and with available resources.

APPRAISAL

One of the most fundamental elements of archival practice is appraisal—the process by which the archivist assesses the value of documents and decides which should be kept and which should be destroyed. Since documentation is a key part of society's ability to preserve and reconstruct the past, it is appraisal that determines which events, people, and facts can be recalled and verified and which will be forgotten or retrievable only in nonverifiable ways.

The core of appraisal is a decision on the value of documents. While appraisal is generally discussed in the context of decisions on what to preserve and what to destroy, it also can be seen in a macrocosmic sense as a fundamental component of all other areas of archival work. The value of a record series, manuscript collection, file, or individual document should govern the level and type of descriptive tool created, the type of storage environment, and the range of preservation activities needed. Perhaps the broadest and best way of viewing appraisal is to consider it as inherent in the decision-making processes used for all aspects of archival operations.

The common use of "appraisal," focusing on its microcosmic sense of deciding whether a particular document or set of documents should be retained or destroyed, has been covered well in the basic archival literature and is the subject of continuing refinement.[3] However, there is an ongoing uneasiness about appraisal—it is seen as an almost mysterious process. The elements of appraisal can be itemized, but the exact method for deciding the value of a given record series remains unclear.

Some recent investigators have suggested that appraisal decisions seem to occur within a "black box" explainable in terms no better than archival intuition. However, attempts to elucidate the process have had only limited success in specifying what causes an archivist to decide to retain or destroy records.[4] This is not particularly surprising, since the essence of appraisal is a subjective judgment on the value of documents. Formulae, flow charts, and checklists can help clarify the elements of the decision process, but they cannot change the fact that appraisal is primarily a decision based on the archivist's knowledge, experience, and instinct. Nevertheless, there is a value in checklists and taxonomies in that they can subdivide appraisal into discrete components. This process helps to isolate the series of decisions that need to be made, which in turn can provide archivists with a sequence of activities to lead them through the work. This book will present a modified version of the traditional taxonomy of appraisal to provide an effective way to understand and implement the process.

Elements of Appraisal

Collecting Information

Appraisal cannot and should not occur within a vacuum. Rather, the first element in appraisal is to examine the context in which the records or manuscripts exist, including the institutional mission of the archives, the nature and history of the parent college or university, and the availability of similar or related documentation. These are critical steps in the process, although they are best understood as background for the microcosmic work of appraising a set of records.[5] A more practical way to approach appraisal is to examine the steps involved in evaluating a single body of records. Appraisal should begin with the collection of information about the records' attributes. These can be divided into characteristics relating to the record's form and characteristics dealing with the record's substance. The first category includes physical form (e.g., paper, film, magnetic tape), volume, age, condition, and type (i.e., office or official record, publication, or personal papers). As one gathers this information, a pattern for the upcoming appraisal process may emerge. For instance, if preliminary review shows that the records include a large volume of very recent machine-readable records, the archivist will have to plan a more intensive appraisal than if they included only a small or medium volume of very old published reports.

Once these fairly straightforward questions are answered, the archivist should move to the more challenging area of identifying the substantive or intrinsic characteristics of records. These relate to content: what kinds of information the records hold, how and why the information was fixed into a physical record, and what uses the record may be able to fulfill beyond its initial purposes. These characteristics can be called functional, evidential, and informational.[6]

Functional characteristics concern the purpose for which a record was created, such as to authorize an action, document an event or condition, or explain a policy. Evidential characteristics focus on what the record tells about the organization and the processes that led to the creation of the record. They can be used to answer questions, such as how the organization is structured, how decisions are made, why a given decision was made, what policies have influenced the organization, and how human beings have effected change within the organization. Some records provide better evidence than others because they contain more synthesis, analysis, or expression of rationale than others. For example, a letter or file note is more likely to explain the reasons for firing (or hiring) an employee than the notification of termination/appointment form in the personnel file.

Informational characteristics relate to the discrete bits of data that a record may provide independent of its revealing the process of the organization. Records have strong informational characteristics if they contain large quantities of specific, individual data (such as in a student-staff directory or a financial aid form). These informational characteristics can make records useful even if they do not explain any overall process, event, or policy (such as what credentials are required to become a student or faculty member).

Readers may note that this categorization of "evidence" and "information" as characteristics is inconsistent with the tendency of archivists to talk about these categories as "values" of records. Following T. R. Schellenberg, many writers have described the decision to retain or discard as one based on the "evidential value" and "informational value" of the records.[7] This book, however, suggests that appraisal is easier and more logical if "evidence" and "information" are treated not as separate values but as overlapping attributes of records. Then an assessment of value can be formed based on a review of the sequence of uses to which records might be put, regardless of their characteristics, as described below under "Assessing Value."

It is important to realize that these intrinsic characteristics—function, evidence, and information—are not
mutually exclusive, and a record may have a high quotient
of all three. For instance, the minutes of meetings of a
board of regents will exist for a certain function (to effect
and to document an action). They can provide evidence on
why a decision was made, and they can contain considerable specific information, such as names of regents and
statistical data about issues under consideration. Although this discussion of records characteristics may
make the process seem rather abstract, identifying and
listing these characteristics is actually a relatively simple
first step in making appraisal decisions.

After determining the intrinsic characteristics of the
records, the archivist should ask how well the records
fulfill each of their purposes. Thus, how well does a set of
files accomplish the function for which it was created? Is
that function important enough to justify retention of the
records concerning its accomplishment? Do the records
provide good evidence of what happened and how and why
it occurred? How much useful information about specific
things and people do the records provide?

The information the archivist assembles about the
records will provide the basis both for the ultimate decision and for the best allocation of staff time to conduct the
appraisal. For example, information on volume or age of
records may enable the archivist to "short-circuit" the
process and move to an immediate decision, such as when
a small volume of ledger books from the college's first
decade are encountered. In this case, the archival value of
the records will be apparent immediately. By the same
token, data showing that the records under consideration
are part of a large series of recent documents with a
uniform informational content (e.g., student financial aid
applications) will suggest that the archivist may need to
plan substantial additional appraisal work before reaching a decision on whether to accession or discard them.

Assessing Value

Determining the functional, evidential, and informational characteristics of records is critical to appraisal, but it is only the first step. The real key to appraisal lies in the next step: determining the value of the records. Before describing this process, however, it is necessary to clarify use of the terms "evidential" and "informational." Following Maynard Brichford, this book considers evidence and information not as values but as characteristics that must be examined before attempting to decide on the value of records.[8] In actual appraisal work, this approach will be useful because the differences between evidence and information often are not clear and may depend on the perspective of the user, rather than on the records themselves, and because the documentation found in academic archives is so diverse. Considering evidence and information as values can create problems for appraisal because they often overlap. In addition, evidential value has too often been treated as inherently superior to informational value because it is more relevant for the narrative, administrative, and diplomatic history that has formed the traditional background for archivists and researchers. With the advent of social and quantitative history and the increased use of archives by social scientists, records with strong informational but weak evidential characteristics (e.g., social-work case files) have become equally important for research.

There is an important, additional reason to treat evidence and information as characteristics rather than as values. It is more logical and efficient to determine first how much evidence or information the records contain than to consider immediately what the value of the evidence or the information is. Once the characteristics of records have been determined, the archivist will be in a stronger position to move to the next step in appraisal—assessing the value of the documents.

The best way to decide on the value of a document is to subdivide the process into a determination of the five kinds of value that records can have: administrative, financial, legal, research, and archival.

Administrative Value

All records have administrative value insofar as they perform the function for which they were created, such as communicating a change in policy, articulating a problem or question, or registering a transaction. They are necessary for the administration of offices because they store information for potential future retrieval and use.

When evaluating records to determine whether they have sufficient administrative value to merit archival retention, one needs to consider the importance of the office in question, the importance of the function accomplished by the particular records, the relevance of the records and function to the main activities of the office, the extent to which this information is available from other sources, and the frequency with which the records are consulted after their creation.

Financial or Fiscal Value

Some records document the monetary value of property held, the receipt or disbursement of funds, or the delivery of goods or services in exchange for funds. These records have financial or fiscal value if they are necessary to account for property, receipts, and expenditures and if they permit later audits to demonstrate that funds were disbursed properly, transactions were made in an orderly way, and goods and services were actually rendered. Not all financial records have the same financial or fiscal value. For example, cancelled checks will have little fiscal value beyond their short-term use for proof of payment, if bank statements or ledgers provide a record of date and amount debited according to each check number.

Legal Value

A record has legal value if it may be used to refute or support a claim relating to a person's or institution's action(s). Areas of law likely to require records include ownership and use of property, employment practices, employee benefits, patents, contractual obligations, civil rights, educational rights, etc. Legal actions requiring use of records are not limited to formal court cases; they can also include legislative and regulatory hearings and reviews, and certification of action and fact by the institution.

Archivists often are nervous about legal values because they may have little expertise in the law, even though they understand the importance of records for an organization's legal needs. The most important principle in appraising for legal value is acknowledging that an archivist is not a lawyer and should not attempt to make the final decision on the legal value of a record. The appropriate role for the archivist is to conduct a careful review of the files, ask the records' custodians about likely or actual legal uses of the records, and then suggest a retention period that appears to cover these needs. If other considerations and values do not recommend the retention of the records in question, the archivist should compare the records and legal issues to similar situations to see if disposal is warranted. If this still does not resolve the legal question, then the archivist must seek the advice of the institution's legal counsel.

While the archivist should not make the final decision on the legally required retention period, he or she should still be able to identify legal values by making a preliminary assessment of the records' potential usefulness in a legal action. To accomplish this, the archivist should be aware of the principles governing the legal need for records and, thus, their legal value. These principles include the following:

- The statute of limitations for each type of legal action determines how long a delay can occur before a claim can be brought and, thus, the maximum period that records may be needed for court action. Common bases for claims are property, labor, and civil rights legislation.
- Some statutes or regulations dictate a specific retention period as a means to control ongoing activities. This may occur especially in cases of public health and safety (e.g., handling of

hazardous wastes) and certification and
accreditation of professionals.
• Contractual obligations require the retention of
records to document the rights and
responsibilities of all parties until the contract is
completed and the statute of limitations for
claims arising from the contract has expired. It is
important to remember that not all contracts are
explicit and formal documents. In a college or
university, there are many implied contracts,
such as that a student will receive a degree if
tuition is paid and academic requirements are
met.
• Income-tax regulations stipulate that
appropriate and detailed records of employees'
income be maintained for certain periods of time.
Moreover, an overall record of expenditures and
income is needed to support the institution's
claims for tax-free status.
• Litigation or other legal action, such as
investigation under subpoena or by commission,
may necessitate the retention of large quantities
of records beyond those specifically covered by
law so that all information needed by either party
will be available.

The final decision on the need to retain records for legal
purposes should be an administrative one. Caution is
necessary, but the archivist, legal counsel, and campus
administrators should recognize that all records likely to
be needed in any possible court case cannot be retained.
In all cases, however, appraisal decisions should be made
in an orderly way so that if subpoenaed records have been
destroyed, it will be possible to demonstrate that the
destruction was neither arbitrary nor accidental but part
of an overall program for administrative efficiency.

Research Value
      A record has research value if it can be used by
individuals engaged in the collection and analysis of data

about one's institution and its property, faculty, students; the activities in which they are involved; and the ideas that are the basis for their actions. The researcher may be looking for evidence, information, or both, but the essence of the research process is a systematic effort to collect data on a given subject, person, or thing in order to answer the questions posed by the researcher. Because the core of the research process is the discovery of new knowledge, definitive determination of research value is illusory, and archivists cannot expect certainty in determining research value. Instead, they must make their best effort to anticipate potential future use by drawing on a thorough knowledge of the records, the creating office, past use patterns, and trends in historical research.

To appraise for research value, the archivist needs to determine what kinds of evidence or information the records hold and what level of the organization they document. A good method is to consider these factors:

- Uniqueness of the record. Are there additional copies in other more/less central locations? Is the information and evidence recorded elsewhere in a more/less summary manner?
- Credibility. Was the information recorded in an objective fashion? Were the records' creators in a good position to have a clear view of what was being recorded? Are the "vested interests" of the creator likely to have influenced the recording of the information? If the objectivity of the record is questionable, is it nonetheless useful to reflect the opinions of its creator?
- Understandability. Is the record legible? Does it need to be "translated" either via language or computer code to be understood? Is machinery necessary, and is it available to examine the record?
- Time span. Does the record cover a narrow or broad time period? Does it provide a good overview over time or an in-depth view of a single year?

• Accessibility. How effectively and efficiently might the records answer the research questions that will be asked of them? Will access need to be restricted?

Once information on these aspects of the records has been assembled, the archivist should move to the most difficult part of appraisal—deciding whether the subjects and activities documented are important enough to merit retention of the records. While the archivist's knowledge of the important events in the institution's history, experience with previous researchers, and awareness of potential new areas of research all contribute to the decision on research value, ultimately it is a value judgment that should reflect the archivist's *weltanschauung*. The responsible archivist will not try to avoid or deny this fact but recognize limits, preferences, and prejudices and then control and exploit them.

Archival Value

Most writings on appraisal include only the previously mentioned values for retention, but Brichford has suggested another, called archival. In essence, this is a combination of all the others. It is included here out of a conviction that an academic archives serves multiple communities—administrative, legal, fiscal, and research. Thus, if a record has sufficient value in any one of the areas above to justify permanent retention, or if it has an important relationship to material already held in an archives or can otherwise contribute to the program's operation, it has an archival value. At the same time, the concept of archival value implies that the decision to accession a record into an archives should be based on a combination of all of the above values and internal considerations relevant to the administration of the archives.[9]

Appraisal in Practice

The core of appraisal work is gathering data about the characteristics of records and answering questions about their potential administrative, fiscal, legal, research, and archival uses. While collecting this information and asking these questions, the archivist gradually will form an opinion about the ultimate value of the records and the likely disposition recommendation. The process will be simplified by the use of a few forms and by regular procedures for consultation with institutional officials and, sometimes, researchers. While these steps can be consolidated into an elaborate flow chart or checklist with each step described in detail, such a treatment would burden the archives unnecessarily. A few appraisal decisions will be complex enough to justify such procedures, but many can be made competently with simple descriptions and unwritten rules based on experience.

The use of formal, written appraisal procedures will be more important and necessary if the archives is large or a number of people must participate in the decision. A small archives, in which the same person inventories and appraises records, may not need the same kind of appraisal reports and recommendations as a large repository, in which the head archivist must reach a decision based solely on inventories and analyses prepared by staff members. Thus, archivists will find it most efficient to design a few basic inventory and appraisal forms and then begin the process without worrying about elaborate procedures for each step in the process.

Appraisal is a dynamic process. The assessment of the five values of records may be five distinct steps or a judgment that is formed and revised continuously as the archivist gathers more information about the records. Assessment begins with an opinion formed during the initial contact with the office that holds the records. It proceeds during the formal inventory process and continues until the records are either accessioned or scheduled for disposal. It also can be reinitiated at any time, once the documents are in custody of the archives. Thus, the reappraisal of records that have long been part of the archives is an appropriate action, indeed a responsibility, for good program management.[10]

While appraisal is a fundamental technique that should permeate an archives' activities, it is performed most commonly at three times: while records are still in the hands of their creators (often through records management); when the records are first received in the repository (as part of accessioning); and in the course of processing. Ideally, the bulk of appraisal is done while the records are still in the hands of their creators because this affords the greatest opportunity to understand the records in the context of their creation and use. Appraisal at this stage also provides a better chance to see all the office's records and thus to insure that other valuable documents are not discarded or disarranged by the records' creators, who often have mistaken notions of which records have the greatest value. When appraisal is conducted while records are still in their creators' custody, the focus of analysis should be at the filing-unit or record-series level so that the decision will cover an entire record series rather than individual folders or documents. If more detailed appraisal is necessary, it should be delayed until it can be incorporated into archival processing. Appraisal of records while they are still in the originator's custody can best be assured by a strong records management program, but it can and should be applied also by archives lacking records management authority.[11]

As a practical matter, the academic archivist needs to recognize that a substantial amount of "appraisal" and disposal will be performed by office staff without any archival guidance or authorization. The administrative and clerical staff (especially where turnover is high) are often unaware of the existence of the archives and institutional requirements for prior archival approval of disposals even where such policies have been published in campus handbooks. While the archivist will never be able to prevent all such disposals, the damage can be limited in three ways. The archivist should publicize the campus records program, cultivate and educate campus administrators and clerical staff through outreach programs, and respond quickly to offices' requests for assistance with records transfers and disposals.

The second major time appraisal occurs is when records are actually accessioned by the archives. If the records arrive unannounced without previous appraisal, it will be necessary to follow the complete process of examination and evaluation, just as would be done during a pre-accession or records management appraisal. Even when an accession has already been appraised, the series should be scanned quickly to determine if it conforms to previous impressions and if it contains any obviously non-archival material that may be discarded to reduce volume prior to storage before processing. Once again, the archivist should focus on decisions to retain or discard entire series, rather than on individual documents and folders.

Even the best cared-for records and the most carefully appraised series may contain files and documents of dubious value, but this often can be detected only after they arrive at the processor's work station. A key part of processing (the series of activities done to prepare records for preservation and use) is to weed out materials that do not have archival value, but appraisal during processing should be limited in several ways. First, it should be the exception more than the rule, since the decision to retain the overall series has already been made. Second, when appraisal does occur during processing, it should focus on the folder level or on overall categories of documents found throughout the series (e.g., junk mail). Decisions on a piece-by-piece basis should be very rare because full appraisal in such detail is prohibitively expensive and very susceptible to the idiosyncracies of each processor unless detailed guidelines are prepared for each series. Except for general weeding guidelines, such as removing all copies of campus publications from office files, formal appraisal during processing is inadvisable.

This review of appraisal has focused on the information gathering needed to reach decisions on whether records or manuscripts should be preserved. It has not delineated how the archivist determines what is historically valuable because those decisions must vary from institution to institution. Such decisions should emerge from a knowledge of the institution's past, trends in historical research, and documentation already available. At the same time, the decision on the retention or destruction of a single record series should be made in reference to the archives' mandate and resources. Thus, the archives' authorizing document, by delineating the program's mission and authority to decide on retention or disposal, will provide the broad framework for appraisal work. Greater specificity on what subjects to document, and levels at which to document, should be embodied in a documentation policy statement, as discussed in the following section.

Despite the importance of professional standards, institutional mandates, collection policies, and advisory committees, there is no escaping the centrality of the individual archivist who must take the primary role in appraisal. The archivist should employ the most systematic appraisal methods available, but ultimately the process is a subjective one that can be improved best through broad knowledge and long experience. There is much merit in the advice often given to beginning archivists—"When in doubt, *do not* throw it out!" Experience and long tenure can make the archivist more conservative, but the greatest asset to the archives' appraisal program will be the breadth and depth of the archivist's experience with the institution, users, and research patterns as a whole.

DOCUMENTATION STRATEGY, FUNCTIONAL ANALYSES, AND DOCUMENTATION POLICIES

The preceding overview of appraisal, incorporating both the basics of archival theory and an outline of practical steps, should be sufficient to help the academic archivist begin evaluating records. Appraisal, however, does not and should not happen in a vacuum. Furthermore, it should be conducted with reference to three theoretical frameworks—documentation strategies, functional analyses of institutions, and "acquisitions" policies. Each of these constructs relates to appraisal goals and methodology because each is concerned with defining the parameters used in deciding which materials should be transferred and preserved in an archives.

These constructs have received great attention in recent years as fresh contributions to archival theory, but they do not supplant the value of traditional archival appraisal. Rather, they represent differences in emphasis, detail, and terminology and reflect useful conceptual approaches to the critical issue of selecting records and manuscripts for retention. They therefore deserve the attention of the academic archivist. Each represents a more complex process than can be fully explained in this book, but the following summary emphasizes the practical contributions they can make to archival practice in colleges and universities.

Documentation Strategies

In recent years, several archivists have argued that traditional descriptions of appraisal, similar to those in the previous section, are insufficient to deal with what they see as the major new challenges of the growing complexity and volume of modern records and the persistence of limited resources for archives. They have explored new approaches to assessing records by emphasizing the need to go beyond analysis of a single institution's records to look systematically at broader areas of documentation. The goal has been to create a strategic approach to documentation that will make the most efficient and effective use of resources while ensuring that records of enduring value are preserved.[12]

The emphasis in traditional explanations of appraisal has generally been on the archivist's role in assessing the value of each specific body of records that he or she encounters. By contrast, the documentation strategy process emphasizes the need for two steps prior to decisions on the value of a body of records: looking at what functions, subjects, persons, and types of records need to be documented, and determining where these are documented and who holds the documents. The method emphasizes that documentation will occur in many sources beyond official records, and it implies cooperative arrangements among several institutions and types of information service agencies in advance of decisions on accessions. Once the documentary area has been defined, a strategy can be then developed to ensure that the documents are preserved and made available through both the local repository and other institutions. To ensure that documentary goals are being met, the process includes steps for reporting and analysis.[13]

This paradigm is quite attractive. It frees the archivist from being dependent only on the records at hand when deciding what will be in the repository. It also provides a systematic model for selecting subjects to be documented and thus emphasizes the centrality of the archivist in controlling the selection and preservation of documents. On the other hand, the importance of going beyond the records at hand when making appraisal decisions is not so new a concept as the documentation strategists would suggest.[14] More importantly, there is a theoretical difference between appraisal and documentation strategies—the former is an inductive process starting with consideration of all records that actually exist; the latter is a deductive process starting with definitions of subject areas and then moving to determining whether records exist to document the subject area. Because college and university archivists start with a defined sphere of responsibility (documenting a single institution), it can be argued that the documentation-strategy approach has less validity in this setting than it would for manuscript curators struggling to define and control collecting areas.[15] Nevertheless, the technical processes used in documentation strategies can be quite useful to the academic archivist in reaching decisions on collecting areas beyond institutional records, handling complex areas of institutional documentation, and developing cooperative arrangements with other repositories.

sizes the differences between "archives" and "manuscripts," and instead emphasizes their commonalities as cultural documentation, refer to Patrick M. Quinn, "Academic Archivists and Their Current Practice," *Georgia Archive* 10:2 (Fall 1982): 18-20.

5. Ernst Posner, *American State Archives* (Chicago: University of Chicago Press, 1964).

6. An overview of the development of academic archives and excellent historical bibliographies can be found in Nicholas C. Burckel and J. Frank Cook, "Profile of College and University Archives in the United States," *American Archivist* 45 (1982): 410-28; and J. Frank Cook, "American Archivists and the SAA, 1938-1979: From Arcana Siwash to the C & U PAG," *American Archivist* 51 (1988): 428-39.

7. A thought-provoking analysis of the roots of academic archives, and a view of their special mission, can be found in Maynard Brichford, "Academic Archives: Überlieferungsbildung," *American Archivist* 43 (1980): 449-60.

8. An understanding of the importance of the archives' age underlies Quinn's pragmatic advice on making choices for archival programs; refer to his "Academic Archivists and Their Current Practice," 14-24.

Functional Analysis

In an attempt to deal with the limitations caused by appraisal's focus on the records at hand and by archival structures designed around institutional hierarchy, Helen W. Samuels, of the Massachusetts Institute of Technology, has suggested that the starting point for appraisal should be an analysis of the functions of a college or university. She argues that institutional collecting programs or documentation plans should begin by looking not at which offices create what records, but by determining the essence of each of the institution's multiple functions and roles. Once such a functional analysis is completed, the archivist can decide which functions to document and at what level. Then, the archivist can assess what documentation exists or should exist and select that portion needed to meet the archives' documentary goals.[16] A particularly interesting feature of the project is that instead of the traditional triad of teaching, research, and public service, Samuels has identified seven functions that cut across many conventional organizational lines. She emphasizes verbs rather than nouns: a college or university sustains itself, confers credentials, advances knowledge, communicates knowledge, preserves culture, and socializes youth. This is an important project that should be examined by all academic archivists because it will give them a new way to analyze their institutions as they consider appraisal and acquisitions policies. Samuel's project articulates the long-recognized phenomena that functions, people, and documentary sources can never be restricted neatly to specific places on organizational charts in the records of "key, central" offices. A broader perspective on appraisal as well as reference service will evolve from this approach's emphasis on functions rather than offices and records.

Documentation Policies

In an effort to make the acquisition of new holdings more systematic, librarians and archivists have long endorsed the practice of preparing a general policy statement to define the criteria for selecting materials for their collections. In recent years, most librarians and many archivists have abandoned the term "acquisitions policy" in favor of "collection development policy" to reflect a broadening of the concept and to focus more on the long-term effect of selecting material than on the one-time act of acquisition. The concepts of collection development, collection management, and the more traditional acquisitions policy can provide important insights to archival work. However, because these concepts were developed first in the library world, archivists should be aware of some important problems in terminology before they adopt these concepts.

The terms "collection" and "acquisition" are problematic for archives because archivists do not collect or acquire records, but rather accession them, meaning that the records are transferred to the archives but their ownership remains with the institution that created them. Thus, acquisitions and collecting policy and collection development are not satisfactory terms for archives, where the core focus should be on organic or regular transfers of material within the parent institution. In practice, however, archives cannot rely solely on passive internal transfers of official records if they hope to document the parent institution properly. In addition, many academic archives have broadened their holdings to include several types of manuscript collections. In these circumstances, the principles embodied in acquisitions or collection development policies can nonetheless be of great value to academic archival work. Fortunately, the broader term of "documentation policy" can be used to cover both core institutional records work and library and manuscript acquisitions. This book, therefore, will use "documentation policy" to refer to the principles that should provide a framework for decisions on whether to accept or reject a given set of records or manuscripts for the archives. The term "acquisition practice" will describe the systematic processes that ensure the regular flow of campus records and, where appropriate, manuscripts to the archives. These are discussed in the following section.

Documentation policy statements can be prepared for different types of materials and at levels ranging from an entire library or archives to a specific subject or collecting area. Regardless of their range, they share the same elements:

- Statement of mission of the repository or purpose of the subject area.
- History of the repository or collection area and summary information on size and scope.
- Summary descriptions of the subjects documented and the types of researchers served.
- Assessment of relation of the repository or subject area to other repositories or forms of documentation.
- Indication of locus of responsibility for acquiring materials.
- Statement of present and desired levels of intensity of coverage for each component of the repository.
- Criteria used in selecting material in each subject area (e.g., dates, origin of documents, geography, types of material).
- Commentary on past and future directions for the repository or subject area.[17]

For most academic archives, such a documentation policy statement requires only two to five pages, although it may be advisable to prepare separate statements for manuscript collecting areas that are beyond the archives' institutional focus (e.g., local political papers, literary manuscripts, or business records).[18] To ensure their accuracy and usefulness, documentation policy statements should be updated on a regular basis—perhaps every five to ten years, depending on how rapidly the archives is growing and altering or refining the scope of its holdings.

Despite the endorsements that such policy statements have received in archival and library literature, they are not without rather serious limitations. Most significantly, they are far less useful for guiding future acquisitions than for articulating a rationale for past decisions. Given the continual changes in record-keeping technologies, institutional activities, and research topics, it is extraordinarily difficult to draft a policy statement that will provide practical detailed guidance for the future. While policy statements provide general guidelines, they cannot incorporate the kind of detail necessary for daily situations the archivist will encounter. It is therefore unwise to specify precise policies for future appraisal or acquisitions decisions.

Given these reservations, a cynic might reject documentation policy statements as a waste of time, but this would ignore three important benefits of the process. First, preparing a statement requires the archivist to analyze the current holdings and reconsider the mission of the archives. The gathering of information and evaluation of the program will provide a basis for understanding what the archives does and does not contain and will lay a foundation for long-range planning. Most importantly, the review and analysis process should implant knowledge of the repository's contents and goals firmly in the mind of the archivist. This knowledge of the archives can then inform future decisions, even if the policy document is not examined during each appraisal.[19]

Second, documentation policy statements can play a critical role in administration of the archives. They help to explain the archives' actions to the outside world and to provide continuity in decision making. While all repositories have anomalies in their holdings, policy statements can demonstrate that the repository's records and manuscript collections are not the result of whim and idiosyncrasy, but the cumulation of many rational decisions on the value of documents. Archivists may not always follow their written documentation policies (and many act as if the policies were written to be broken), but such statements are essential summaries of the systematic approach that should underlie archival work. Even though documentation policy statements may not be detailed charts of the future, they should provide sufficient discipline to preclude the most undesirable fluctuations in selection decisions. They can also be very useful in providing continuity when there are changes in the archives' personnel.

The third and perhaps most practical value of documentation policy statements is that they provide a solid basis for rejecting material offered to the archives. They can be a particularly useful tool when archivists are asked to accept material that they do not want or cannot afford to accession, process, and preserve because it is clearly insignificant or out of scope. Being able to argue that the potential accession is outside of the repository's established scope will be an important supplement to the archivist's other reasons for rejecting the material. This practical value alone should repay the archivist for the effort of preparing a policy.

Understanding documentation strategies and functional analysis and developing a documentation policy will contribute to the success of the academic archivist—not by superceding traditional appraisal work, but by providing a systematic means to find the context for decisions on the value of records. Documentation strategies and functional analyses will be most useful for contributing the broadest possible context and providing a basis for the periodic long-range planning that every archives should conduct. Documentation policies provide an excellent means to review and articulate program goals for holdings of records and manuscripts.

As a practical matter, traditional appraisal methods, modified and informed by these perspectives, will remain central to what the archivist must do when facing records and responding to institutional concerns about its documentary heritage. While archivists might engage in lengthy discussions about whether appraisal should follow or precede documentation strategies, functional analysis, or writing of documentation policies, daily practice will demonstrate that all of these techniques for selection are closely related and occur in a tight matrix rather than a linear sequence.

ACQUISITIONS PRACTICES

Academic archivists need carefully developed procedures to assist in obtaining physical custody of the records and manuscripts needed to fulfill the repository's documentary mission. These procedures can be called acquisitions practices even though the term "acquisitions" has no distinct basis in archival theory.[20] In the allied field of library science, "acquisitions" is used to describe the activities that follow selection and that are designed to physically obtain materials for an information center.[21] Analogous activities are necessary in an archives even though institutional records are accessioned by internal transfer, rather than "acquired." Regardless of terminology, archivists can benefit from attention to the technical processes needed to ensure the flow of documents to the archives.

The most basic elements of acquisition work for archives and manuscripts are found in appraisal and in the development and implementation of a documentation policy, both of which are complex processes with their own theoretical foundations. The subject foci in a documentation policy for official records will be determined by the nature of the archives' parent institution. The specifics of such policy, especially elements focusing on the level to which institutional units and subjects are to be documented, relationships to other information sources, and the scope of non-institutional manuscripts collecting, must be worked out by each archivist in relation to available resources, level of use, and available documentation. In daily archival operations, however, much acquisitions work will proceed independent of, and often in spite of, a formally developed documentation policy. Once the archives is established and becomes known on campus, large quantities of material will arrive unsolicited and without the benefit of previous archival review of their long-term research value. In these cases, solicitation work per se is not necessary, and the archivist can proceed immediately to the application of standard archival practices of appraisal, accessioning, arrangement, description, and pres-

ervation. In a well-run archives, such a passive acquisitions program is the result of sound processes established in the early years of the repository and reinforced
through regular records management and publicity programs.

Office Records and Publications

The most important prerequisite for acquisitions work
is to possess authority to accession all records of the parent
institution. Thus, as noted in the chapter on "Fundamentals of Academic Archives," the first step should be to
secure an authorizing document designating the archives
as the institution's official repository for its records. If the
archives has the role of collecting manuscripts on subjects
other than the institution (e.g., local history, political
papers, business records), this should be stipulated clearly
in the authorizing document. Once official institutional
approval of this document has been granted, the details of
a documentation policy can be developed so that the archivist will be able to respond systematically to each potential
acquisition.

A crucial element in the authorizing document will be
authority to review all records before they can be destroyed. The nature of such records-disposition authority
may vary depending on legislation and the presence of a
records-management program, but procedures always
should ensure that the campus archivist has veto power
over recommendations for disposal. Where a well-designed records management program is operating, acquisitions work for official records can be held to a minimum,
since many transfers and disposals will be based on schedules developed after careful appraisals. Another important structural element facilitating acquisitions is the
promulgation of a policy that one copy of all campus
publications, broadly defined, be deposited in the archives.
Arrangements with central graphics design and printing
or copy centers will provide a means to gather such deposits on a regular basis, even though much material will still
need to be gathered from individual departments.

In a well-ordered world, records and publications policies would enable the archivist to be passive for most
accessions, but there are many times when more active
work is essential to ensure that all records needed for
adequate documentation of the institution are acquired.
Thus, most archivists will find that the approaches used
in manuscript solicitation can be quite useful for institutional records. These techniques are neither mysterious
nor beyond the realm of common sense—phone calls and
letters reminding offices of the archives' existence, its
institutional mission and authority, the space savings
resulting from archival storage, and so on. Such solicitation campaigns should be planned carefully and be based
on the archivist's identification of key units under-repre-
sented in the archives. A useful first step is to compare the
institution's telephone directories, organizational charts,
and the archives' own classification guide with the archives' finding aids and accession lists to determine which
offices have not yet transferred records for important
periods of their operations. A large wall chart or time-line,
with columns for offices and rows for decades of the institution's history, can be useful in mapping holdings and
gaps. From this, the archivist can prepare a list of record
types and dates needed to fill in gaps, and then systematically contact the underrepresented offices.

Sometimes the archivist will not need to take the
initiative in securing the office staff's interest in transferring records. Campus moves and space shortages often
lead to telephone calls and unsolicited deliveries of boxes.
A particularly useful tool in dealing with such questions
about archival transfer will be a short flier or brochure
explaining the archives' purpose and operations and listing records commonly transferred and commonly destroyed. For example, see the "University Archives Transfer
Guidelines for Noncurrent Office Records" in Figure 1.

Unfortunately, there are some conditions of academic
life that cannot be addressed through procedure manuals,
rules, or guidelines. For instance, how does one deal with
the most common problems in acquisition of records: persuading protective clerical staff in some offices to relin-

quish control over records; convincing less careful offices to consult with the archives before disposing of their records; dealing with large unscheduled transfers when space and staff are not available to accommodate them; and responding to the sudden necessity to accession records under the "threatening" circumstances that arise when offices are closed or moved, or lose storage space. Success will depend on the archivist's skill in working with people and ability to accept frustration when things do not follow textbook paths to happy conclusions. Only patience and persistence in contacts with office personnel will produce the long-term successes that will overshadow the inevitable defeats and losses of records.

Personal Papers

An area presenting further challenges is that of acquiring personal papers of students, staff, and faculty.[22] The first step toward regularized acquisition of these papers is the combination of a documentation policy and broad visibility within the university community as the sole unit responsible for historical documentation of the institution. Faculty, staff, and students may not perceive the clear distinction between an archives and other campus information centers, such as libraries and alumni offices. Thus, it is important for the archives to have good relations with such offices so that their staff regularly route campus publications and all student and faculty manuscripts to the archives. Given the close ties that often exist between branch librarians or bibliographers and faculty, archivists should exploit this network as a way of extending their reach. Once these elements are in place, a number of collections of faculty, staff, and student papers should find their way to the archives with little additional effort.

Frequently, however, an active solicitation program is necessary to meet documentation goals and obtain balanced coverage, especially in a new archives. By comparing the archives' holdings with biographical directories of the institution, the archivist can identify individuals or entire departments and colleges that are under-repre-

TRANSFER GUIDELINES FOR NON-CURRENT OFFICE RECORDS

The official University Records Policy contains three provisions:

1. University records are all documents produced or received by any agency, officer, or employee of the university in the conduct of its business. Documents encompass all forms of recorded information.

2. All records produced or received by any agency or employee of the university in the transaction of university business are university property and subject to university policy for retention or disposal.

3. No university records can be discarded or destroyed except upon the prior written approval of the University Archivist.

The University Archives is the repository for all non-current, inactive official university records that have sufficient value to warrant their preservation. Records commonly transferred to the Archives include:

1) Constitutions and by-laws, minutes and proceedings, transcripts, lists of officers of University corporate bodies;

2) Office files: correspondence and memoranda (incoming and outgoing) and subject files concerning projects, activities and functions;

3) Historical files documenting policies, decisions, committee and task force reports, questionnaires;

4) Publications: one record copy of all programs, journals, monographs, newsletters, brochures, posters, and announcements issued by the University or its subdivisions; the Archives should be placed on college, departmental, and office mailing lists to receive all future publications;

5) Audio-visuals: photographs, films, and sound and video recordings;

(continued on next page)

Figure 1. Transfer Guidelines for Non-current Office Records
(1 of 2)

6) Personal papers of students, faculty, and staff which relate to the university's work;

Records which should not be transferred but scheduled for disposal <u>after consultation with the Archivist</u> include:

1) Records of specific financial transactions;

2) Routine letters of transmittal and acknowledgement;

3) Non-personally addressed correspondence such as "Deans and Directors" memoranda (except for one record copy from the issuing officer);

4) Requests for publications or information after the requests have been filled;

5) Replies to questionnaires if the results are recorded and preserved either in the Archives or in a published report.

Items which may be discarded directly from the office when they are no longer needed for administrative purposes include:

1) All blank forms and unused printed or duplicated materials;

2) All other duplicate material: keep only the original copy and annotated copies;

3) Papers, reports, workpapers and drafts, which have been published;

4) Artifacts and memorabilia. The archives does not collect non-documentary objects related to the university's history except in cases of great importance and manageable physical size and condition. Please call the Archivist to discuss options for preservation of such objects.

Materials should be transferred in the order in which the records' creator maintained them. A letter briefly identifying the material and describing the activity to which it relates should accompany the transfer.

This list is intended as a general guide. If there are questions about records not listed here or questions about the retention or disposal of specific record series, please telephone the Archivist at _____ .

WHEN IN DOUBT, DO NOT THROW IT OUT!

Figure 1. Transfer Guidelines for Non-current Office Records
(2 of 2)

sented in the archives. Then, a series of solicitation letters can be sent to targeted individuals. To make this process manageable, the archivist might focus on one college or department each year. Another useful form of solicitation is to examine the institution's annual list of retirees to locate important faculty and staff who have not yet made arrangements to deposit their papers in the archives. Similarly, letters should be sent to the next of kin at a decent interval after the archivist learns of the death of a faculty or staff member.

Useful elements of all solicitation letters are a description of the archives' role in documenting the institution; a note on the importance of personal papers for full coverage of the college or university; an acknowledgment of the academic and professional accomplishments of the individual being approached; a broad outline of the kinds of records and subjects of interest to the archives; and an offer to assist in reviewing the person's papers. The archivist may also find it useful to develop a simple flier to characterize the kinds of documents relevant for faculty papers collections. For example see the "University Archives Transfer Guidelines for Personal Papers of Faculty and Staff" in Figure 2. In addition, the inclusion of sample finding aids and references to related collections already in the archives can be quite effective in demonstrating the research value of personal papers and their importance to the institutional archives.

The acquisition of student and alumni papers, as well as records of their organizations, will present greater challenges for the archivist because the universe of available materials is so large that systematic coverage is difficult. For students, the community is so transitory that constant attention is necessary just to acquire a small quantity of material. In addition, it is difficult to predict which records and papers will best document student life at any given time in an institution's life. Thus, the archivist should be aware of the inherent limits of any static listing of which kinds of student materials should be solicited and how these documents can best be obtained. Useful student documents include course notes, exams,

diaries, photographs and scrapbook albums, and correspondence. However, changes in personal writing habits
and the elusiveness of what is called student life suggest
that one must be realistic and accept that much of student
life will go undocumented. One may suspect that chance
will bring in as many high-quality collections of student
papers as a systematic solicitation program, but a safer
strategy is to have an active outreach and reference-ser-
vice program to ensure that large numbers of students and
alumni know of the archives' existence and purpose. From
such awareness can come contacts leading to the donation
of a number of student-papers collections from those who
are historically minded. For those who are not historically
minded, no amount of systematic work will guarantee
even a minimally useful record. In these cases, a vigorous
oral history program may be the only way to document
these individuals, and that is beyond the means of many
archives.

Perhaps a more productive area for the archivist's
attention in documenting student and campus life is a
regularized campaign for acquiring records of student and
faculty organizations. While not all student interests and
energies will be channeled into organizations, records of
these groups can provide a good barometer of changing
mores, attitudes, and preoccupations from year to year,
even though the fluidity of such organizations and the
shortness of students' tenure makes such collecting quite
difficult. Useful solicitation mechanisms include: placing
notices about the archives' collecting interests in the student newspaper each semester; mounting exhibits on topics of guaranteed student interest (e.g., athletics and
campus life); and corresponding directly with officers of
organizations. Acquisition of student publications and
broadsides can also be based on regular archival "raids" of
bulletin boards and literature stands in student unions
and campus libraries. Finally, the archives might consider
its student employees as field agents for this work by
asking them to bring in copies of publications for organizations in which they are involved. At best, the results will

TRANSFER GUIDELINES FOR
PERSONAL PAPERS OF FACULTY AND STAFF

The University Archives is the repository for the non-current records of the University as well as for the personal papers of faculty and staff. The Archives preserves and makes these documents available to aid in research on the history of the institution and on the development of academic disciplines. The personal papers of faculty and staff provide a rich source for historical research. The following guidelines will assist faculty and staff in identifying those portions of their files that are appropriate for transfer to the Archives.

Items likely to be of archival interest include:

1) Biographical information: resumes, vitae, bibliographies, memoirs, genealogies, published and manuscript biographical sketches;

2) University official correspondence and files: outgoing and incoming letters and memoranda relating to departmental and University business, committee minutes, reports, and files;

3) Professional correspondence (outgoing and incoming) with colleagues, publishers, professional organizations, and former students;

4) Teaching material: one copy of lecture notes, syllabi, course outlines, reading lists, examinations, and correspondence with students;

5) Publications: one copy of all articles, books, reviews, or works of art;

6) Audio-visuals: photographs, films, and sound and video recordings;

7) Personal and family correspondence, diaries, photographs.

(continued on next page)

Figure 2. Transfer Guidelines for Personal Papers of Faculty and Staff (1 of 2)

TRANSFER GUIDELINES FOR
PERSONAL PAPERS OF FACULTY AND STAFF

Documents which generally should not be transferred without prior consultation with the Archivist include:

1) Detailed financial records, canceled checks, and receipts;

2) Routine correspondence especially non-personally addressed mail and routine letters of transmittal and acknowledgement;

3) Grade books and class rosters;

4) Duplicates and multiple copies of publications, course materials; all other duplicate material: keep only the original and heavily annotated copies;

5) Typescripts, drafts, and galleys of publications and speeches unless the final publication or presentation copy is unavailable;

6) Books, research papers, journal articles, and reprints written by other persons;

7) Research notes and data if a summary of the data is available and transferred; bibliographic notes and notes on reading. Because of wide variations in the nature of research data, it is best to consult with the Archivist before discarding research notes and data.

8) Artifacts and memorabilia. The Archives does not collect non-documentary objects except in cases of great importance and manageable physical size and condition. Please call the Archivist to discuss options for preservation of such objects.

Materials should be transferred in the order in which the faculty or staff member maintained them. A letter briefly identifying the materials and describing the activity to which they relate should accompany the transfer.

This list is intended as a general guide. Because of broad variations in personal papers, it is advisable to consult with the Archivist to determine how your own files relate to these guidelines. Exceptions often are made after a review of the conditions under which the documents were generated and their potential usefulness. Please telephone the Archivist at _____.

WHEN IN DOUBT, DO NOT THROW IT OUT!

Figure 2. Transfer Guidelines for Personal Papers of Faculty and Staff (2 of 2)

be mixed and the process will have to be repeated regularly.

Another frequently effective device for documenting student organizations is available on campuses where offices administering student activity fees maintain records on all officially recognized and registered organizations. Case files from these offices, as well as from the campus offices assigning space to student groups, can provide a base level of documentation for a very broad range of student groups. Even though the individual files may not provide much information about any single organization, they can be quite useful for examining patterns in student interests, establishing founding dates, and providing lists of officers. They can be especially valuable if the archives also maintains a file of publications and literature from these organizations. Individually, many publications are little more than broadsides and announcements, which may contain little substantive evidence of a particular student event, but the accumulation of such publications, especially in combination with organization registration records, can contribute substantially to research on student activities. They can also provide minimal information to satisfy inquiries when better documentation is not available.

In the case of papers of alumni, many archives encounter little difficulty in acquiring at least a few of these collections, since the donation of papers to one's alma mater is a hallowed tradition among graduates and often exploited by campus fund-raising offices. The greater problem will be to create a rational collecting scope for alumni papers. Since it is neither possible nor desirable to solicit and acquire more than a sampling of alumni papers, the first step in their acquisition should be the careful definition of a collecting scope. Once this is done, specialized solicitation techniques, tailored to the targeted groups, will have to be developed. These might include working with specific departments to identify leading alumni whose careers merit archival documentation. It is not advisable for the archives to send a generalized solicitation letter to all alumni to request their papers. Rather, the archivist should develop a set of criteria for selecting and soliciting alumni papers based on subject-area interests (e.g., politics, business, entertainment); general prominence in their post-college career; or continued involvement in the alma mater.

To reach alumni, the archivist should work with the alumni office to obtain addresses and names of field contacts, as well as to make arrangements for participating in alumni gatherings. Useful contacts with alumni include correspondence, invitations to exhibits, general presentations to alumni meetings, and notices in the alumni newspaper. In generalized solicitations of alumni, it is advisable to focus requests on those documents covering the graduate's student days. While the repository should be careful to accession only those alumni papers of archival value and that are related to the repository's overall documentation policy, exceptions are inevitable—especially in cases of alumni with deep loyalties and ties to the institution. In fact, the alum's or institution's ulterior motives can be the greatest risk in the acquisition of alumni papers. Many archivists have been persuaded to accept a particular collection of alumni papers when university officials believe there are prospects for financial contributions to the institution, even if the funds would benefit the football team rather than the archives. While these compromises are inevitable, the problem underscores the fact that the most important elements in managing all acquisitions will be to have a carefully developed documentation policy for the archives so that the archivist can respond to such pressures systematically.

ACCESSIONING

All archives need a system to establish initial control over documents as soon as they arrive in the archives. Commonly called accessioning, this process lays the basis for most of the subsequent handling of records and manuscripts. Its primary purposes are to identify the materials, establish preliminary control, and inform the donor of receipt. Accessioning is especially useful for clarifying source and ownership and enabling the archivist to track the material before it has been arranged and described. Except for receipt of regular mailings of campus publications, accessioning is necessary for all arriving material. It is particularly important when, as so often happens, the material arrives without the benefit of formal appraisal, which would have produced a brief written description of the records and thus precluded most further work until actual processing. In reality, only a few of the records received by the academic archives will have been evaluated at their original site, and most often they arrive without notice or clear identification.

Accessioning should not only permit the archivist to identify records as they are received, but also provide enough information to facilitate the formulation of processing plans and retrieval of documents before they are fully processed. Since new acquisitions are likely to remain unprocessed for at least a few months, careful accessioning procedures are important because they will provide the only access points until the material is processed. As in so many other areas of archival practice, there is no end to the amount of information that might be collected on incoming records and manuscripts, and accessioning procedures can easily become elaborate and time consuming. Overly detailed systems are unlikely to be maintained uniformly, and the time spent on detailed accessioning would be better spent on preliminary or final processing. Therefore, it is important to develop a simple system to accession material quickly since accessioning is intended to be a provisional level of control.

The first part of accessioning is to identify the materials and determine their appropriate record group, subgroup, and record series. Second, the archivist should record summary information on dates, volume, and source. Third, the archivist should send a transmittal notice to the office of origin or conclude a deposit agreement/deed of gift with the donor of the manuscript collection.[23]

Accessioning also involves steps to establish physical control over the material, including reboxing and placement in an interim storage area. Perhaps the most important step will be a brief survey of the incoming material to locate critical preservation problems, especially insects, rodents and mildew, or large quantities of deteriorated nitrate negatives. If any such problems are found, immediate steps should be taken to ensure that the new accession will not endanger documents already held in the archives.

Appraisal and preliminary weeding also can play a role in accessioning. The archivist should scan the boxes quickly to determine if they contain notable quantities of records that fit into a general disposal policy and should not have been transferred. For example, large quantities of routine financial records, stocks of publications, or library materials often can be spotted easily. If such material can be weeded before the accession is stored, the space demands for unprocessed material will be reduced. Sometimes, the archivist may determine that the accession contains material that does not have archival value but is not yet old enough to be destroyed. Unless the archives is operating a records center, the archivist should return the material to the originating office and use the occasion to encourage better records-management practices.

Preliminary review of the materials during accessioning might also include basic arrangement and description. When it seems unlikely that the material will be processed in less than twelve months, the archivist should take the time to reestablish the original order if it has been clearly destroyed during the transfer by careless office or physical plant personnel. In addition, a preliminary box list might be prepared to establish initial control so that the contents can be accessible while awaiting processing. However, time devoted to these activities should be monitored closely because the efforts would be expended more appropriately on final processing than on creating systems that can encourage staff to countenance processing backlogs.

To facilitate accessioning, the archivist should use a simple form to record basic information on each body of materials received. Whether the form stands alone or is linked to a microcomputer database, it should include the following:[24]

Elements of an Accession Inventory Form

Essential:

> Date received
> Source
> Address of source
> Probable record group and subgroup
> Temporary title
> Brief note on content (if not apparent from title)
> Volume
> Number and type of containers
> Storage location

Useful but optional:

> Name or initials of person recording accession
> Critical needs: _____appraisal _____preservation
> _____arrangement or identification
> Date that receipt or acknowledgment was sent to source
> Is a formal deed of gift necessary?
> Related series now in archives
> Related series on records schedules

When records are received in good order from campus offices, or when a complex manuscript acquisition leaves a separate paper trail, many of these details, e.g., names and addresses, may be eliminated from this summary record. The information from such forms can be converted into a simple, automated database using commercial software. Bibliographic utilities supporting the MARC-AMC format also include the capability of tracking accessions, but given the costs of creating records for the MARC format and the fact that accessioning should be a temporary level of control, they may not offer a significant advantage. A simple local database or set of handwritten

UNIVERSITY ARCHIVES ACCESSION REGISTER

Date Received	Title of Record Series/Collection	Rec. Group Number	Physical Description	Volume	Location	Source and Notes
9-5-90	Seabaard + Blade Record Book	41/63	1 envelope	.1	UA 39-2	Anne Kennamon
7-16-90	Plant Pathology Personnel File	8/13	2 boxes	1.8	UA 40-2	J.B. Lindsey
7-24-90	Student Trustee File	1/1	4 boxes	4.0	UA 40-1	Todd Sebroff
7-25-90	Steven Hoscall Farm Records	8/4/7x	2 binders	.3	UA 39-2	William Edell
7-30-90	"Harker Years" Video	011/811	1 cassette	.2	UA 39-1	Ray Justice (U-matic tape)
8-6-90	Student Trustee File	1/1	3 boxes	3.0	UA 40-1	Todd Sebroff
8-10-90	President's Films + Videos	2/14	2 boxes	1.3	UA 39-3	Jane Konklin (5 films, 3 quad tapes)
8-29-90	Football Programs	28/5/811	1 stack	.4	UA 39-4	Sports Publicity
9-7-90	Alumni Files	26/4/1	2 envelopes	.3	UA 39-1	Beth Reinhard
9-12-90	Hockey Club Records	41/68	1 envelope	.2	UA 39-3	Hugh Peotone (restricted)

Figure 3. Accession Register

forms should meet the basic accessioning needs of most college and university archives.

To ensure proper control of accessions, much of the information listed above should be recorded in three places: on an accession register or log; on an accession or preliminary inventory sheet stored with the materials; and in a donor/accession file, arranged by office of origin or donor's name. For the first step, a sample accession register or log is shown in Figure 3.

For the second and third step, archivists can use a "Records Inventory Worksheet" similar to that used for records management work.

These traditional paper forms have great value even though they may be less sophisticated than modern relational and bibliographic databases that support multiple access points. The paper forms provide portable and readily retrievable documentation of functionally distinct aspects of accessioning. They can be very important in tracking material and avoiding embarrassing "losses" of material or information about documents or donors before the records and manuscripts are brought under full control. The most important element of an accessioning system, however, is that it be simple enough for a non-professional staff member to maintain. Assuming no additional appraisal or preservation work is needed, it should be possible to enter all the necessary information on accessions in less than five minutes for all but the most difficult materials. This simplicity is paramount because new materials frequently arrive when the search room is full of users, the telephone is ringing, and the rest of the staff is on vacation, at a meeting, or concentrating on the more critical archival functions of arrangement and description.

ARRANGEMENT

One of the most distinctive characteristics of archival work, separating it from other information disciplines, is the way it approaches the arrangement of documents. In its simplest form, the archival theory of arrangement states that documents should be arranged or ordered in a way that reflects exactly how they were held and used by the office or person creating the records. This approach is embodied in the three closely related principles of *respect des fonds,* provenance, and the sanctity of the original order. While the documentary problems faced by archivists do not always follow such neat theoretical lines, a brief explanation of each principle will provide a useful foundation for how the documentation of colleges and universities should be arranged and managed.

In the early nineteenth century, following unsuccessful attempts to impose chronological and subject classification on records, French archivists concluded that archival arrangement must not mix the records of one office with those of another office. Each deposit, or *fonds,* of records, they decided, should be respected as a separate entity, even if several *fonds* covered the same or similar subjects. In other words, *respect des fonds* requires archivists to respect the integrity of the body of records at the time it is deposited in the archives. In the late nineteenth century, German archivists refined and extended the idea of *respect des fonds* with the concept of provenance. This principle directed that each deposit of records be placed within an overall arrangement or classification scheme to reflect its origin and relation to other deposits from the same administrative body. At the same time, they emphasized the necessity of not disturbing the internal order of each body of records. This latter principle is so important to archival practice that it is often referred to as the sanctity of original order.[25]

While it is important to understand the chronological sequence of the development of these three principles, it is also appropriate to recognize that each is most relevant at a different phase of arrangement. Provenance applies most to how an overall classification scheme is established to show the relationship of one office and its records to all others within an organization. *Respect des fonds* is most usefully understood as dictating that a specific body of records not be mixed with other records from the same or other offices. Finally, "sanctity of the original order" is best seen as the principle guiding the internal arrangement of a given set of files. Understanding these distinctions is important, but there is little harm in the fact that the terms are often used interchangeably in daily practice. Their cumulative impact is that archivists do not re-arrange the material they receive to create the illusion of greater accessibility or rationality in the records because doing so would violate the integrity and meaning of the records.

A review of these principles can leave the impression that the archivist need not do much work in arrangement beyond receiving and maintaining each set of files exactly as it was held in the creating office. Were this the case, there would be little to distinguish archivists from warehouse and inventory personnel. In fact, arrangement represents one of the fundamental challenges of archival work because the principles may be straightforward, but their execution is not. First, explaining the relationship of one body of records to all others and to the overarching institution can be quite complex since organizations are living bodies undergoing constant change, and since each organization is a unique mix of mission, resources, people, and environment. Second, the evidence of a file's origins and its internal arrangement is often lost or badly muddled by the time the material arrives in the archives. This is true for many campus offices because colleges and universities frequently lack the time, interest, and personnel to maintain highly structured files and because personal papers and manuscript collections, which are generally far less organized than office records, are often an important component of the documentation of the parent institution.

Almost as important as the basic principles of arrangement is the concept of levels of arrangement, which was best articulated by Oliver W. Holmes based on experience at the National Archives.[26] While Holmes wrote strictly from the experience of a large governmental archives, his key point was that arrangement occurred at different levels in a general hierarchy of units: depository or institution, record groups, record subgroups, record series, filing units within series, and documents within filing units. The value of this approach for colleges and universities, even if they have much simpler records systems than the U.S. government, is that it provides both a way to organize an institution's records and a principle for structuring work throughout the archives. For example, a new archival program may choose to concentrate on appraisal, description, or preservation activities at the record-group level, whereas a long-established archives with modest resources might choose specific record series or filing units, for which it will prepare detailed name and subject indices.

As important as it is for academic archivists to understand the basic theories and principles of arrangement, they also should recognize that principles and practice often conflict. In addition, archivists should realize that the principles originally evolved, and will continue to evolve, from the daily experience of archivists like themselves confronting changing information technologies and the growing complexity of filing systems. Arrangement principles and practices should be understood as flexible responses to the changes in the nature of records systems and administrative information-handling practices.[27]

Regardless of evolution in theories and techniques of arrangement, the process has two key goals that dictate its centrality to archives and can thus serve as benchmarks for daily implementation. First, the arrangement system must simplify the placement of each new accession within a larger framework reflecting the relationship of the new material to previously received records. Second, arrangement should facilitate retrieval of both the bodies of records and the individual documents after they have been placed in the archives for preservation. No arrangement system alone can accomplish both these goals—their fulfillment requires descriptive systems far more elaborate than simple outlines of the arrangement sequence.

Thus, arrangement and description are inextricably linked, but the basic arrangement system should suffice for finding a proper "home" for each new accession as well as for supporting considerable information retrieval. While the following outline of arrangement refers to a few descriptive tools, its primary focus is the conceptual sequence for creating and maintaining arrangement in academic archives. Details on descriptive tools will be discussed later in this book.

Record Group and Subgroup Level

Classification Systems

Holmes's emphasis on the fact that arrangement occurs in a parallel fashion at each of his levels provides an excellent starting point for understanding how to approach arrangement. The first level of arrangement, that of the repository, has usually been established as an operating assumption of the program before the first archivist has been hired. That is, the records of the parent institution have been conceived as a single body to be placed only within its own archival repository. While academic archives sometimes also contain the records of other institutions, the archives' primary focus should be the records of the parent organization.

Within an academic archives, the first major step in arrangement will be to group all the offices likely to create records into an overall scheme designed to reflect the administrative structure of the institution. This can be accomplished most simply by creating a classification system that uses numerical notation as a shorthand to reflect the major and intermediate campus organizational units likely to generate records. With such a system, the archivist will be able to assign control numbers quickly to each accession and thereby illustrate their organizational origin.

The purpose of archival classification is to provide an efficient means of arranging (at least on paper) the records based on their source. In using the term "classification," archivists need to distinguish their practice clearly from that of librarians, who arrange books by the subject category or "class" thought to be most central to the books' contents. Both kinds of classification system are descriptive mechanisms to permit both physical and intellectual sequencing of information, but in archival classification, the emphasis is on the origin of material rather than contents.

To expedite the arrangement of archival material, it is best to create a classification system before records arrive or before beginning work on arrangement or description of any documents already in the archives. Ideally, an archival classification system would be a hierarchical scheme that structures the archives' holdings to mirror or parallel the administrative organization and reporting lines of the parent institution. Unfortunately, the accuracy of the mirror image often will blur in practice as lines of authority become crossed and functions are transferred from one reporting line to another. While archival classification is best understood as providing only a rough reflection of the complexity of the organization's structure, the model provides a solid theoretical basis for a pragmatic system to facilitate arrangement.[28]

The classification system should attempt to reflect the institution's hierarchy and chain of command but avoid the impulse to illustrate these in precise detail. In view of the various levels of authority, the varying lengths and crossings of chains of command, and the frequency of turnover in higher education, the system should be kept simple. For most institutions, the classification scheme needs to reflect only two, possibly three, levels of authority over each unit that creates records.

In most colleges and universities, a three-level system will suffice: record group, record subgroup, and record series. For extensive and complex record series, it may also be necessary to recognize a fourth and subordinate level, the record subseries. The levels can be defined as follows:[29]

• Record Group: A body of organizationally related records, normally large in size and established on the basis of provenance to accommodate the records of major organizational units and functions of an institution. In an academic archives, a separate record group will encompass the records of each major administrative unit, such as chancellor's office, colleges, and business office. A record group may also represent a synthetic collective body created by the archivist to group the records of several smaller bodies with similar functions or organizational characteristics, such as campus committees, student organizations, or nonuniversity sources of information about the university.

• Record Subgroups: Smaller bodies of organizationally related records placed within a record group to correspond to the subordinate administrative units that collectively form the record group. Subgroups can be delimited by lines of authority, function, geography, or chronology. Record subgroups are secondary units, such as academic departments, divisions of major administrative offices, and bureaus. Examples might include the Spanish department, auditing division, and married student housing.[30]

• Record Series: A systematic gathering of documents that have a common arrangement and common relationship to the functions of the office that created them. Record series are the filing units created by offices at all levels in an institutional hierarchy. Each series will be arranged internally according to a system established and modified by its creators. Boundaries between one record series and the next are sometimes razor-sharp and sometimes fuzzy. Typical record series include subject files, project files, chronological correspondence files, student advising files, faculty applicant files, financial records files, voucher files, and minutes and agenda files.

While archivists will generally agree on the names and relative order of these levels, there is great variation in which is used as a repository's primary level of control and in what constitutes a record group, subgroup, or series. This book emphasizes that the record series or office filing unit should be the primary level of control for academic archives. Futhermore, the terminology of record series is the clearest and most useful way to identify these organizationally and functionally related filing units held by offices.

A uniform classification system for all colleges and universities will not be proposed since it could not reflect adequately the complexity and diversity of their structures. Rather each archivist must play the central role in establishing the sequence of record groups, subgroups, and series that best reflects the parent institution's structure and the nature of the archival transfers. To simplify the maintenance of such a system, the archivist should start by developing a classification guide to outline distinct record groups and subgroups, along with a numbering system for each sequence.

Classification Guide

The classification guide is a fundamental tool for the administrative and intellectual control of archival holdings. It should consist of

1. A list of the names (and corresponding numbers) of all record groups for all major administrative units, whether or not records exist for these units.

2. A list of all major record subgroups within each record group to correspond to individual offices and programs generating records.

3. A numerically arranged sequence of administrative histories for each record group and all major subgroups.

4. An alphabetical index referring the user from the names of major, intermediate, and minor administrative units to the number of the corresponding record group or subgroup.

The classification guide is an important means of reflecting the institutional structure that creates the records that eventually will come to the archives. It also expresses the relationship of each record unit or series to all others. The outline of administrative structure can be built from a variety of sources, including the institution's organizational and flow charts, telephone directories, governing statutes, constitutions and bylaws, administrative handbooks, and accounting and budgetary statements.

Given the constantly changing nature of university administration, no numbering scheme or hierarchical arrangement will provide for all contingencies. The fact that the system is only an imperfect mirror should limit the archivist's worries in identifying which offices should be designated as record groups, which should be subgroups, and which should be subordinated or combined with others in a single subgroup. In a college or university, useful record groups will include trustees or board of governors; president; chief academic officer (e.g., provost); faculty senate; each of the colleges, schools, and institutes; major administrative units, such as the business office, admissions and records, student affairs, public relations, alumni office, and so on. The exact sequence of numbers assigned to each unit is not critical, and it should not attempt to follow institutional hierarchy. Instead, it can utilize logical groupings of similar units (e.g., governing officers, colleges, and services) as in the following sample list:

Record Group

0/	External Sources of Information about the University
1/	Board of Regents
2/	President's Office
3/	University Senate
4/	Campus Committees and Boards
5/	Financial and Business Affairs
6/	Provost
7/	Graduate College
8/	Public Affairs

9/	[Vacant]
10/	Chancellor or Dean of Faculties
11/	College of Art and Architecture
12/	College of Business Administration
13/	College of Communication
14/	College of Engineering
15/	College of Law
16/	College of Liberal Arts and Sciences
17/	College of Medicine
18/	School of Social Work
19/	[Vacant]
20/	Physical Plant
21/	Housing
22/	Student Union
23/	Student Affairs
24/	Student Organizations
etc.	

While the creation or deletion of major administrative units is not a frequent occurrence, there are enough changes in university structures to justify leaving gaps in the sequence to accommodate new record groups in logical places as new colleges or administrative units are created. When there are major changes in the administrative hierarchy, it is best to continue the existing record groups unless those groups later prove to be totally inadequate to handle the complexity of new records.

Once the names and numbers of record groups are determined, there should be a similar development of subgroups for the records of the subordinate units and offices that belong to each group. There should be enough similarities from record group to record group that parallel numbering schemes can be used for subgroups throughout the classification scheme. For example, the first subgroup under each college could be for the dean's office, the second through fourth for other administrative offices, and the tenth and so on for each department. Thus:

16   Liberal Arts and Sciences, College of
        16/1 Dean's Office
        16/2 Assistant dean for faculty
        16/3 Assistant dean for students
        16/4 to 16/9
              vacant—for future expansion of
              administrative offices and records
              systems (e.g., disciplinary schools,
              recruitment, development, public
              programs)
        16/11 Anthropology
        16/12 Biology
        16/13 Chemistry
        etc.

Since the nature of university administration will vary
from large units to small and from administrative offices
to academic programs, there can be no single model for
subgroup numbers. The archivist should avoid attempts
at overly precise systems and instead look for convenient
schemes, or rules of thumb, to simplify the maintenance
of a classification and arrangement system. Unless staff
resources are unlimited or the institution's structure
ceases to evolve, elaborate and precise systems will be
impossible to maintain.[31]

Administrative Histories

More important than detailed numbering schemes for
the classification guide will be administrative histories to
provide organizational background on the campus units
designated as record groups and subgroups. These administrative histories, normally about one-half to one page in
length, should be prepared for each unit that is likely to
create records. The purpose of including administrative
histories in the classification guide is to define the function
of each unit/record group and office/subgroup, and note its
date of creation, authorizing documents, subordinate
units, and major changes in purpose, reporting lines, and
programmatic functions. Its purpose is not interpretative,
and it should avoid attempts to assess the significance of

the office or sift through various explanations of how it evolved. Rather, its purpose is to provide background on the administrative structure and scope of authority and responsibility of offices so that the archivist can place accessions appropriately.

For major units/record groups such as colleges or key administrative offices, one single-spaced page may be appropriate. For offices/subgroups, a half a page may suffice. In all cases, footnotes should be used liberally to provide careful citations to sources of information on founding, dates, and changes in name and mission. The footnotes can also contain references to additional sources of information, and notes on related record groups and subgroups, as needed with departmental mergers or separations. With the frequent changes in administrative structure, these histories can be a highly efficient means to keep the classification system and guide current, but since it is not possible to keep all administrative histories up to date, it is useful to note the date of the last revision at the end of each history.

The following sample administrative history for a large academic department at the University of Illinois illustrates many features of a model entry in a classification guide:

13/ College of Communications (Record Group)

13/3 Department of Journalism (Record Subgroup)

The University began instruction in journalism in 1902 with a course in business writing offered under the English Department's program in rhetoric and oratory.[1] In 1915, the Trustees provided funds for a Department of Journalism and in 1927 it became a separate administrative unit, the School of Journalism.[2] In 1950, its name was changed to the School of Journalism and Communications, with divisions of journalism, radio, and advertising,[3] and it became part of the Division of Communications.[4] In 1954, it was restored to independent status.[5] The School was given College status in

1957.[6] In 1959, its three divisions were designated as departments.[7] The Department of Journalism offers a two-year undergraduate major in the fields of newspaper, magazine and technical writing and editing; community journalism and news broadcasting,[8] and a two-year Masters of Science program.[9]

1. *Catalogs and Registers, 1902-03,* p. 274.

2. *Board of Trustees Transactions, 28th Report,* September 27, 1915, p. 830; 34th Report, July 14, 1927, pp. 416-17.

3. *Board of Trustees Transactions, 45th Report,* February 16, 1950, p. 992.

4. Ibid., p. 988.

5. *Board of Trustees Transactions, 47th Report,* April 21, 1954, pp. 1322-23.

6. *Board of Trustees Transactions, 49th Report,* June 20, 1957, p. 435.

7. *Board of Trustees Transactions, 50th Report,* February 19, 1959, p. 301.

8. *Undergraduate Study Catalog, 1960-61,* p. 229. *Undergraduate Programs, 1985-87,* pp. 155-156.

9. *Graduate Programs, 1984-86,* pp. 122-123.

updated 1/15/87

The overall classification system, including the administrative histories, will serve a dual purpose. First, it facilitates basic tasks of archival administration, including appraisal, arrangement, and description of incoming records. Second, because administrative histories contain historical information, they can function as a reference tool that sometimes answers a researcher's questions without requiring further searches.

Limits of Provenance-based Classification Systems

Archivists are not always comfortable with provenance-based classification systems and guides. They frequently become frustrated with using different classifications for a given institutional function (e.g., foreign-student financial aid) as it is moved from one administrative unit (e.g., Student Affairs) to a second (e.g., International Programs) and often to a third (e.g., Registrar), all within a twenty-year period. Equally problematic is the common academic practice of shared responsibility for programs, such as the interdisciplinary centers created by naming faculty from four different departments, establishing two dozen cross-listed courses, and hiring one secretary to handle the center's business and files. Then the archivist is faced with such difficulties as appropriate classification of related records from different offices and the possibility that the classification scheme will never be accurate unless it is highly detailed and constantly revised.

The archivist should remember, however, that a major goal of provenance-based classification is simplicity to permit rapid classification and arrangement of filing units. It is not intended as a definitive or comprehensive description and retrieval system. Thus, when faced with the records of the above-mentioned center, the archivist needs to make a quick choice and assign the documents to a single place in the system based on logical criteria, such as placing the center's files with those of the department of its first director. If the center is a major unit with many records, the archivist may create a new subgroup within the record group that most nearly approximates its parent. Most importantly, the archivist should manipulate the classification system with the realization that it will never be perfect or exact, and that other descriptive access mechanisms, such as indices, can be used to note the functional connections of related records.

Contributors to recent archival literature have argued that problems like these suggest that provenance-oriented classification is obsolete and should be replaced with new technology and archival theory.[32] One possibility is to rely on certain fields in the MARC format for Archives and Manuscripts (MARC-AMC) to index the layers of administrative origin as well as the records' links to other records from the institution.[33] With appropriate programming and application development, the hierarchy of each record series and its relationship to other bodies of records can be displayed. This use of the MARC format has great promise as an aid in reference service for archives lacking adequate arrangement and indexing systems. Nevertheless, the access points provided by the MARC format cannot substitute for the ability of a provenance-based classification system to outline organizational structure and rapidly illustrate relationships of records. Furthermore, the first step will still need to be the development of a conceptual arrangement of records and records creators so that the automated system can be taught which links to illustrate. Unless one starts with a structured and controlled classification system, reliance on such descriptive tools to answer provenance questions can give the impression that each accession is an isolated body of information, which would hinder analysis of records in relation to the structure that created them.

There are practical advantages to provenance-based classification systems that should also be considered. They allow the construction and use of identification numbers for each record series that illustrate, albeit only in broad strokes, the origins and relationships of each accession. Because such numbers can carry far more meaning than control numbers based solely on date or sequence of receipt, they are enormously useful in many administrative tasks, such as filing and retrieving acquisitions correspondence, recording use of records, tracking documents charged out for exhibits, or expediting a researcher's bibliographic citations. Thus, there is a broad value to the conventional three- or four-level classification guide, with administrative histories explaining how the levels interact and how the classification system's outline of structure differs from reality.

Record Series Level

The arrangement system and classification guide for record groups and subgroups focuses on identification of the institutional units that create records, rather than on actual arrangement of any given body of records. This latter function will occur at the next lower level in the structure—the record series, which is the most basic element in archival arrangement. As each accession is examined, it should not be difficult to identify its office of origin, thereby establishing its provenance in order to assign it to the proper record group and subgroup. Further examination will be needed to identify each distinct record series, since a given transfer of records could include several record series. This work can require considerable skill and experience since one transfer could be a single new series, several new series, or an addition to one or more record series already in the archives. Often, identification will not be possible until the records have been examined and described at the folder level.

Once a series has been identified and given a tentative title, the archivist will need to assign an appropriate number to place it in the classification system. To reflect the three levels of arrangement recommended for use by academic archives, the number would have three parts, or fields. The first two fields would represent the record group and subgroup, and the third would be used to create a unique number for the record series. For example, a new accession is found to be a subject file from the physics department, a unit of the College of Engineering. A number of 14/11/1 is chosen to reflect its place in the structure of institutional records: College of Engineering (Record Group 14), Department of Physics (Subgroup 11), the first series of records received from that department. The number for the specific series (the third field) could be either serial (with numbers assigned successively as materials arrive) or relational (with certain numbers reserved for certain common types of files, such as "1's" for subject files, "6's" for budget files, "4's" for personnel files, and "42's" for examination questions). For example:

14/ College of Engineering
    14/11 Department of Physics
        14/11/1 Subject File
        14/11/6 Budget File
        14/11/8 Particle Accelerator Laboratory Records

14/11/25 Physics Alumni Files
14/11/42 Physics 108 Examination Questions
14/11/100 to 299
    Personal Papers of Physics Faculty and Staff
14/11/300 to 14/11/499
    Physics-related manuscript collections from
    nonuniversity sources
14/11/500-14/11/799 [Vacant]
14/11/800-14/11/999
    Publications, e.g., 14/11/801 Newsletters;
    14/11/802 Brochures and Announcements;
    14/11/820 Particle Accelerator Research
    Reports, E-Series; 14/11/825 NSF Contract
    Reports

This scheme has the advantage of articulating some of the functional relationships and similarities between record series, and it can be used as a model for the creation of record series within subgroups for offices throughout the institution. While it is preferred to one which would assign the series number solely on the basis of when it was received, it must be used flexibly since some departments will generate substantially more complex records requiring more series than others.

In view of the principle of *respect des fonds,* the archivist should not attempt to divide or merge incoming records that were organically related during their active use merely to fit a pre-arranged classification scheme. It is, however, appropriate for the archivist to examine each accession and determine if it should be the first installment of a new record series, an addition to one or more existing series, a group of several record series that must be subdivided, or some combination of these.

Arrangement Within Series

Once the archivist has identified a record series and its place in the overall classification scheme, attention can turn to the arrangement of documents within the series. There has been considerable discussion of work at this level in institutional processing manuals as well as in David B. Gracy's manual on arrangement and description. The following discussion focuses on the theoretical basis for arrangement at the series level and provides practical suggestions for fitting this work into the resources of a college and university archives.

The fundamental principle in the arrangement of documents within record series is respect for the sanctity of the original order. At the series level, in particular, great efforts should be taken to maintain the documents in the same order as that in which they were generated and used by the creating office or person. This principle is based on both theoretical and practical considerations. First, rearrangement of the documents into any other sequence destroys the evidential characteristics of the file and hinders examination of contextual and relational issues. Second, rearrangement to create a supposedly more usable order is often presumptuous and short-sighted and ultimately can be an endless task as later groups of users approach old records with new questions.

While the principle of original order is a fundamental archival concept that should guide everyday practice, questions of arrangement at the series level are not always cast in such clear-cut terms. Often, it can be difficult to determine the original order of a file, since the order at the time of transfer can reflect the disarrangement of documents as files were moved from active use to inactive filing cabinets, then to boxes in storage closets, and eventually to the archives. In other cases, files from small offices without strong clerical staff often reflect unsystematic and nearly unusable arrangement schemes. In these cases, the archivist must make a careful assessment of the file to decide whether to reconstruct the original order or to devise an arrangement scheme that facilitates access. These schemes are best if based on simple arrangement sequences, such as chronologically or alphabetically by folder title.

A useful device for arrangement within complex record series is to create subseries that group documents according to distinct functions or activities of the originating office. Subseries may be unnecessary in small record series and even in large series with simple arrangement schemes (such as alphabetical subject files), but they can be most valuable when dealing with complex filing systems that were created and maintained by a large clerical staff. If subseries are necessary, their summary descriptions are best kept to one or two paragraphs. Numbering of subseries should be avoided, but if it is necessary, the numbers should not be included in the classification guide or in the access system used to describe all archival holdings at the record series level. Attempts to develop an access system that uses subseries numbers for some, but not all, record series can give the impression of arbitrariness and will be particularly frustrating if the archives tries to automate access. Computers do not welcome such inconsistencies because they often represent logical inconsistencies and "jumps" of human judgment that can be automated only by the use of complex rules.

The record series is a flexible unit to which additional material can be added from later transfers. When each new accession is examined, the archivist should determine if it is a new record series or an addition to an existing series by considering whether the new accession is from the same or a successor unit; whether it contains similar types of documents covering similar subjects; and most importantly, whether the documents it contains have the same functional relationship to the activities of the office as did the original record series. In adding new accessions to old series, the archivist must find a middle ground between diluting the concept of the record series by merging unrelated material, and fragmenting the documentation of the institution by creating a new series for nearly every accession.

Box- and Folder-Level Arrangement

A major component of arrangement occurs when the archivist determines the proper sequence, generally of folders, within each series. The principle of the sanctity of the original order dictates that the sequence created by the originating office should be maintained, but the archivist must analyze the records to see if this order has been disturbed and if not, whether it is adequate for administrative and research purposes. Even if files appear to be in good and accessible order, the archivist still needs to analyze the accuracy, completeness, and consistency of the folder titles. Thus, if the processor locates similar files under both "Family Housing" and "Married Student Housing," a decision should be made about which is the more appropriate heading, and the other folder should be moved. It may also be necessary to merge folders where the present distinctions are purely arbitrary and when the merging would reduce supply costs or facilitate access (e.g., merging folders for "Associate Professor Inquiries, A-E" and "Associate Professor Inquiries, M-Z" into one folder, or merging thin folders for "Construction Plans 1965-66" with "Construction Plans 1966-67"). While this and other modifications of the sequence of folders can be made, the sanctity of the order of documents within folders should be regarded as absolute and should not be altered, except to correct obvious filing errors or create order when all traces of original order have disappeared. In all work at the folder level, the archivist should balance the labor involved against supply costs, staff time, and ease of access.[34]

A question that arises when adding to existing series is whether to interfile the new folders with the old. For example, should the 1970-75 alphabetical subject file of the Dean of Art and Architecture be interfiled with the existing files covering 1928-69? In most cases, such interfiling should be avoided since it is labor-intensive, requires considerable reboxing, and can destroy evidence of filing systems that may have significance for the informational content of the files. Moreover, research access to all boxes with folders of a given title (e.g., Art and Design Curriculum) can be simplified by creating an index to the container list. In the case of biographical files, such as alumni and personnel files, with long-term research value and likely frequent retrievals, periodic mergers of all alphabetical sequences are appropriate. These mergers will be most beneficial where the office's filing is dependent solely on accidental characteristics (e.g., filing alphabetically by proper name of correspondent) rather than on discretionary language (e.g., filing documents on residence halls under "Student Housing" because that is the office's preferred term).

Practical Considerations

Those seeking to link broad principles of arrangement with detailed flow charts and guidelines for work on documents will find a large gap between theory and practice. Certainly long lists of instructions and examples could be developed, but such guidelines will have little practical value because of variations in the nature of the records, resources, and institutional practice. No set of instructions can substitute for the archivist's own professional expertise in interpreting archival principles in practice. The best archivists will be those able to make case-by-case decisions that vary the amount of work in proportion to the value of the material. Thus, one returns to the fact that appraisal is the fundamental archival function that underlies all others.

A second practical difficulty arises from the tendency to discuss arrangement theoretically, in a top-to-bottom sequence, as in this manual. In actual practice, however, problems of arrangement are addressed in varying sequences. In many cases, larger arrangement questions can be answered only by moving directly to work at the series level. For example, a new accession may be determined to be a distinct series but of uncertain provenance. In such a case, it should be processed, folder by folder, with only those modifications in the sequence of folders that are consistent with the apparent original order. Then, following preparation of a summary record series description, the proper record group and subgroup should be discernible so that the archivist can determine the series' final place in the classification system. Given the limited time available, the focus of the academic archivist should be on the establishment of a general structure that permits the expeditious arrangement of new accessions and relies on the archives' descriptive systems to resolve anomalies in provenance.

Manuscript Collections

The preceding principles and procedures should provide considerable practical direction in handling official institutional records—the core responsibility of the academic archivist. Once these basic arrangement issues have been addressed, the archivist can move on to considering the arrangement of the manuscript collections that so often are an integral part of an academic archives' mission.

Arrangement of manuscripts can provide greater challenges because manuscript collections often represent the gathering of documents based on their relation to a person or subject, rather than on their relation to a function or purpose assigned to an office. The contrast is particularly striking when one compares the condition of an accession of archival records from a well-staffed campus office with the condition of a deposit of personal papers from a long-term faculty member, documenting a diverse career and having been maintained without clerical assistance. With such personal papers or manuscript collections, the archivist may need to go beyond the simple archival dictum of maintaining the original order.

Arrangement practices within manuscript collections often need to be quite complex and vary from collection to collection. The academic archivist should attempt to apply many of the general principles outlined for archival records. This is sometimes as simple as recreating the original order or establishing a logical sequence of folders to organize the material in a way that would have been efficient for the creators of the documents if they had only taken the time to do so. For modern manuscript collections, this archival approach has a great deal of merit because it can greatly reduce the time required to make collections accessible, compared to practices followed for pre-twentieth-century manuscripts.

The archivist can find considerable guidance in the literature on arrangement of manuscripts, but the many recommendations should be assessed carefully.[35] Unfortunately, manuscript practice has often focused on meticulous definitions of narrow subject areas, which lead to the fragmentation of information within collections by dividing documents into an excessive number of artificial series or subseries created by the curator. Because there are important conceptual differences between archives and manuscripts, the archivist must recognize that arrangement schemes designed for archival records are not necessarily appropriate for manuscripts.

An important problem for academic archivists is how to integrate manuscript collections into the overall arrangement system of the archives. For example, should the collections' control numbers be based on origin, subject, or date of receipt? One way to answer this question is to consider four broad categories of manuscript collections commonly found in university archives. These categories are:

1. University-related collections of personal papers and records of faculty and student organizations.

2. Papers unrelated to the institution but emanating from its faculty, students, or alumni.

3. Personal papers of individuals with no connection to the institution.

4. Records of outside organizations.

Given the frequency with which faculty and staff papers contain documents on institutional policy and development, they should be classified or arranged according to provenance. Thus, a physics professor's papers should be placed in the record group and subgroup for physics department records. To differentiate between such papers and the official publications and records for that department, the archivist might reserve certain sets of series numbers in each record group for such collections. Student and alumni papers can be placed in record groups or subgroups specially designed for these purposes because these papers do not emanate from any single department already reflected in the classification system.[36]

Because academic archives frequently acquire personal papers and manuscript collections with little or no organizational connection to the institution (e.g., political papers, business records, association archives, and local history collections), additional arrangement questions are raised. It is not necessary, from the standpoint of intellectual control, to place these within the archives' overall classification system, but there is a need for a notational system to facilitate physical and indexing control. Such collections could be numbered successively "MSS 1," "MSS 2," and onward, but a multilevel numbering scheme parallel to, or part of, that used for institutional records could also be used. Thus, all nonuniversity manuscript collections might be given a "record group" number of "99/," and subgroup fields could be used to reflect broad subject or collecting areas, such as "99/1" for professional organizations, "99/2" local history, and "99/3" business records. More precise definitions of subject areas are likely to be unproductive because most manuscript collections will document several subjects. Moreover, such subject classifications should be used sparingly and only for those collections that have no clear connection to units reflected in the institutional classification system. Otherwise, they can create the temptation to divide material by subject regardless of provenance. The archivist should recognize that such a numbering system is synthetic, intended more for administrative and physical control than subject access. More important for access will be the development of a thorough description system with appropriate indexing to provide leads to collections wherever they are placed.[37]

This account of arrangement can easily give the impression that the process is an elaborate task that occupies a large and distinct block of the archivist's time on a daily basis. Arrangement is an integral part of archival operations, but once the archives has established an overall arrangement scheme and rules and procedures for placing newly processed accessions into that scheme, the system should be quite simple to maintain. Daily attention to arrangement will focus on identification of the creators of records received and the assignment of proper record groups and subgroups based on the overall classification system. In practice, archivists will find that the majority of their time spent on arrangement work will be in the processing of individual record series and manuscript collections and that this work will be integrated closely with the description of holdings. Thus, the principles of arrangement are important theoretical constructs that help organize how archivists go about their work, but they are only one element in the battery of tools archivists use to establish control over, and access to, the documentary record of their institutions.

DESCRIPTION

Principles of Archival Description

Of the three great archival functions—appraisal, arrangement, and description—description is the least dictated by theory and the least likely to determine how other archival activities are conducted. Still, description is the function most able to address the problems left unanswered by other archival practices. To the users of an archives, description is often the most visible and possibly the most important archival activity. While archivists have recognized the importance of description, failing to recognize the limits within which it must be applied will lead to excessively lavish descriptive tools. In fact, because it can absorb so many program resources, the efficient management of description is critical to the success of academic archives, and it will be essential to recognize the distinction between the archivist's role and the researcher's responsibilities.

As with arrangement, library science has developed its own approach to analogous, but essentially different, problems. Understanding the serviceability of library cataloging for library material can be a useful starting point for understanding archival description. The archivist should not, however, attempt to replicate the functions of library-based cataloging systems because librarians focus on single or discrete items and create very brief descriptions in preordained formats. In addition, because of the frequent institutional proximity of academic archives to libraries, the archivist must understand that a descriptive system should be based on archival theory, needs, resources, and goals. The following discussion should help in that process by outlining the basic elements of the descriptive systems required in an academic archives.

Description is commonly done in conjunction with arrangement as part of what is called processing. Logically, description follows arrangement work, but it can be conducted simultaneously to create the finding aids needed to overcome access problems posed by the original order of records and manuscripts. The purpose of description is to provide a structured but flexible language that establishes intellectual and administrative control over archival and manuscript holdings, thereby facilitating research and administrative access to this material. The underlying principle should be that it is an access and control system, not an exercise in the interpretation of historical documents. Thus, archival finding aids should guard against the strong temptation to place narrative text into descriptions. Instead, they should focus on summarizing briefly and listing accurately the content of collections, with a minimum of analysis and evaluation. To do otherwise moves the archivist from the role of custodian and facilitator of research to that of interpolator between the documents and the researcher. Interpretation and analysis may be satisfying to archivists who come from an historical research background, but it is a misuse of valuable resources and, worse, a nuisance, if not a disservice, to researchers. Wherever possible, descriptive work should be limited to summary statements of content coupled with appropriate container lists.

The most efficient way to establish this descriptive control over holdings is to employ different tools at different levels. While it is theoretically possible to devise a single tool to describe all materials at all levels, in practice the archivist will find that such systems are very complex and eventually will fail as certain kinds of collections or records require specialized and nonstandard finding aids to deal with the specialized material they contain. Nevertheless, it is both possible and appropriate for the archivist to aim at a standardization of format and scope at any given level of description.

In an academic archives, the most useful tools for description are the classification guide with administrative histories (at the record group and subgroup level); summary descriptions in the catalog or primary finding aid (at the record series and manuscript collection level); detailed finding aids and container listings (within record series and manuscript collections); and specialized indices and finding aids to meet research needs identified through analysis of use. Because these tools have been fully explained elsewhere in the archival literature, this book will focus on how each tool can be related to the others to create a balanced and workable system.[38]

Classification Guide

As a descriptive tool, the classification guide's key function is to outline the record groups and subgroups used to establish the overall scheme in which the archival holdings are arranged. The classification guide provides a model of the hierarchy and relationships of university functions and records, even though such models sometimes break down when examined in detail. As noted previously, the guide can stand alone as a descriptive tool that provides an outline of the institution's pattern of administration and documentation while functioning as a resource for research. Parts of the classification guide, especially administrative histories, can be photocopied and placed in the detailed finding aids or container lists for individual record series. The judicious archivist, however, will assiduously adhere to size limits because more detailed and interpretative histories are the responsibility of the archives' users, not its staff.

The Catalog or Primary Finding Aid

The most important descriptive tool will be a catalog arranged by provenance and containing a summary description of each record series and manuscript collection held by the repository. These descriptions are the primary finding aids because they represent a uniform level of description for all archival holdings regardless of the size and complexity of each series or collection. Efficiency in developing the catalog of primary finding aids is most important, but flexibility must be maintained. Some repositories find that a manual card (5" x 8") or binder system is adequate and most manageable, others find that local applications of commercial textbase or database systems work best, and still others have the resources to take advantage of a system based on the MARC Archives and Manuscripts Control (MARC-AMC) format operating on a bibliographic utility. More important than the specific system chosen, however, will be rigorous consistency in its use. Finally, regardless of system, a key element in preparing entries for the primary finding aids will be the recognition that archival description is an art rather than a technical process of applying rules and completing fields in catalog records. Clear communication should be its paramount goal, and discipline over the urge toward detail should be a central operating principle.

The catalog of primary finding aids will be most effective and efficient if it contains a fixed number of fields (i.e., discrete categories of information) and if the total length of the catalog entry is limited to a manageable size that can be skimmed quickly by users. Whether this catalog is maintained and searched in machine-readable or hard-copy form, or both, the basic categories of information are the same for all primary finding aids: name and number of record group and subgroup, title of record series or manuscript collection, inclusive dates, physical volume, notes on availability of more detailed finding aids, physical location, access restrictions, dates acquired, and a summary narrative description.

These data elements should be quite short except the narrative description, which must vary in length from series to series and collection to collection. For small and simple series of office records or publications, it may be no more than a few lines long. For larger series, it will need to note the names of the principal records creators, their titles and dates of responsibility for the functions documented in the materials, the chief functions, the records covered, physical types of documents, major correspondents, and important subjects covered.

The following example of a primary finding aid from the University of Illinois at Urbana-Champaign illustrates how these features are developed to provide a summary description of a record series:

15/1/35 Associate & Assistant Deans Subject File, 1948-72
[Record Series number and title]

Record Group: Liberal Arts & Sciences
Subgroup: Dean's Office

Assistant Dean's Subject File including correspondence, memoranda, agenda, minutes, and reports regarding admissions (1959-71), advance enrollment (1962-71), affirmative action, assistant and associate deans (1962-71), budgets, committees, building programs, courses & curricula (1957-70), registration (1960-69), SEOP (1968-70), space utilization, summer sessions (1958-71), teacher education (1956-65), and other functions of the Dean's Office, including Foreign Language Building construction and planning (1966-70), space requests and assignments (1957-69), and the committee on motorcycle safety (1966-68). Principal correspondents include assistant deans F. J. Koenig (1948-65) and Roger E. Martin (1965-69) & associate deans Bruce Harkness (1964-66) and Robert A. Waller (1967-72).

(11 page unpublished finding aid in the Archives)

Volume: 17.3 cubic feet
Dates received: 8/1/78; 7/1/85

A half-size sheet, 5" x 8" card, or the equivalent of one or two 80-column by 26-line computer screens should suffice for each series or collection. Strict limits on the size of primary finding aids are important because they permit the efficient management of resources for description. Without such yardsticks, control over time for description can be lost quickly, and the result will be both uneven finding aids and backlogs of unprocessed material. Some archivists and manuscript curators may argue that such size limits are insensitive to the unique descriptive requirements of each record series or collection, if not also antediluvian because of the opportunities offered by computer-based systems to handle records of varying length. Admittedly, a small series of institutional publications or office records will not need so much description as a collection of faculty papers documenting a 35-year career in teaching, research, and university and professional service. In the latter case, additional narrative and analytical descriptions will be necessary. However, the vast majority of archival record series, and most manuscript collections in academic archives, can be made quite accessible with very brief primary finding aids. In the few cases where greater description is necessary, it can be incorporated into the introduction to the detailed finding aid.

Detailed Finding Aids and Container Lists

The primary finding aids, prepared for all series and collections, provide a uniform level and format of description and will suffice for many modern record series and manuscript collections, especially those smaller than one cubic foot. More detailed finding aids, however, play a crucial role in describing the holdings of academic archives, especially for series and collections larger than one cubic foot. The most common of such finding aids is the container list, which provides an inventory of the entire series or collection, generally at the level of box and folder title. It is often useful for the container list to include background information, such as provenance notes, detailed administrative history of the parent office, biographical information, or summary descriptions of subseries and any other information needed to understand the documentation.[39]

To facilitate research use, a photocopy of the primary finding aid or the complete MARC-AMC record for the series should be a prominent part of the detailed finding aid. This should be followed by brief notes on the arrangement of documents within the series or collection if that is not readily apparent from the container list. The largest sections of these detailed finding aids, however, will be inventory-like lists, generally at the level of folder titles. Only rarely will it be desirable to list more than the title and dates of each folder.[40] For personnel and other case files, the container list often need not go beyond identifying the first and last folder in each box. Thus, the overall principle is that detailed finding aids are intended to provide generalized administrative and intellectual control of records and manuscripts, normally at the folder level; more detailed description should be avoided in all but the most complex and demanding circumstances.

Specialized Indices and Finding Aids

In addition to tools that describe each series or collection independent of the rest of the archives' holdings, many repositories develop specialized finding aids and indices to facilitate access to material on related subjects. The most common special finding aids are repository-wide subject indices that guide researchers to the titles and series or collection numbers of all holdings related to a given subject. These can be derived from MARC-AMC cataloging records through subject access points in bibliographic databases. They can also be developed locally using commercial computer software or a manual card-index system. Regardless of approach, the most challenging aspect of such subject indices is the development of a thesaurus of subject terms. Development of thesauri and indices are complex tasks beyond the scope of this book, but academic archivists will find such descriptive tools invaluable to reference work.[41]

Repository-wide subject indices can provide good summary access for an encyclopedic array of topics, but often the strengths of an archives' holdings, as well as user demands for specific research areas, require other specialized and detailed indices to groups of series or collections. These might include a consolidated index to literary or presidential manuscripts; a guide or index to biographical information in several series of student and alumni case files from different administrative units; guides to specific subjects (e.g., cultural anthropology, urban politics, civil rights) documented in several series and collections; and listings of motion pictures or architectural records in series from several campus offices. The development of these specialized finding aids should follow assessments of repository strengths, researchers' needs, and use patterns rather than any predetermined theories of archival description. The nature of the records may readily suggest a consolidated finding aid, for example, to simplify access to information in a file of student organization constitutions and a file of student organization publications. In most cases, however, specialized finding aids should wait until use patterns demonstrate the need for the tool.

Administrative Guidelines for Description

Through the exercise of professional expertise, the archivist will determine which descriptive tools are most appropriate for each record series or manuscript collection and thereby ensure the efficient use of program resources. These decisions should utilize appraisal criteria to establish the appropriate level of description, its length and detail at that level, and the circumstances in which the level of description can be varied to meet the needs of the documents and users. Generally speaking, less is better, with most material described in fixed-length summary finding aids followed by folder-title lists for those series larger than one cubic foot. Fortunately, refinements can be added later, if the initial level of description proves to be inadequate. A flexible approach that alters description to meet the research needs and historical value of documents is what distinguishes archival practice from the more rigid and formalistic methods of librarians.

Traditionally, there has been a great deal of variation in the format of descriptive approaches from one institution to the next. The resultant variety of tools for description has made exchanges of information about archival and manuscript holdings cumbersome. A recent development, which provides a basis for standardization of archival description, is the creation of a MARC format for manuscripts and archives. Like other MARC formats developed by the Library of Congress, the MARC-AMC format consists of a standard sequence of fields and subfields to describe different aspects (e.g., date, language, author, and title) of units of information (e.g., books, films, newspapers, or manuscript collections) in a regular fashion. This regularity facilitates the automated control of the resultant description. Since the format divides description into segments and requires standard forms for entering such information as names, subjects, and dates, interinstitutional exchange of data can be supported by use of computer networks.[42]

Availability of the MARC-AMC format and the supporting computer software can be seen as revolutionizing archival and manuscript descriptive practice, but the academic archivist's decision on how to use them should be made in the context of maintaining balance of all program resources. While the MARC-AMC format can be used for any and all levels of description (from an item to an entire repository), the academic archivist will find it most manageable when used at the series (archival records) or collection (manuscripts) level. Cataloging entries prepared in the MARC-AMC format and loaded into a network such as OCLC or RLIN or a microcomputer application such as MicroMARC:amc or Minaret can provide better subject and name access than that permitted by the traditional manual finding aids at the series or collection level. Nevertheless, one must also consider the substantial time required to catalog according to standardized rules so that the MARC-AMC records will be acceptable to network or software guidelines.[43] In addition, the MARC-AMC format can be more cumbersome in displaying hierarchical informational and organizational relationships that are well handled by conventional archival record group, subgroup, and series classification systems and by commercial relational database programs such as dBase or R:Base.

This is not to deny the great value of the MARC format; rather, the archivist needs to choose carefully how the format is used. It should supplement but not replace the traditional archival descriptive tools—classification guide, administrative histories, primary finding aids, container lists, and registers. Academic archives with limited resources may find it functions best as a rear-end technology—that is, as a supplement prepared after collections and records have been described via conventional mechanisms.

Decision on use of the MARC format should be determined by balancing the value of the collections and record series against the resources available. Repositories with inexpensive access to utilities or software and sufficient staff to prepare MARC records for all holdings should rely on those records for their primary finding aids. At other institutions, without these resources or where allocation of staff resources to cataloging might aggravate processing backlogs, archivists may need to limit their use of the MARC format to the most important collections that need to be reported to national bibliographic databases. As in so much other archival work, the key will be appraisal—appraisal of each new accession to determine whether it merits full cataloging and MARC tagging as well as appraisal of the overall information needs and resources of the repository. This conservative approach is based on a concern that the academic archivist needs to be holistic, keeping all resources in balance lest processing, reference service, or preservation suffer.

Manuscripts Description

This discussion of description has not hitherto distinguished between archival records and manuscript collections because archives and manuscripts need to be considered together as parts of the larger entity of institutional documentation and because many archival descriptive practices are directly usable for manuscripts. Thus, the archives' overall arrangement and description systems should group both archival and closely related manuscript holdings into a single catalog or primary finding aid. This system should operate at the common level of record series or manuscript collection so that a single file of primary finding aids can show the broad relationships of all archival record series and manuscript collections.

However, given the subject diversity, organizational characteristics, and provenance of many manuscript collections, both primary and detailed finding aids may need to be more complex than those for archival record series. In addition to the box and folder lists that generally suffice for archival records, the detailed finding aids for manuscript collections may need to include scope and content note; biographical note or career chronology; brief administrative history, if the collection concerns a nonuniversity organization; and provenance note explaining how the collection came to exist and was acquired by the university archives. Since many manuscript collections may be divided into subseries, brief descriptions of the scope and content of each subseries may be useful additions to the manuscript finding aid. Kenneth Duckett, David B. Gracy, and Richard Berner have covered the intricacies of manuscript finding aids quite thoroughly, although some discretion will be needed to adapt their models to what is realistic for available resources and for collections with lower research value.[44]

In working with finding aids for manuscripts, the archivist needs to be particularly careful that the description does not become overly interpretative. This is a particular danger when archivists trained in history or another subject specialty encounter records and manuscripts that provide many interesting research possibilities. Controlling the length of description can be difficult. Finding aids may need to reflect judgments about the relative strengths of an accession, but evaluative comments should be kept to the minimum necessary to inform the researcher of the kinds of documents in the accession and the subjects that are well represented. Too many finding aids attempt to interpret the organization's history or the person's life for the researcher. Instead, a simple description of the scope of the records, a physical inventory of the filing units, and a brief chronology will often be of greater help to the researcher and far less expensive to prepare. The finding aid's purpose is only to serve as a guide and access tool.

In addition to the previously mentioned descriptive devices, the academic archivist needs to consider a number of specialized tools to make information on holdings broadly available. An important responsibility will be reporting information on collections of broad research significance to national databases, especially the *National Union Catalog of Manuscript Collections* (NUCMC) published by the Manuscripts Division of the Library of Congress and now being prepared for entry into the RLIN database. Repositories using the MARC format through the bibliographic utilities may assume that entry of their cataloging data into the OCLC or RLIN databases will promote the national accessibility of information on holdings, but the limited use and availability of these databases means that other national access points, such as NUCMC and subject-area surveys and guides, are still of value. A recently developed national access tool is Chadwyck-Healey's *National Inventory of Documentary Sources: Part IV—College and University Archives* (Alexandria, Va., 1984), a microfiche edition of finding aids from repositories throughout the United States accompanied by a hard-copy index.

National reporting of information on holdings is an important activity, but the archivist should avoid rewriting finding aids or creating new ones for such reports. Instead, useful reports to national access tools can and should be compiled from the existing descriptive tools, especially the primary finding aids. The work involved in description is simply too great to justify extensive reworking for each new reporting place.

Another descriptive tool that can be useful in academic archives is a published repository guide to describe the entire contents of the archives, generally at the record series or collection level. Given the dynamics of new accessions, however, printed guides can become outdated quickly. If the guide is created and stored in a machine-readable form (e.g., via word processing or database software), it can be updated and reprinted at regular intervals or when existing supplies are depleted. An analogous tool is the in-house subject and name index noted earlier. While the temptation to produce a subject index or guide to aid in reference service early in an archival program may be strong, it should be resisted. Such guides and indices become practical and necessary only when a critical mass of records has been accessioned and several years of reference service have suggested the range of research possible from the archives' holdings.[45]

To ensure efficient use of resources, the system of descriptive tools employed should emerge from careful management choices. The decisive factors should be the significance of the materials, the access offered by their existing arrangement, their current and potential future use, and the share of the repository's overall resources that can be devoted to description. All the descriptive tools should have common elements but flexibility in response to the needs of each collection or series is fundamental to all archival practice. Often as important as guidelines for uniformity in descriptive practice will be sound judgments on how the descriptive needs of each accession can be balanced with all other archival needs.

PRESERVATION

Preservation is one of the broadest goals of archival theory and practice, although it is often perceived as a narrow and specialized component of archival work. It is an all-encompassing concern because the underlying purpose of archives is the preservation of documents for the future, and it needs to be a central focus of archival activity because of the impermanence of the media on which information is recorded. At the same time, the diversity in information-recording technology and the increasingly frequent use of unstable media have made the task of preservation complex and intimidating to the general archivist. While there are a few general principles that should guide preservation policies and practices, the greatest challenge to the academic archivist will be to develop and maintain expertise regarding several technical problems (such as impermanence of paper or instability of nitrate negatives) and processes (such as microfilm, deacidification, and encapsulation).

This discussion of preservation will focus on the broader question of what the academic archivist must do to make sure that preservation issues are addressed and integrated into overall program management. As such, it will focus more on preservation (the range of practices that deal with the environments surrounding archival materials) than on conservation (the specialized techniques that alter the physical or chemical condition of the items).[46] The literature of preservation and conservation is extensive, complex, and does not always yield clear answers on important technical issues. This manual does not purport to provide definitive details on preservation practice. Rather, it will identify the conditions influencing the longevity of materials and suggest preservation actions to deal with impermanence of materials, as well as administrative processes for handling preservation problems and solutions.[47]

The conditions influencing the longevity of materials, and thus the extent of the threat to preservation, are diverse, but can be divided into two basic categories:

internal and external.[48] Internal causes are those arising
from the nature of the material on which information is
recorded. The longevity of paper is heavily dependent on
the stability of inks and the papermaking processes. The
latter, in particular, has been the primary offender for
documents dating since the mid to late nineteenth century—the period during which wood pulp was introduced
as the predominant component for paper manufacturing.
The lignin in wood fibers and the chemicals used to process
the wood into paper are unstable and deteriorate to form
acid compounds that break down the paper's fibers and
cause it to become brittle, stained, and fragile. Other
information storage media, such as photographic prints
and negatives, sound recordings, videotapes and computer
tapes, disks, cards, and perforated tape, present a range
of different problems. It is particularly common for college
and university archives to hold a great variety of photographic, audiovisual, and other machine-dependent records, all of which have different storage requirements.[49]
Thus, in terms of preservation, the academic archivist's
primary responsibility is to become knowledgeable in two
areas: the technical characteristics of the storage media in
order to determine which materials need special attention
to survive for future generations of users and the storage
conditions needed to prevent further deterioration. The
archivist can generally do little about the internal or
inherent characteristics of the documents, other than replace them through expensive and often imperfect methods of recopying or perform major chemical and physical
treatments, such as deacidification and encapsulation.

However, major threats to the permanence of documentary materials often come from external sources. For
instance, light can fade inks and photographic images,
especially if it contains ultraviolet radiation. Heat can
accelerate the acidification of paper and plastic-based
materials. Fluctuations in temperature, even as little as
ten degrees on a daily basis, can cause considerable stress
on the chemical and physical structure of documents.
Considerable damage is caused by excessive moisture,
whether atmospheric or by surface contact. It can cause

inks to run and papers and photographs to fuse together. While less obvious than leaky pipes, floods, and efforts to extinguish fires, daily atmospheric moisture serves as a major catalyst for the acidification of paper.

Air pollution can cause damage both through particulate and gaseous fumes. At a minimum, airborne particles soil documents and leave harmful deposits that can corrode the surface of documents, especially of plastic and photographic materials. Much of the danger from airborne particulate pollution can be alleviated through storage of documents in closed containers, sealing or elimination of windows, filtration of air, and good custodial services. Also threatening to the permanence of materials are gaseous pollutants, such as sulphur dioxide and nitrogen dioxide, which result from industrial processes and transportation systems and are far more difficult to control.

Insects (especially silverfish and roaches) and rodents can cause considerable damage to documents, but they can often be controlled through good housekeeping, regular but careful use of institutional pesticides, close examination of incoming materials, and fumigation where necessary.[50] Significant damage to all information-recording media can result from adjacent materials, such as newsprint clippings, paper clips, staples, pressure-sensitive tape, rubber bands that can rot onto paper, inadequately sealed wood cabinets or shelving (especially for photographic materials), and magnetic fields, which can weaken and destroy information on tape recordings or computer diskettes.

Perhaps the greatest external danger to documents is posed by humans. Before documents are transferred to an archives, people often expose records to many of the dangers listed previously. Active and inactive files may be poorly handled, left exposed to light and heat, crammed into storage cabinets, and housed in damp basements, dirty attics, and overheated closets. Once records are transferred to the archives, the threat from people can be controlled but not eliminated. Archival staff are not always so careful as they should be and sometimes expose documents to excessive light and handling during processing. Once processed, the documents may be damaged by users and may have to be stored in substandard space. It is important for the staff to be able to observe users to ensure that documents are handled carefully, kept in proper order, not left exposed to light, not subjected to the risk of spilled beverages or food crumbs, and not lost or stolen. A graphic illustration of proper and improper handling of archival documents can be found in a booklet from the Public Archives of Canada, *Handle With Care: Fragile.* This publication should be purchased and made available for staff and users in the search room.[51]

If any one of these conditions is not enough to worry the archivist about the permanence of documents, the many combinations of problems that occur in everyday practice certainly will be intimidating. For example, an archivist may be faced with a rich correspondence file from the dean of students regarding campus unrest in the late 1960s. The file contains fading Thermofax photocopies, newsclippings, and handbills interspersed with incoming and outgoing correspondence. Because the originating office was closed in 1972, the orphaned files were moved several times before they found a home in a leaky attic, which they shared with a brood of pigeons. While transfer to the archives and routine processing can solve many problems, the aging of the files has already been accelerated, and the mix of physical materials requires special attention to ensure that important ephemeral documents do not disintegrate. As if these problems were not enough, the archivist knows that many potential users are likely to be careless as they search for single documents or subjects in the records. These conditions are daunting and the archivist might be inclined to neglect preservation and focus instead on other aspects of the program, but this would be to shirk a core professional responsibility.

Practical Preservation Actions

Regardless of how limited resources may be for active preservation work, there are a number of things the academic archivist can and should do. The most fundamental is to educate the staff. A thorough knowledge of the physical nature and longevity of information-recording media, as well as an understanding of the broad range of threats to each type of document, should be part of the background of all archival actions. This knowledge should guide staff in daily operations so that the myriad of details contributing to a document's longevity can be handled sensitively and intelligently. Beyond this, archivists should view preservation as a series of actions that are employed at different times and levels. Preservation actions should be preceded by an assessment of the archival value of the documents involved, their physical condition, and the resources available for their care. When preservation is divided into components, archivists will have a process for making daily decisions, as well as for preparing overall preservation plans.

The first and most basic component of preservation is the transfer of records and manuscripts from their creators or custodians to the archives. Even the poorest archival environment for unprocessed materials is likely to be superior to the office or home areas used for storage of inactive records and manuscripts. More importantly, transfer to the archives removes documents from the risk of accidental or deliberate destruction or damage by persons unable to appraise and handle them properly. Accessioning generally presupposes that the documents will receive at least the minimal level of preservation represented by the repository's processing guidelines. At accessioning, the key preservation step should be a thorough examination of each container to determine if immediate fumigation is necessary to prevent insects, rodents, or mold from continuing to damage the documents and from spreading to the rest of the archives.

The second step in preservation occurs through basic archival processing. Even though practices will vary for each institution and for each series or collection, the key preservation components include rudimentary cleaning of documents; removal or replacement of harmful materials, such as rust-free paper clips and staples, rubber bands and fasteners; replacement of conventional file folders with acid-neutral ones; relabeling of folders; reboxing of documents into acid-neutral archival or records boxes; weeding of duplicate and nonarchival documents; division of documents into physically manageable units (e.g., dividing a three-inch-thick folder into three one-inch folders); preparation of special boxes for irregularly shaped material; placement of oversized material in separate oversize files and writing of cross-reference sheets; and final boxing, labeling, and shelving of the accession following preparation of the descriptive finding aid.[52]

Judgment and evaluation are important at each stage in processing. One always needs to consider the archival value of the material, its inherent physical properties, its current condition, and the likely costs. For example, refoldering may be eliminated if the existing folders are in excellent condition and the documents are of paper quality that is inferior to the folders, and if the existing folders provide adequate structural strength to support the documents. Some records (e.g., a series of thousands of cards on student majors over thirty years) may be of sufficiently limited archival value that a minimum of work should be performed. Reboxing into sturdy containers may be all such records merit, unless information from use analysis suggests otherwise. Common sense should dictate most of these decisions, provided the staff starts with a careful appraisal of the value of the documents.

An important managerial control will be to defer many preservation actions until processing is underway or completed. Processing permits the folder-by-folder, if not piece by piece examination of the entire accession. This examination, in combination with appraisal, will suggest which areas of each series or collection need specialized preservation procedures, such as microfilming, deacidification, and encapsulation.

The third major preservation action for archivists is careful monitoring and regulation of the environment in which documents are stored and used. Because academic archives often must share space with other units, they may be limited in the environmental control they can exercise, but they should monitor and make adjustments whenever possible to achieve optimal conditions for humidity and heat, lighting, and use.

The most basic preservation requirement for storage is sufficient space in structurally sound buildings with shelving equipment capable of holding the documents without danger to the documents or staff. For example, attic storage areas with rickety wooden shelving and inadequate control over fire hazards should be avoided. The structure should provide adequate security, with limited numbers of doors and windows, all of which should be securable. In some cases, intrusion alarms will be desirable. There should be adequate fire protection, such as fireproof construction, smoke- and flame-alarm systems, portable fire extinguishers, and water or gas fire-extinguishing systems.

Perhaps the most important factor in maintaining the proper environment to protect holdings is that the archives should be the sole user and occupant of the facility. If shared space or occupancy in multipurpose buildings can be avoided, many problems may not develop. Rules on smoking, eating, and drinking can be enforced more easily, authorized access to collection storage areas can be limited, and environmental controls can be set to meet archival requirements.

These fundamental structural components need to be supplemented by control of the heating, ventilation, and air-conditioning systems. For storage areas, the temperature ideally should be maintained at 67 degrees Fahrenheit, or less, and the relative humidity held at 47 percent. The ventilation system should include filters, and these should be changed at frequent intervals to reduce airborne dust and dirt. Filtering systems to remove gaseous pollutants, while desirable, are likely to be beyond the reach of most archives. Lighting in stacks, reference, and exhibit areas should be carefully controlled so that damage from natural and artificial light is minimized through a combination of controls, such as ultraviolet filter sleeves for fluorescent lights, ultraviolet filtering on windows and exhibit cases, switchable lights (perhaps timed) in each stack aisle, blinds or shades, and boxing of documents.

Maintaining the performance of heating, ventilation, air-conditioning, and lighting systems can be a constant challenge. Frequently, thermostats are located elsewhere, and building-maintenance personnel set air-conditioning and heating systems on seasonal schedules that are focused on occupant comfort or energy conservation rather than document preservation. The archivist, therefore, may have to expend much time educating maintenance personnel as well as administrators about the need for special environmental controls for the archives.

To limit damage from insects and vermin, regular cleaning and dusting are needed. Depending on the local conditions, regular spraying should be scheduled, and rodent poison should be distributed. Given the human health hazards these chemicals present, they should only be applied by maintenance staff or contractors trained in their proper use, but these specialists will need to be informed of the need for careful application of chemicals so that boxes and documents are not sprayed. Similar careful monitoring of custodial staff is necessary when floors are cleaned and shelving is dusted. Plastic-based documents, which are particularly sensitive to many chemicals used in cleaners, should be shelved where they will be least exposed to such hazards.

The fourth major preservation action within the reach of all archivists is control of environmental conditions during use. The key will be a series of systematically enforced rules, including:

- Materials should be used only in a supervised reference room.
- Eating, drinking, and smoking should not be permitted in the reference room or adjacent offices.
- The number of boxes retrieved for a patron at one time should be limited to what can be reasonably examined in a daily research session.
- Only one box and one folder should be opened and used at any one time.

- Fountain, felt tip, and ballpoint pens should be prohibited.
- Documents should be returned to folders and boxes in their proper order at the end of each session.
- Out cards or substitution cards should be placed in boxes as markers when folders are removed for use.
- Photocopying should be limited to documents of such size and condition that they can be placed on copiers without damage.

The types of users, holdings, and circumstances of each repository will dictate the level of enforcement of each rule, but posting detailed user regulations is a basic requirement since it provides a yardstick to monitor and enforce preservation conditions in the reference room. Announcement of the rules for use often can be coupled with user registration forms.

Advanced Preservation Techniques

Basic preservation actions, once incorporated into the archives' policy, environment, and daily practice, will contribute significantly to the survival of its holdings. For a large portion of the archives, these actions will suffice or be all that can be undertaken realistically with available resources. In some cases, however, advanced preservation work may be needed, and academic archivists should be aware of these techniques and procedures even if they lack the expertise, equipment, and resources to perform all of them. If environmental conditions, kinds of materials, or use have led to the deterioration of archivally valuable documents, the first course of action may be reproduction of the original through photocopying, photography, rerecording, or microfilming. When a file of documents in otherwise excellent condition contains a few deteriorating, or soon to deteriorate, documents, selective electrostatic photocopying onto acid-neutral bond paper and disposal of the original will often be the most efficient way to preserve the information content of the original. This practice can be readily incorporated into regular archival processing, but the staff should follow preestablished guidelines based on appraisal criteria so that overuse of this technique does not inflate processing time and supply costs.

When the volume of deteriorating, but archivally valuable, documents increases so that photocopying of entire files or boxes would be necessary, microfilm should be considered. Experienced archivists know that the costs and work involved in producing preservation-quality microfilm are quite substantial and that microfilming is not the technological "quick-fix" for space and preservation needs that campus officials, ranging from janitors to chancellors, often think it is. Nevertheless, when an entire series or collection is in badly deteriorating condition, microfilming may well be preferable to the specialized conservation techniques needed to guarantee survival of the documents. The criteria for such microfilming include

1. A large number of the documents are deteriorating or are recorded on materials of very limited life.
2. The documents have considerable long-term research value.
3. Frequent use of the originals would damage the documents.
4. Microfilm would permit much broader use without damage to the originals.
5. Filming problems would be minimal (e.g., relatively few oversize documents, good contrast in the originals, uniformity of colors and types of papers).

In an academic archives, good candidates for filming can include long runs of case files, such as student transcripts and campus-wide personnel files, well-organized modern office correspondence files, and alumni biographical files. Before microfilming is planned, however, the full range of regular processing for arrangement and description should be conducted. This will weed out non-archival material and suggest areas where appraisal might be performed in greater depth to reduce the amount to be filmed. Most important are proper arrangement and good finding aids to facilitate access. Unless these last two steps are completed, the archives risks generating a useless microfilm.

The filming can be done on the archives' own or leased equipment. Alternatively, the archivist can utilize a photoduplication unit elsewhere in the parent institution or contract for services through a commercial vendor or nonprofit conservation center. When working with commercial vendors and conservation centers, extra care must be taken to ensure that archival standards are met. Before undertaking such a project, the archivist should become familiar with the standards of the American National Standards Institute for producing the film and for storing the negatives and positives once the film is generated.[53]

Photographic reproduction may be more appropriate than microfilming when individual documents have a high visual value, such as posters and handbills, photographs, founding charters, and maps. This will be particularly true when the miniaturization inherent in microfilming would impede the retrieval of some of the original information. With photographs, a frequent preservation technique is to recopy images onto archival-quality film and paper, followed by storage in archival-quality containers. Where better image quality is needed, original negatives should be copied using either direct duplicating film or the film interpositive process. Least desirable is the too common practice of creating a new negative by printing from the original negative and then rephotographing the print to create the new negative.[54] A technique to make such visual material more accessible while supporting preservation of the original image is to have the photos microfiched.[55]

While microfilming, photocopying, or photographing are convenient means of preserving the informational content of documents, they do not preserve the document itself. When physical or chemical actions are necessary to alter the condition of the documents themselves, a broad range of rather complex conservation techniques can be brought to bear. These include fumigation, cleaning, mending, deacidification, encapsulation, and construction of specialized protective storage containers. It is unlikely that all these procedures would be applied to any particular document or that any would be used for more than a small quantity of an academic archives' holdings. While these techniques can be fairly complex and should not be undertaken by untrained staff, the academic archivist should be familiar with their purposes and basic elements and can refer to the technical literature for detailed instructions.[56]

Fumigation of new accessions to kill insects, rodents, and molds is often necessary to ensure they do not introduce new preservation hazards into the repository. In some cases, these hazards may not be discovered until the collections are being processed or used, but they always require prompt treatment. Because of the dangerous and toxic chemicals involved and because of the risk to documents from improperly applied chemicals, such procedures should be conducted only by staff who are familiar with the equipment and chemicals and follow proper personal and environmental safeguards.

Less hazardous is the cleaning of documents during processing. Since airborne dirt can damage and obscure documents, soft brushes, erasers (e.g., Art Gum® or Magic Rub®), vacuum cleaners, and treated dusting cloths (One-Wipe® or Stretch 'N Dust®) should be available for use as necessary. Removal of stains and such harmful materials as adhesive tapes is more complex and should be undertaken only by the trained conservator. If regular dusting of shelves and boxes is not possible, reference procedures should require dusting each box before it is brought to the search room. Placing clean boxes in the hands of the researcher is as much a conservation technique as a public relations measure, and it is within the means of every repository.

Deacidification is a chemical process to neutralize the acid and thereby raise the alkalinity of paper. It enables the archivist to arrest the harmful processes that result in embrittlement, discoloration, and eventual disintegration. It can be accomplished with a two-step aqueous-based or a one-step solvent-based solution process (e.g., Wei T'o®). These processes (the Wei T'o method has become most common and available in recent years) require advanced training. Testing of the solubility of inks, strength of paper, and current pH level should precede any attempts at deacidification. Each document should be examined carefully and, where possible, photocopied before treatment to ensure that valuable information is not lost during efforts to save the document. While recent experiments with mass deacidification hold promise for reduced costs, many technical problems must be solved before it will be readily available to academic archives.[57]

Whether deacidification is necessary or not, the archivist must frequently repair tears and breaks in paper. Again, considerable technical expertise is required in using various mending techniques, such as Japanese paper, filling with paper pulp, tissue, and silk, or heat-set tissue, before this work should be attempted. Common pressure-sensitive tapes should be avoided in all circumstances. Even those advertised to be of archival quality may not be able to meet all of the manufacturer's claims, and they should be used judiciously until there is more research on their permanence and safety. For many less critical documents, however, these "archival quality" tapes may be adequate.[58]

To strengthen documents and solve problems caused by tears, breaks, and general weakness of the paper, two techniques have been developed: lamination and encapsulation. With lamination, the document is sandwiched between sheets of cellulose acetate and tissue and then placed in a special press under heat and pressure to bond the elements into a single piece. While lamination has been available and used for several decades, conservationists and archivists are increasingly advising against its use. First, lamination goes against the basic conservation principle of "never do what you cannot undo" because the process generally is irreversible. Furthermore the heat, pressure, and lamination materials can cause permanent changes in the documents, such as discoloration and distortion of the paper.

A less expensive and far more advisable approach for academic archives is encapsulation. In this process, the document is placed between two sheets of polyester. Static electricity holds it in place while the edges of the polyester are bonded together with a special double-faced tape (3M Scotch Brand No. 415), heat, or ultrasonic sealing.[59] This approach has several advantages: it requires only a small initial investment in tools and supplies (unless one purchases an ultrasonic sealer); it does not physically alter the document; and, most importantly, it is reversible. Thus, if additional conservation work is needed, the sleeve can be cut open easily and the document removed for treatment. Often the sleeve can be reused. A major disadvantage is that the encapsulation enclosure adds significantly to the size and bulk of the document. The document first should be prepared carefully so that harmful substances (e.g., mold, dirt, or acid content) are removed. Since encapsulation is reversible, even documents that are slightly acidic may be encapsulated to protect them from tears and abrasion. Ideally, however, documents should have an acceptable pH (7.0 or higher) before encapsulation.

This overview of conservation practices suggests the more extensive techniques for protecting, repairing, and restoring documents. Before embarking on specific procedures, the archivist should not only consult the technical literature, but also consider some basic principles. First, the archivist should accept the fact that conservation techniques are the province of specialists and require careful training and hands-on experience. Without a thorough knowledge of a given technique, its possible consequences, and some practical experience, the archivist is better advised to do nothing rather than risk doing irreparable damage while intending to conserve. Most archives might well decide to rely on commercial conservation laboratories or those managed by the parent institution's library for specialized procedures. Secondly, both archivists and conservators should always look for techniques that are reversible and represent the least work appropriate for the archival value of the document. The most important role for the archivist may be that of appraising the value of the informational and artifactual characteristics of the document to determine what level of conservation activity is appropriate. Given the size and diversity of holdings in a modern academic archives, conservation work must be highly selective, but only an archivist knowledgeable about both holdings and conservation technologies can make these decisions wisely.

Disaster Preparedness

A critical component of the preservation program for each college or university archives is the development of a disaster plan to outline procedures and resources to be used in the case of sudden structural failures or environmental crises caused primarily by water, fire, and storms.[60] The essential elements of the plan are to define levels and types of disasters; describe the dangers presented by fire and water; provide telephone trees of contact people; list area resources (such as freezing facilities); mandate the stockpiling of basic supplies (e.g., dehumidifiers, wet vacuums, plastic sheeting, paper towels, and drying racks); identify sources of supplies and equipment that cannot be stockpiled; and designate the key people to decide on the value of damaged materials, as well as the appropriate procedures. Work on a disaster plan should also include preparing an annotated list of the archives' holdings to identify those records that must be salvaged at all costs, those that should be salvaged if possible, and those that can be passed over as staff use their time to salvage other materials. Thus, the disaster plan requires both compiling considerable technical information and obtaining advance assurances of cooperation from main on- and off-campus offices (e.g., physical plant, fire, and police department). If the plan is to be useful, it must be disseminated to all staff members and updated regularly.

It is equally important for the archives staff to monitor its storage and use locations regularly for present or developing hazards. Given the frequency with which water accompanies most disasters, all archives should secure a good supply of plastic sheeting, waterproof tape (such as duct tape) to secure the plastic, and large containers, such as plastic garbage cans, to collect runoff. Above all, the staff should be well-informed of dangers to documents as well as basic remedies. A well-trained archives staff, not an outside conservation service or library disaster team, will be the best insurance that the damage from the inevitable disasters will be kept to a minimum.

Preservation must be an all-embracing concern. While several conservation techniques will be beyond the means of many academic archives, all archivists should understand the nature, benefits, and limitations of major conservation practices. In academic archives, the first step should be to incorporate the goal of preservation into the repository's management philosophy and policies. This step should be joined with instruction and self-education in hazards and solutions. When faced with the vastness of the preservation problem, it is easy for the archivist either to despair of any solution or to expend tremendous time and resources in minute preservation of unsystematically chosen documents. Neither is a productive approach. Rather, the archivist should identify the several levels of preservation treatment possible, ranging from boxing and shelving to deacidification and encapsulation, and then make appraisal decisions to establish how much can be done for each accession in relation to the archives' overall goals and resources.

USE

A major focus of attention in all academic archives should be a series of activities aimed at facilitating and supporting use of the repository's holdings. Use can be defined as the retrieval of information from archival and manuscript holdings, finding aids, reference tools, and staff memories. Regardless of purpose, such as administrative action, publication of a book, preparation of a

course paper, genealogy, or personal curiosity, any retrieval of information should be considered as use. The
process by which archival staff assist persons in obtaining
information from archives is commonly called reference
service.[61] Beyond the premise that use should be paramount, the administration of use is less dependent on a
body of archival theory than are appraisal, arrangement,
and description. In fact, the specifics of administering use
are defined predominantly by pragmatic responses to the
needs of users and documents. However, because the intellectual and interpersonal elements of reference service
are quite demanding, the archivist needs to plan carefully
to ensure the most efficient utilization of resources.

Use is central to the mission and core purpose of all
archives and manuscript repositories. It is particularly
important in colleges and universities because it illustrates the key role of archives in supporting research,
which is so highly valued in academic settings. Thus,
understanding and being able to explain the use of one's
repository is a fundamental responsibility because use is
a core archival goal and because it provides a tangible and
comprehensible indication of the value and purpose of the
archival program. Not only will a clear understanding of
the nature and extent of use permit stronger justifications
of the program, but it also will enable the archivist to
improve the quality of service to users.[62]

Direct and Indirect Use

Use of archival material can be categorized as direct
or indirect. Direct use of archives consists of the examination of documents to extract information or develop an
interpretation of an event. This type of use occurs whenever a person seeking information asks questions about or
examines archives and manuscript holdings, primarily in
the research room. It can also occur when files are returned to originating offices or when photocopied or microfilmed documents are sent to off-site users.

Before direct use of the archives can occur, however, staff intervention is necessary. The archivist will usually ask a series of questions and provide background information, often from memory and experience, to help users move from their initial inquiry to relevant records and manuscripts. In many cases, especially those involving simple reference questions on popular topics, this interpretative and explanatory work may be all that is necessary to answer users' questions. In other cases, it is but one step in assisting researchers to exploit the archives' resources. More extensive interpretative work is especially common in responses to mail and telephone inquiries, but it should enter into all types of reference service.

Other components of service for direct use include supplying copies of finding aids; advising on research methodologies and strategies; suggesting alternative sources of information; providing names of third parties to do the research; supplying photocopies or microfilm of records; and referring users to other offices, archives, or manuscript repositories for further information.

Assisting researchers and administrators who request specific documents or data may be the most tangible aspect of archival reference service, but archivists must also recognize the importance of indirect, or secondary and tertiary, use of their programs. Indirect use can be defined as the entire range of results of direct use of archives and is best understood by examples. It would include the administrative staff meeting that hears a colleague's report utilizing documents in the archives to clarify why student visitation hours were changed in 1969. It would include the hundreds of students, faculty, and members of the public who view an archives exhibit on campus architecture, or the thousands of individuals who examine the cover of the student-staff directory reproducing a photograph of the campus in 1890. Indirect users also include the readers of scholarly monographs that are based in part on information extracted from archival documents. These are the terms in which archivists should view use, rather than focusing only on traditional categories such as "serious" or scholarly researchers, genealogists, students, or administrators who visit or write to the archives. While it may be impractical to quantify indirect use, an appreciation for it should be central to the archivist's management of historical documentation and articulation of the value and purpose of the archival program.[63] Such indirect use, or outcomes of use, may not loom large in daily reference service, but reference practices and policies should be built upon this broader understanding of use to provide the best service goals and strongest justifications for an archival program.

Administering Use

The promotion and management of use of archives and manuscripts requires considerable attention to physical facilities, reference tools, staff, procedures, and access policies. There needs to be a great deal of local variation in these elements, depending on staff size, space and facilities, holdings, and use level, but the following discussion supplies general guidance on providing for use and users.

Space and Equipment

The basic facilities needed to support use include a reference room large enough to comfortably house researchers and the archival and manuscript material they are using, and whatever equipment is needed to support research. Even the smallest academic archives should have adequate table space for six to nine researchers simultaneously, and a few large tables (e.g., 3' x 6') can provide the greatest flexibility and efficiency. The area will need to be well lighted, but artificial and natural light should be filtered to limit damage from ultraviolet rays. In ideal conditions, the reference area might be subdivided into sections for types of use, such as class assignments, long-term research projects, and certain formats of materials, such as photographs, maps, and audiovisuals. All archives should provide access to a photocopy machine in or immediately adjoining the reference room, although it may be necessary to require that some sensitive or fragile materials be photocopied only by staff members.

In smaller repositories, especially those with only one or two full-time staff, it may be appropriate to forego a separate reference room. A single large room could be divided into three distinct areas for reference, processing, and office work. If the areas can be clearly demarcated with glass partitions, such an arrangement can enable a small staff to complete processing and office work while also monitoring users to ensure security and good reference service. In repositories with three or more staff members, however, the creation of a separate room for researchers, perhaps combined with a glass-enclosed office space, is clearly preferable.

Equipment needed in the reference room will depend on the nature of the archives' holdings as well as its proximity to other units to which material can be checked for use or from which equipment can be borrowed when needed. Equipment needs will be related to the extent of microfilm, photographic, and audiovisual holdings. When equipment needed to examine holdings is not immediately available, the archives should develop policies and procedures for charging out such machine-dependent records to places where the necessary equipment is available (e.g., a campus audiovisual center). When equipment is used in the archives, care should be taken to ensure that its use does not disturb other researchers or staff. Earphones can solve this problem for audio equipment, but a special room may be necessary for video and projection equipment.

An important design consideration for the reference area is that it must enable staff to monitor use so that documents are not damaged, stolen, or disarranged during use. The entrance area should include racks and lockers for coats and briefcases, and it should be easy to view and control so that arriving users can be assisted immediately and departing users can be monitored to ensure that they are not removing documents. The space should be designed so that staff can help arriving users without distracting those already conducting research. A reception area with a small desk and a glass partition to separate it from the body of the reference room can accomplish this quite effectively. To minimize disruptions to users and staff, the reference room should be reserved for research-ers—other program functions, such as processing, typing, and administration should be located elsewhere, if at all possible.

Reference Tools

The reference room should contain information re-source tools to facilitate use of the archives' holdings. Most important are working copies of the classification guide, administrative histories, the catalog of primary finding aids, and the detailed finding aids, such as container lists, collection guides, and registers. Additional tools, which should be readily accessible to users, include the repos-itory's subject index; indices to the student newspaper; faculty senate minutes, or chief executive's correspon-dence; and computer workstations, if some finding aids are available only in automated form. To assist in reference service on popular topics, the archivist should develop a vertical ready-reference file containing duplicates and photocopies of documents and publications that provide particularly good summaries on topics that are frequently in demand. These ready-reference folders can be arranged alphabetically by subject, and they should concern topics such as campus traditions, popular buildings, major con-troversies, key historical figures, and campus firsts. A substantial portion of these files can be built from campus publications, newsclippings, anniversary announce-ments, building dedication programs, and internal histo-ries. To maintain the files' usefulness, the archivist will need to add new material, delete material on inactive subjects, and add new files as new subjects and research areas emerge. One filing cabinet of ready-reference folders should suffice.

Most archives find it convenient to maintain a refer-ence set of the institution's major publications in the search room. These might include the proceedings of the governing body (when published), annual reports of the president or chancellor, course catalogs and academic program descriptions, yearbooks, student newspapers, alumni newspapers and magazines, alumni and faculty biographical directories, staff and student address and telephone directories, commencement programs, and financial reports. Experience with use will enable the archivist to add to or subtract from this list.

To assist both user and staff reference work, archives should include a small library of reference books and secondary sources relevant to the repository's interests. A number of basic reference works (such as dictionaries, atlases, encyclopedias, and "who's who" directories) can often be obtained from campus library units when older editions are superseded. In addition, the archives should have the tools needed to help both beginning and experienced researchers find source material at other repositories. National archival and manuscript directories and guides, such as the NHPRC *Directory of Archives and Manuscript Repositories* and a recent edition of the American Association for State and Local History's *Directory of Historical Agencies in North America,* are core reference tools for archives aspiring to be resources for those doing historical research on topics beyond campus history. If budgets allow, the archives should also have copies of the *National Union Catalog of Manuscript Collections,* published guides from other repositories, and subject guides, such as *Women's History Sources.* Finally, recently superseded copies of general reference tools such as the *American Library Directory* might be obtained from the parent institution's library.

In addition to general reference works and guides to archives, the reference room should include noncirculating copies of secondary works on the institution and the major subjects documented in the archives. These may include dissertations on the institution's founding or major events in its life, biographies of its leading figures, architectural guides, and monographs examining issues that figure prominently in the institution (e.g., the underground railroad for Oberlin College). Such secondary works may range from scholarly monographs and dissertations to short public relations "histories" and unpublished student essays or alumni memoirs. While the quality of the works will vary, they can often provide ready answers to frequently asked questions and an excellent starting point for advanced studies.

Reference Staff

Regardless of physical facilities, equipment, and reference tools, the most important element in reference service is a responsive staff. The amount and kind of staff must vary depending on the repository's size, volume of use, and extent of resources. Only a few institutions will be able to support a full-time professional archivist whose sole duty is reference service. In many institutions, the archives will rely on the full range of regular and student employees to perform reference service in addition to their many other responsibilities. The exact mix should be determined through assessment of each staff member's communication skills, subject expertise, personality, length of service, and knowledge of archival holdings. In a larger repository, a clerk or paraprofessional can play an important role by handling the large volume of routine questions as well as the initial stages of more complex inquiries. When hiring and training such a reference reception person, a most important skill is the ability to perceive when the more advanced assistance of a professional archivist is needed as well as when inquiries do not merit professional attention. Regardless of rank or functional role, all staff members, from processors and clerks to the director of the archives, should take an active role in reference activity. The cynic might say that this is merely making virtue out of the inability of institutions with small staffs to specialize, but sharing reference responsibilities can provide valuable insights into appraisal, arrangement, description, preservation, automation, and administration.

The Reference Process

The complex issues in reference service have received considerable attention in the library and information science fields, and many of these findings are transferrable to archives.[64] The major difference will be that far more orientation and interviewing of archival users is necessary before placing them in contact with documents that address their information need. The key steps in archival reference service are:

- Querying the researcher to draw out the specific nature of the subject as well as secondary aspects of the subject that can serve as leads to documentation sources.[65]
- Translating the terms and concepts of the inquiry into the terms and concepts of the archives' reference apparatus.
- Explaining finding aids, archival methodology, and the nature of manuscripts and records documentation.
- Guiding the researcher to the appropriate finding aids and/or records.
- Retrieving the records that appear to be relevant to the researcher's inquiry.
- Informing the researcher of policies and practices for making copies and handling documents to ensure that the records are not damaged or disarranged.
- Consulting with the researcher during and after the visit to determine how well the records answered the question or led to new questions.

Not all these steps will be necessary for each user, but all staff involved in reference services should be able to communicate clearly in each phase.

An important responsibility of reference service is staff follow-up to determine if researchers' questions have been answered, what the answers were, and whether the investigation has suggested additional lines of inquiry. This procedure has an additional staff development benefit. The reference staff's effectiveness will depend on familiarity not just with the archives' subject matter, but also with the diverse research methods used by archival researchers. Brief, unobtrusive interviews of users therefore should be conducted whenever time permits. Archivists should take the opportunity to discuss research methodologies with all types and levels of users to improve their understanding of use and how inquiries develop and conclude.[66]

With this broad range of responsibilities and archivists' predisposition to research, it is important to have working limits on the amount of time staff spend on each inquiry. For example, a guideline of ten minutes for in-person inquiries, fifteen minutes for telephone inquiries, and twenty minutes for correspondence inquiries could be used. This is often enough time to identify the scope of the question, the likelihood of holding relevant material, and the need for additional research time. These times should be used only as targets, and there are many occasions when more than an hour of sleuthing by an experienced archivist is necessary before the reference staff can turn the question over to the researcher again. In addition, in a new or small archives with low reference use, or on a slow day in a normally busy archives, more time can be allocated. Likewise, if finding aids are not yet fully developed, additional time will be needed.

When complex inquiries require extensive work, it can be useful to recommend that users visit the archives in person or make arrangements to hire someone, such as a graduate student, to perform research for them. Archivists often will make exceptions for special classes of users whom they may be courting or whose abrasive manner demands more attention. Nevertheless, it is a reasonable administrative practice to have general guidelines for minimal service to ensure fair distribution of resources. In reference work, archivists need to remember that their role is to be facilitators of research, not interpreters, beyond what is necessary to locate information. Instead, they should limit their work to that which is necessary to answer simple questions and facilitate access to documents. The act of interpretation and analysis is best left to the users.

The efficient delivery of reference service requires explicit procedures. All archives should have printed user regulations and post them prominently in the reference room, and users should be requested to read the regulations before documents are provided. The user regulations should address care in handling original documents, copyright regulations, procedures for obtaining copies of documents, and rules for citation of archival materials. For example, the form shown in Figure 4 might be modified for local use.

Measuring Reference Use

To monitor and understand the volume and type of reference service provided by the archives, there should be simple procedures for collecting data on each reference inquiry. This data collection can be accomplished through an index card for each user, whether in-person or by mail or telephone. Each user card should record the date; the user's name, address, and institutional affiliation; a brief statement of the subject of study; check-off boxes to show purpose of use (e.g., publication, dissertation, course paper, administration) and type of user (e.g., administrator, faculty, undergraduate, public); and what records are used, generally represented by listing the numbers of all record series or manuscript collections consulted. A sample user (reference) card is reproduced in Figure 5.

To simplify compilation of statistics, the card may be kept separate from the larger user-registration and agreement forms that many archives maintain. The information on user cards should be collated and summarized on a monthly and/or annual basis to produce statistical tables illustrating the volume of use by purpose, type of user, and record groups or series and manuscript collections used. These cards also will provide the basis for surveys of trends in research topics and allow archivists to retrieve information that can assist future researchers working in the same topic area.[67] Finally, data on use can facilitate administrative decisions on reference books, staffing loads, shelf locations for heavily used materials, priorities for microfilming, and appraisals of new accessions.

Reference and Access Policies

Each archives should develop a general access policy to define the conditions of use and outline how restrictions should be handled when they are necessary. Ideally, the vast majority of the archives' holdings in both public and private universities and colleges should be open and available for use by all researchers who are willing to submit to the archives' general user regulations concerning decorum and proper care for the records and manuscripts.[68]

Inevitably, however, most academic archives include at least a few series of records and manuscripts that require restrictions on access to protect the privacy rights of individuals about whom the information was collected. The most common types of these records are student academic records; disciplinary and counseling records; student financial aid files; faculty and staff personnel files; promotion, tenure, and grievance files; and medical and legal counsel's case files. In some cases, the privacy of such information is protected by federal, state, or local statutes, such as the federal Family Educational Records and Privacy Act. In other cases, the records must be restricted to protect privacy that was promised or implied when the information was originally collected. In all cases, however, any special access provisions should be developed during appraisal, accessioning, and processing, rather than waiting until a researcher requests access.[69]

It is not uncommon for archives to have restrictions on a few record series of central administrative records (e.g., Chancellor's Office Subject File), which are often seen as particularly sensitive. This practice is unfortunate, but may be unavoidable at some institutions, especially at private colleges and universities. When it cannot be avoided, it should be limited to central offices (president, chancellor, and deans); the restriction periods should be limited to no more than ten to twenty-five years after the creation of the documents; and there should be procedures for researchers to apply for access before the end of the restriction period. Occasionally, it will be necessary to establish restrictions for series about controversial and

Rules for the Use of University Archives

To safeguard unique and valuable archival and manuscript material, researchers are requested to observe the following rules:

HOURS: The Archives are open from 8:00 a.m. to 5:00 p.m., Monday through Friday except for campus holidays.

MATERIALS BROUGHT TO THE READING ROOM: Users are to bring into the search room only those materials needed for research. Coats, books, briefcases, and other items should be placed in lockers unless otherwise permitted by Archives staff.

REGISTRATION: Each user must fill out a reference card on his/her first visit, and on succeeding visits when requested. Separate registration forms may be required for the use of certain series/collections.

SMOKING, EATING, AND DRINKING: are not permitted in the University Archives under any circumstances.

EQUIPMENT: Portable computers, typewriters, and photographic, video, and audio equipment may be used with permission of the Archivist. Please see room attendant in choosing seating to avoid disturbing other researchers. Users are responsible for the security of equipment and materials they bring to the search room.

HANDLING OF MATERIALS: Materials must be handled with care. DO NOT:
1) mark on material or erase existing marks;
2) use fountain pens, felt-tipped pens, or similar writing instruments;
3) write notes on top of material;
4) fold, tear, or cut documents;
5) make tracings or rubbings;
6) rest books or other objects on the surface of items;
7) touch the surface of loose sheets or book pages if they can be handled by their edges;
8) apply paper clips, fasteners, tape, "Post it" notes or rubber bands.

(continued on next page)

Figure 4. Rules for the Use of University Archives (1 of 2)

MAINTAINING ORIGINAL ORDER: To safeguard the integrity of archival documents, the original order must be maintained by:

1) Requesting only one record series/collection at a time and use no more than two boxes at a time.
2) Using one folder from a box at a time.
3) Maintaining the existing order of material within each folder and box. If there is any doubt as to the order please notify the room attendant.

CIRCULATION: No material will circulate. Exceptions may be made for offices or persons requiring use of material they have transferred/donated to the Archives provided they have prior approval of the Archivist.

REPRODUCTION: Material may be photocopied in accordance with the limits of the copyright act and the Archives' policies. The Archives may set restrictions to protect fragile or damaged materials.

RESTRICTED MATERIALS: The use of certain documents may be restricted by statute or the office of origin/donor. The researcher must assume full responsibility for fulfilling the terms connected with the use of restricted material. For the protection of its holdings, the Archives also reserves the right to restrict the use of materials which are not arranged or are in the process of being arranged, materials of exceptional value, and fragile materials.

PUBLICATION: Permission from the Archives must be obtained before any unpublished documents can be published. In giving permission to copy, quote from, or publish, the Archives does not surrender its own right to publish such material or to grant permission to others to do so. The researcher assumes full responsibility for use of material and for conformity to the laws of defamation, privacy, and copyright, and shall indemnify and hold harmless the University and the Archives from claims arising as a result of use of the material so obtained. If the donors have retained literary rights, the researcher must obtain their permission before publication.

CITATION: If permission to publish is granted, location of the material must be indicated in the work. Examples of footnote citations are available on request from the Archivist.

Figure 4. Rules for the Use of University Archives (2 of 2)

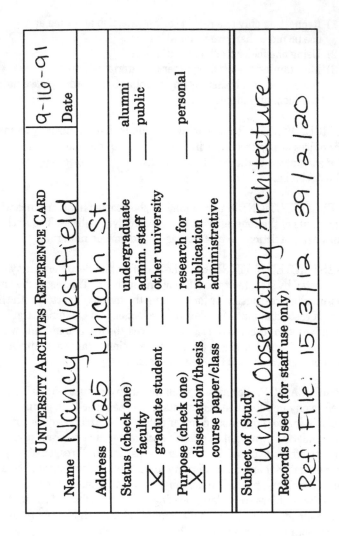

Figure 5. Reference Card

sensitive subjects, such as campus demonstrations, athletic scandals, and fraternity/sorority disturbances. Accepting restrictions may be a precondition of acquiring such material, but the archivist should work to limit these restrictions to the period normally required for passions about the incident to subside. Generally a decade is adequate. However, student, faculty, or staff case files containing information about their academic record, personnel evaluations, counseling, or other sensitive incidents may need to be restricted for significantly longer periods of time.

Manuscript collections may contain research notes on human subjects that need to be restricted to protect the privacy of information collected for studies. Far less defensible are restrictions placed on the use of a manuscript collection to provide exclusive access to a researcher designated by the donor. Such use restrictions should be avoided whenever possible, and when not avoidable, the restriction should be limited to a time in which the research might be reasonably completed, e.g., three to six years.

While access restrictions are easiest to administer when they apply to entire record series or collections, the nature of record-keeping does not always permit such neat distinctions. Documents of a sensitive nature may be found within general correspondence files in personal papers and office records. Identifying such material should be part of routine archival processing. If entire folders of sensitive materials (e.g., a professor's grade books and reports, or personnel grievance documents) are located, they should be segregated, returned to the records creator, or placed under an appropriate restriction policy.

Nevertheless, the archival staff should not become overly cautious about material that wary administrators may see as sensitive. Many records creators, if asked point blank about whether they want their correspondence on major policy and program issues to be made available to the public, are likely to hesitate and suggest a restriction. Archivists know that the vast majority of users are not looking to damage the reputation of an administrator, but to obtain the full background to past actions, and they need to convey this to the records creators. In fact, archivists normally can reassure such administrators by noting the procedures and regulations that archives users must accept before materials are provided in the search room. The archivist should accept the restrictions if, and only if, the files contain information about private lives or are clearly covered by legislative or regulatory privacy provisions. The archivist, however, should resist efforts to restrict files merely to obscure the nature of campus operations or the official conduct of college administrators.

When establishing restriction periods for documents and files specifically covered by federal, state, and local legislation, or regulation, the archivist should work with campus personnel who specialize in these areas. These would include the originating office, the legal counsel, admissions, medical, and counseling personnel, and the institution's freedom-of-information officer if one exists. In working with such representatives, it is important for the archivist to ensure that institutional caution and wariness do not lead to overly long restrictions for entire series of records merely to avoid the possibility of controversy. At a maximum, personnel and academic records might be restricted until the death of the individual in question. A simpler policy might be restrictions of seventy-five years for student records and fifty years for personnel records from the date of last entry in the files. Given the sensitivity of counseling and disciplinary files, such time periods may need modification based on the content of the particular record series.[70]

Administering restricted materials will require more than a simple list of time periods for each restricted series or collection. For each restricted group of materials, there also should be a brief description of what is restricted, a statement of the reason, a clearly defined restriction period, and a note on who is allowed access without special clearance (e.g., personnel from the originating office). There should always be provisions by which researchers can apply for permission to use the documents before the end of the restricted period. For example, the restriction on faculty personnel files should indicate that researchers who have written permission of the faculty member may use the documents upon approval of the archivist, and users researching deceased faculty should apply to the appropriate dean or vice-chancellor for permission. The archives should not accept any records or manuscripts that are restricted from examination by the archives staff or for which the donors are unwilling to accept a policy outlining the end of restrictions and procedures for access.

Ideally, users of restricted materials should sign an agreement form stating that they will not disclose confidential or sensitive information found in restricted series without obtaining appropriate approvals. While such stipulations may hinder a few studies, most research can proceed quite successfully within these limits. However, the occasional study of campus controversies, such as the firing of a faculty member, will present problems that can only be resolved on an *ad hoc* basis. In providing access to restricted materials, the archivist needs to make sure that the policy is administered fairly and that no group or individual researcher is given preferential treatment or access that is denied to others.

It is important not to let anticipated restrictions interfere with appraisal decisions. If a body of documents is determined to have long-term research or archival value but is likely to be subject to restrictions, the archivist should accession it and then work to secure reasonable conditions to govern use. If this is not possible but the records have clear archival value, they should be retained. In the case of manuscript collections for which donors have insisted on clearly unreasonable restriction periods, the archivist may need to refuse the manuscripts. To capitulate to unreasonable restrictions will only open the archives to further compromises on basic archival principles.

In addition to considering access issues, the archivist needs to be aware of legal and ethical issues related to how researchers use the information they derive from the materials they examine. These are concerned primarily with libel and copyright. Conforming to these laws is largely the responsibility of the user; still, the archivist

needs to understand these issues and inform the researcher of their general contours.

Libel is the malicious publication, or other dissemination, of information to impugn the memory or reputation
of a living or dead person. Use of archival and manuscript
material could lead to the libeling of an individual, but
several features of legal practice make it highly unlikely
that an archivist would directly become involved in a libel
case. For such a suit to be effective, the injured party
would need to demonstrate not only that the archivist, in
making information available to a researcher, had previous knowledge of the untruth of the information, but also
that the archivist's intention was malicious in making it
available while not disclosing its untruthfulness. In the
case of deceased persons, the heirs would need to prove
that the libelous material impugned their own reputations
as well. If the archivist reminds the researcher of the need
to determine the document's accuracy before disseminat-
ing information critical of another person's reputation, the
danger of action for libel is limited.[71]

Copyright also requires archivists to inform researchers of the need to be careful in how information from
research is disseminated. Copyright has evolved gradually
in Anglo-American law since the mid-eighteenth century
to reward intellectual creativity by protecting the property
rights of the creator. Virtually all types of materials held
by archives—publications, manuscripts, photographs,
and audiovisual documents—fall under the protection of
the copyright law. Recent revisions, primarily in 1976,
have expanded the act's coverage and modified time limits
on copyright protection. The law now protects the author
of a document against its unauthorized reproduction and
dissemination for the life of the author plus fifty years,
with no material to be removed from copyright protection
until 2002.

Although most archives' holdings are under copyright
protection, this should not limit their availability to researchers. Under the common-law concept of fair use,
incorporated in the 1976 act, the use of copyrighted material for scholarship, research, news reporting, or teaching

does not represent an infringement.[72] Furthermore, many of the copyright restrictions do not apply to use of short quotations and excerpts. In addition, the most recent act permits archives and libraries to copy works for preservation, security, replacement, and reference purposes.

Copyright does, however, become a concern if the use involves copying the document beyond that necessary for individual reference use. Repositories can fulfill their responsibilities by placing copyright notices on photocopying machines, user registration forms, and photocopy order forms, and by taking reasonable care that requested copying is for one-time research use only. Beyond these measures, the archives should make clear to researchers that permission to use is not permission to publish and that obtaining copyright clearance before publication is the responsibility of the researcher and not the repository.[73]

In considering the literary rights of all the documents found in official files or private papers, an important underlying concept is that physical ownership does not necessarily include ownership of copyright. In an academic archives, copyright for outgoing and internal correspondence of the parent institution would belong to the parent institution, but copyright for incoming correspondence or documents generally would belong to those documents' authors. Similar distinctions are even more important in manuscript collections. Unless a donation of manuscripts included not only physical title (or custody) but also transfer of copyright, the ownership of copyright (or literary rights) would still reside with the author(s) of the documents. Even if the donor transferred copyright, it would apply only to those documents for which the donor held copyright—generally his or her own correspondence and documents. Thus, copyright for incoming correspondence by the literati in an English professor's papers would still be held by the literati or their estates.

Assessing Limits on Use

This outline of privacy, libel, and copyright limitations does not cover the most basic "restriction" archivists inevitably place on reference service. It is simply realistic to acknowledge that value judgments of users and their questions form part of the archivist's response to each inquiry and that these evaluations enter into decisions on the types of service and access provided. These judgments are both subconscious and conscious, and although they are sometimes accurate and helpful, they are often wrong and a hindrance to the archives and the user. Recognizing that evaluation of users is fraught with perils, the archivist should be willing to form and revise opinions about the depth of researchers' information needs and interests; their experience with research in original source material; the care with which they handle the documents; bias in their approach to the subject matter; and the likely impact of the user and research project on the archives. The suggestion that such judgments influence the quality and quantity of archival reference service can be very troubling to some archivists. However, efficient management of resources and provision of quality reference service will require not only such evaluations but also the realization that archivists are fallible and one's judgments of users are subject to error and prejudice. Thus, the best reference archivists will be those who not only assess their users, but who also constantly critique their responses to each user.

The key to evaluating both users and reference archivists is to judge how the use relates to the overall goals of archival work—preservation and examination of historical documentation to provide a better understanding of the past and to suggest future action building on past successes and failures. If these goals are paramount, archivists should find that evaluation of users will lead to greater and better reference service.

It is unfortunate that discussions of access and use so often move into a review of conditions limiting access and use. By noting a few of the areas for possible restriction, this outline should help the academic archivist see that the vast majority of reference work can be completed without concerns about restrictions. If one accepts the principle that the preeminent purpose of preservation is use, it becomes clear that the archivist should be a champion of the researcher. When restriction of newly accessioned material is proposed, or when research inquiries are made that could benefit from the use of restricted material, it is the responsibility of the archivist to advocate the broadest possible access to the records without infringing on the privacy of the documented individuals or the legitimate operations of the parent institution. Thus, rather than being an apologist for closing materials, the archivist should be a proponent of responsible use of the repository's holdings. This can lead to an inherent tension between archivists' institutional responsibilities and their role as information providers to a broader community. Unfortunately, there are no specific guidelines to resolving these tensions for each case. Rather, mastering this dual responsibility will depend on each archivist's careful application of his or her own professional ethics and vision to each reference inquiry.

SPACE, FACILITIES, AND EQUIPMENT

In discussing the technical elements of archival practice, this book has emphasized both the basic goals of each activity and the minimum performance needed in each area. Space, facilities, and equipment, however, do not lend themselves to this approach, and it is impractical to lay out norms. On the one hand, the ideal level is beyond the resources of most institutions. On the other hand, an outline of "acceptable" but substandard facilities would only undermine the archivist's arguments for adequate facilities. More problematic is the fact that the textbook ideal for one institution will be quite different from the ideal for another institution. Thus, a delineation of and specific goals for space and facilities at a college or university archives is likely to be both discouraging and of limited utility. Fortunately, the archival and library literature on buildings and preservation identify the ideal specifications for such characteristics as: temperature, humidity, lighting, and floor loads. Those involved in planning new or renovated facilities, or justifying requests for improved facilities, are well advised to review this literature.[74] This discussion will focus instead on a functional description of space.

Considerations in Planning Space and Facilities

The level and type of facilities needed by college and university archives will vary greatly depending on such factors as volume and age of holdings, level of use, and size of staff. Equally important may be the availability of specialized technical facilities elsewhere in the parent institution. Ideally, the archives will have its own facilities for each of its needs, except perhaps for a few highly technical and specialized areas. The organizational relationships at many institutions, however, will make the use of shared facilities a necessity. For example, if an archives has ready access to the university library's conservation and photoduplication laboratory or remote storage facility, the need for such facilities of its own will be decreased. An archives housed in a library's special collections department may share its reference room and exhibit area with the rare books and manuscripts unit. Such compromises can range from highly satisfactory to stifling and inefficient.

While a delineation of the exact space and facilities needs for an academic archives is impractical, a description of the functional needs of an archives can provide a clear set of goals. The quality and quantity of facilities will vary, but the basic functional needs in each of three areas—public service, staff, and storage—will remain the same.

Public Service Facilities

If public service facilities are well designed, they will accomplish the following goals whether they are in a warehouse or a walnut-paneled residence:

1. Provide a quiet area for research and reading.
2. Facilitate staff monitoring of users to ensure the security of repository holdings.
3. Promote ready access to finding aids and storage areas so that staff can provide appropriate support to researchers.
4. Permit the archives to present a good public image of its programs and encourage public confidence in the archives' ability to care for documents.

Public facilities can be divided into four functional components: reference interviewing and orientation, research and reading, exhibits, and conference or meeting rooms. In larger archives, a separate room for each is highly desirable, but in smaller operations, some functions can be combined without harm. In the best of settings, a separate area should be maintained for reception and interviewing of users so that the conversations, which are so crucial to this process, do not become noise that disturbs researchers already examining documents. In addition, a separate room or soundproof partition is desirable for microfilm and audiovisual equipment areas.

Staff Facilities

Regardless of design or size of staff, facilities for staff should accomplish the following goals:

1. Provide a pleasant work environment that does not diminish staff morale (thus, natural light and climate controls are "in," and clanging pipes, rodents, and birds caught in ventilation ducts are "out").
2. Support the efficient processing of records. Thus, large open spaces for spreading out collections are preferable to cubicles, study carrels, or dormitory rooms.
3. Provide sufficient office space to permit the separation of administrative activities from processing and reference service, even if all functions are performed by the same person.
4. Provide space and equipment needed to support technical preservation processes and photographic duplication.

There should be a separate office for each professional staff member (100 to 200 square feet is a reasonable guideline). Work stations for clerical personnel can be distributed throughout the archives, depending on available space and the need for clerical staff to perform other functions, such as reference and reception. Because of frequent reliance on student staffing, care should be taken to ensure that each student has a clearly identifiable work station rather than space shared with other staff. This is essential to monitor the quality and progress of their work.

Facilities for conservation and photographic duplication may quickly exhaust even the most ample of budgets. Wherever possible, archivists should make arrangements with other institutional or commercial facilities for this work. However, basic archival processing will require a minimal conservation work area with plumbing and equipment to allow cleaning and flattening of documents, minor repairs, simple encapsulation, and perhaps small-scale deacidification.

Storage Facilities

Archival storage facilities are not highly specialized, but securing sufficient environmentally adequate space for records and manuscripts can be an archives' greatest challenge. Regardless of size, storage space should accomplish the same goals:

1. Provide security and environmental controls sufficient to guarantee the integrity and preservation of the archive's holdings.

2. Permit the efficient storage and retrieval of documents for research use.

3. Provide enough room for expansion to permit retention of all records and manuscripts the archivist may determine to be appropriate.

A central challenge will be obtaining space to allow the archives to grow. While some academic archivists may encounter little problem finding space for their future accessions, many others will have such large volumes of annual accessions, such limited space, or both, that obtaining space may become a major administrative activity. Given budget constraints at most institutions, it may be unrealistic to request more than five to ten years' of expansion space, but in all cases a basic goal should be to have at least two years of "breathing room" to prevent space limits from precluding accessioning important records.

Frequently, academic archivists find that the available storage space was designed for other purposes, most commonly books, and does not house records containers efficiently. When using such space, a practical planning guide is that one square foot of floor space is needed to house each cubic foot of documents. When space is customed-designed for records, far greater storage efficiency can be obtained by use of records-center or compact shelving.

As holdings grow, the only way to increase an archives' capacity may be to accept off-site storage. The quality of such space can range from unused basements and attics in campus buildings to well-designed commercial or institutionally owned facilities. If remote storage is used, additional problems arise, including supervision, retrieval, monitoring of environmental and security controls, and selection of which material should be stored there. Off-site space is inherently less desirable than adequate space at the archives' headquarters, but it may become unavoidable. If properly planned and sufficiently staffed, it can provide a good working solution to the space problem.

In addition to regular stack space, most academic archives will need access to specialized storage facilities—generally vaults—for a few core records and highly valuable items. A vault or other specialized facility is highly desirable to store vital records, such as security microfilms of core documents (e.g., student transcripts, property records, trustees proceedings, and other records needed to maintain the institution's basic operations). A vault might also be needed for artifacts with high monetary value and collectibles, such as the coins, stamps, or literary manuscripts sometimes found in archival and manuscripts collections.

Environmental Conditions

All storage, staff, and public areas should meet environmental standards to protect the documents. These ideal conditions, summarized in the section on preservation, include constant temperature and humidity, ventilation systems capable of filtering the air, tightly sealed windows, ultraviolet filters on windows and lights, smoke and flame detectors, fire extinguishers, freedom from insects and vermin, basic security, and good janitorial services. Since the needs of each repository will vary and expert opinions are constantly evolving, the academic archivist should adjust local resources periodically to best approach the latest recommendations in the preservation literature.[75]

While it is extremely difficult to achieve optimal environmental conditions, the protection of documents is so fundamental to the archivist's mission that great efforts should be made to achieve the best control possible. These efforts should focus on those activities that will have the broadest effect on stabilizing the documents and on those smaller steps that can be implemented easily. Thus, the archives should attempt to regulate temperature and humidity, at least to human comfort levels, through its own controls of heating and air-conditioning systems. In most regions, a room dehumidifier and fan will be an appropriate acquisition to permit localized control of one of the greatest sources of environmental damage. The smaller steps include enforcing prohibitions on food, securing doors and windows, and ensuring that lights can be, and are, turned off when not needed.

In most academic archives, major changes in space and environmental conditions, no matter how desperately needed, will be beyond the reach of the archivist. Efforts to obtain first-rate facilities can be frustrating and unproductive except in those uncommon times when substantial institutional and private funds become available for new facilities or renovation. Given these limits, sound management and the need for peace of mind suggest doing one's best and then moving on to the daily work of appraisal, arrangement, description, and use.

Equipment

To meet the basic operational needs of the archives' public, staff, and storage, several equipment items are required. In the public area, the key equipment will be tables and chairs for users, and bookshelves and filing cabinets for reference volumes, finding aids, and heavily used record series. In planning a workspace for researchers, it is best to base estimates on peak use periods and to choose conference tables, rather than individual desks or carrels. The larger tables can accommodate more users and provide greater flexibility by allowing use for other purposes when necessary, such as spreading out collections to dry following a water emergency or seating class or public orientation sessions. The reference area may also include a photocopy machine in a location visible to the staff responsible for reference service. Audio and video playback equipment, microfilm readers, and slide and motion picture projectors may be needed if it is not feasible to use equipment elsewhere in the institution. Beginning programs and smaller repositories are best advised, however, to make full use of shared equipment whenever possible so that these expensive purchases can be avoided. As the archives moves into increased use of computers for finding aids, catalogs, and networks, a terminal or microcomputer will be needed in the reference area. When possible, the public area also should include exhibit cases for display of documents and conference rooms to meet with classes and groups of researchers and staff.

Staff space will need the usual complement of office furniture, typewriters, large processing tables, and clerical work stations. Depending on the level of automation, terminals or microcomputers may be substituted for typewriters to aid in accessioning, processing, correspondence, administrative planning, and reporting. Basic equipment will also include book trucks, two-wheeled hand trucks for moving boxes, and a sink to support basic conservation work.

Equipment needs in the storage area will consist almost entirely of shelving to house, and trucks to move, boxed material. A variety of cabinets, map cases, and plan files will be needed to handle oversize and odd-sized items. When funds are not available for such specialized equipment, large documents can be placed on open shelves, but should be in oversize boxes and folders to protect them from dust and light.

In addition to this basic space and equipment, all archives will need access to support services from the parent institution, including telecommunications, equipment repair, building maintenance and housekeeping, library resources, and computing services or advice. Basic service in these areas may not be a problem in most institutions, but quality service can be quite difficult to obtain. Particularly problematic is that the archives may not be a high priority and may thus have to live with poor custodial service or long turnaround times for repair of equipment. Even more frustrating is that as higher-education budgets have become tighter, housekeeping service has deteriorated, and there is often little the archivist or most other institutional personnel can do about the problem.

For greatest efficiency, effectiveness, and convenience, the space for the archives should be designed from scratch to meet specific archival needs, but many programs have flourished by adapting existing facilities. Except in a relatively few large or well-established archives, the core of the archivist's job will be learning to cope with space and facilities designed for other purposes. The archivist's success will depend on a willingness to devote time to good management so that space usage can be measured and future needs projected. To improve facilities, a great deal of diplomacy and patience will be necessary to ensure that the archives' functions are understood. This communications task can be particularly challenging since faculty, administrators, library staff, and physical-plant personnel are unlikely to understand the relation between the archives' physical needs and its multifaceted role in administrative service, research support, education, and outreach. Thus, the archivist will find that the essential issues in securing space and facilities are knowing how to adapt to available resources and being able to convince campus administrators of the importance of archival functions to the institution's mission.

Notes

1. T. R. Schellenberg, *The Management of Archives* (New York: Columbia University Press, 1965). Kenneth W. Duckett, *Modern Manuscripts: A Practical Manual for Their Management, Care, and Use* (Nashville, Tenn.: American Association for State and Local History, 1975). Ann Pederson, ed., *Keeping Archives* (Sydney: Australian Society of Archivists, 1987).

2. Both sets of manuals are critical sources for archivists. Refer to the "Bibliography" for complete citations.

3. Maynard Brichford, *Archives & Manuscripts: Appraisal and Accessioning* (Chicago: Society of American Archivists, 1977); T. R. Schellenberg, *Modern Archives: Principles and Techniques* (Chicago: University of Chicago Press, 1956), 133-60; T. R. Schellenberg, "The Appraisal of Modern Public Records," *National Archives Bulletin* 8 (Washington, D.C.: National Archives and Records Service, 1956), reprinted by Maygene F. Daniels and Timothy Walch, eds., *A Modern Archives Reader* (Washington, D.C.: National Archives and Records Service, 1984), 57-70.

4. Frank Boles, "Exploring the Black Box: The Appraisal of University Administrative Records," *American Archivist* 48 (1985): 121-40; and Frank Boles and Julia Marks Young, "The Archival Selection Process: Report of the Boles-Young Appraisal Project," preliminary draft, 1988.

5. Refer to the chapter on "Documentation Strategies, Functional Analyses, and Documentation Policies."

6. Brichford, *Appraisal and Accessioning,* 2-5.

7. The classic description of evidence and information as values is Schellenberg, *Modern Archives,* 15-16, 139-40, 148-49.

8. Brichford, *Appraisal and Accessioning,* 5.

9. To a large degree, the components of archival value have been recognized by Frank Boles and Julia Young, especially in their discussion of "Policy Considerations" that contribute to the selection/appraisal process. Particularly welcome is their clear statement of how important "political" considerations can be in the appraisal process. Boles and Young, "The Archival Selection Process." Also, refer to Frank Boles, "Understanding Contemporary Records Selection Processes," *American Archivist* 50 (1987): 356-68.

10. An excellent introduction to reappraisal is Leonard Rapport, "No Grandfather Clause: Reappraising Accessioned Records," *American Archivist* 44 (1981): 143-50.

11. Refer to the chapter on "Records Management" for a detailed discussion of these issues.

12. Helen W. Samuels, "Who Controls the Past," *American Archivist* 49 (1986): 109-24; Larry Hackman and Joan Warnow-Blewett, "The Documentation Strategy Process: A Model and a Case Study," *American Archivist* 50 (1987): 12-47.

13. Hackman, "Documentation Strategy," 19, 22, 24-25, 27.

14. For example, refer to Brichford, *Appraisal and Accessioning,* 12-13 *et in passim.* Also, refer to Maynard Brichford, *Scientific and Technical Documentation* (Urbana, Ill.: University of Illinois, 1969), 4-6. Brichford does not, however, explain how one can systematize the process, and these practicalities may be the greatest contributions of the documentation strategists.

15. An opposing viewpoint is argued by Richard J. Cox and Helen W. Samuels, "The Archivist's First Responsibility: A Research Agenda to Improve the Identification and Retention of Records of Enduring Value," *American Archivist* 51 (1988), especially 33-35, 39-40.

16. Helen W. Samuels, *Varsity Letters: Documenting Modern Colleges and Universities* (Chicago: Society of American Archivists, forthcoming).

17. A good outline of how library-acquisitions policy statements are prepared can be found in Richard D. Gardner, *Library*

Collections: Their Origin, Selection and Development (New York: McGraw-Hill, 1981), and David L. Perkins, ed., *Guidelines for Collection Development* (Chicago: American Library Association, 1979). Translating these models into archival needs can be quite simple, especially in light of considerations presented in Mary Lynn McCree, "Defining Collections," *Drexel Library Quarterly* 11 (January 1975): 27-33.

18. Linda J. Henry, "Collecting Policies of Special-Subject Repositories," *American Archivist* 43 (1980): 57-63.

19. Judith Endelman, "Looking Backward to Plan for the Future: Collection Analysis for Manuscript Repositories," *American Archivist* 50 (1987): 340-55. Equally valuable on the principles of collection analysis is Paul Mosher, "Collection Evaluation: Matching Library Acquisitions to Library Needs," in *Collection Development in Libraries,* ed. Robert D. Stueart and George B. Miller. Published as *Foundations in Library and Information Science* 10 (JAI, 1980): 527-46.

20. "Acquisitions" implies that ownership of the documents is transferred from their current holder to the repository. Since no transer of ownership occurs when records are merely relocated from an office within an institution to the archives of that same institution, the term *acquisitions* is inappropriate for archives. "Accession" is more appropriate because it implies the action of taking in and establishing preliminary control over records, but the term *acquisitions* may be used here to describe the pre-accession activities needed to ensure the transfer/acquisition of both archives and manuscripts.

21. Richard D. Gardner, *Library Collections: Their Origin, Selection and Development* (New York: McGraw-Hill, 1981).

22. The rationale for and purposes of acquiring faculty and student papers are covered in the sections on "Managing the Documents of Student and Faculty Organizations" and "Manuscripts Collecting."

23. For a sample deed of gift, refer to Gary M. Peterson and Trudy Huskamp Peterson, *Archives & Manuscripts: Law* (Chicago: Society of American Archivists, 1985), 28-29.

24. The "Records Inventory Worksheet" included in the section on "Records Management" can function quite well as an accession form.

25. S. Muller, J. A. Feith, and R. Fruin, *Manual for the Arrangement and Description of Archives,* trans. from the 2d ed. by Arthur H. Leavitt (New York: H. W. Wilson, 1940), 48-90. T. R. Schellenberg, *Modern Archives: Principles and Techniques* (Chicago: University of Chicago Press, 1956), 168-76. Recent research suggests that the development of the concepts of *respect des fonds* and provenance is more complex than the simple linear sequence described here. See Maynard Brichford, "Provenance of Provenance in Germanic Areas," *Provenance* 7 (Fall 1989): 54-70; and Nancy Bartlett, "Respect des Fonds: The Origins of the Modern Archival Principle of Provenance," *Primary Sources and Original Works* 1 (1991): forthcoming.

26. Oliver W. Holmes, "Archival Arrangement—Five Different Operations at Five Different Levels," *American Archivist* 27 (1964): 21-42.

27. Regarding recent discussions of the need for archivists to rethink provenance and traditional arrangement practices, refer to section on "Limits of Provenance-based Classification Systems."

28. When sufficient resources are available, the archivist might consider the alternative of using components of the MARC Archives and Manuscripts Control (MARC-AMC) format to reflect provenance through the descriptive rather than the arrangement system. Refer to the section on "Limits of Provenance-based Classifications Systems."

29. These definitions represent a merging of practical experience with definitions in Holmes, "Archival Arrangement," 23-33; Society of American Archivists, "Basic Glossary for Archivists, Manuscript Curators, and Record Managers," *American Archivist* 37 (1974):428, 430-31; and David B. Gracy, *Archives & Manuscripts: Arrangement and Description* (Chicago: Society of American Archivists, 1977), 4-5.

30. This definition of the record subgroup follows the model of Holmes's five levels arrangement and the SAA *Glossary.* It

disagrees with Richard Berner's use of subgroup as a unit subordinate to the record series or collection. Richard C. Berner, "Perspectives on the Record Group Concept," *Georgia Archive* 4 (Winter 1976): 48-55.

31. For a more detailed discussion of how the archivist can reconcile an archival classification system to a complex and changing organization, refer to the section on "Institutional Change and Archival Classification Systems."

32. Max J. Evans, "Authority Control: An Alternative to the Record Group Concept," *American Archivist* 49 (1986): 249-61. Lawrence J. McCrank, "The Impact of Automation: Integrating Archival and Bibliographic Systems," in *Archives and Library Administration: Divergent Traditions and Common Concerns,* ed. Lawrence J. McCrank (New York: Haworth Press, 1986), 74-75, 77-81, 84-86.

33. For more information on the MARC-AMC format, refer to pages 106-7.

34. For a discussion of the physical elements of processing, refer to pages 115-16.

35. Ruth B. Bordin and Robert M. Warner, *The Modern Manuscript Library* (New York: Scarecrow Press, 1966), 41-46, 72-74. While Bordin and Warner's recommendations are useful for pre-twentieth-century collections, they overlook many of the advantages that modern archival arrangement can bring to more recent personal papers. For these, the archivist might consult Richard C. Berner, "Arrangement and Description of Manuscripts," *Drexel Library Quarterly* 11 (January 1975): 34-54, and Kenneth W. Duckett, *Modern Manuscripts: A Practical Manual for Their Management, Care and Use* (Nashville, Tenn.: American Association for State and Local History, 1975), 118-21.

36. Recommendations for record group classification of records of student and faculty organizations can be found in the section on "Managing the Documents of Student and Faculty Organizations."

37. There may be political reasons for *not* creating separate record groups for all manuscript collections. Having distinct record groups for categories of manuscript collections can leave

the archivist more vulnerable to criticism, however ill-informed, for collecting indiscriminately when items with no institutional connection are labelled so clearly. At the same time, the archives might be more vulnerable to loss of these collections to library special-collections units when reorganizations occur. If these are likely concerns, the archivist may wish to place the manuscript collections within the record group and subgroup that reflects the campus department that provided the first contact about the collection or that is concerned with the subject content of the collection.

38. For examples of description, refer to *Inventories and Registers: A Handbook of Techniques and Examples* (Chicago: Society of American Archivists, 1976); David B. Gracy, *Archives & Manuscripts: Arrangement and Description* (Chicago: Society of American Archivists, 1977); and the appendices to Richard C. Berner, *Archival Theory and Practice in the United States: A Historical Analysis* (Seattle: University of Washington Press, 1983). Care is needed in using such compilations because most writers publish only the best examples of finding aids, and most academic archivists will find that not all of their finding aids need to be so excellent.

39. Detailed finding aids are extremely varied, and even their names can be confusing. They may be called collection guides, inventories, registers, and container lists, depending on their format and content. Because they need to adapt to the nature of the material being described, no single sample can adequately reflect the needs of an academic archives. Instead, academic archivists should examine the few samples provided in works by David B. Gracy, Richard Berner, and Kenneth Duckett. Perhaps more important will be to look at good and bad examples found only by making visits to other repositories.

40. Good descriptive practice, however, will dictate that the archivist examine the contents of each folder and revise folder titles when necessary to reflect accurately the folder's content. If sufficient staff and space are available, the archives might consider extensive retitling of folders so that consistent terminology is used throughout the archives. This approach was the basis for Jill Tatem and Jeff Rollinson's *Thesaurus of University Terms* (Cleveland, Ohio: Case Western Reserve University,

1986), available from the Society of American Archivists. Nevertheless, some archivists question whether such a systematic reworking of original records is consistent with basic principles of arrangement, and others cannot justify the time this would take.

41. For an example of an outline of terms that many have found useful in indexing college and university records, refer to Tatem and Rollinson, *Thesaurus of University Terms*. For an introduction to index and thesaurus construction, refer to F. W. Lancaster, *Indexing and Abstracting in Theory and Practice* (Champaign, Ill.: University of Illinois Graduate School of Library and Information Science, 1991); and Jean Aitchison and Alan Gilchrist, *Thesaurus Construction*, 2d ed. (London: Association for Information Management, 1986).

42. Nancy A. Sahli, "Interpretation and Application of the AMC Format," *American Archivist* 49 (1986): 9-20; Steven L. Hensen, "The Use of Standards in the Application of the AMC Format," *American Archivist* 49 (1986): 31-40.

43. For example, archivists using OCLC for MARC-AMC control would need to ensure that their entries conform to standards in *Anglo-American Cataloging Rules Second Edition 1988 Revision*; Steven Hensen, *Archives, Personal Papers and Manuscripts: A Cataloging Manual*, 2d ed. (Chicago: Society of American Archivists, 1989); and the most recent edition of *Online Systems: Archives and Manuscripts Control Format* from OCLC.

44. Kenneth W. Duckett, *Modern Manuscripts: A Practical Manual for Their Management, Care and Use* (Nashville, Tenn.: American Association for State and Local History, 1975), 135-36, 146-47; Gracy, *Arrangement and Description*, 21-30; Berner, "Arrangement and Description of Manuscripts," *Drexel Library Quarterly* 11 (1975): 34-54.

45. In considering the publication of a guide, archivists should not expect that the guide will significantly change how users approach the archives. In fact, archivists may find that the primary benefits of preparing a guide will be for the archives' internal development; refer to Roy C. Turnbaugh, "Living with a Guide," *American Archivist* 46 (1983): 449-52.

46. Preservation can also be seen as the broader and more generic concern that incorporates all issues related to guaranteeing longevity, while conservation can be seen as the processes necessary to repair or restore individual documents.

47. For bibliographic guidance on preservation issues, refer to Paul N. Banks, *A Selective Bibliography on the Conservation of Research Library Materials* (Chicago: Newberry Library, 1981); Carolyn Clark Morrow and Steven B. Schoenly, *A Conservation Bibliography for Librarians, Archivists, and Administrators* (Troy, N.Y.: Whitston Publishing Company, 1979). Also refer to the annual bibliographies in the July (beginning in 1982) issues of *Library Resources and Technical Services.*

48. For an introduction to archival preservation issues, refer to Mary Lynn Ritzenthaler, *Archives & Manuscripts: Conservation* (Chicago: Society of American Archivists, 1983). The archivist's technical reading should include at least one preservation journal or newsletter, such as *Conservation Administration News.*

49. Archivists with photographs should begin their work with Mary Lynn Ritzenthaler, Gerald J. Munoff, and Margery S. Long, *Archives & Manuscripts: Administration of Photographic Collections* (Chicago: Society of American Archivists, 1984); and Robert A. Weinstein and Larry Booth, *Collection, Use, and Care of Historical Photographs* (Nashville, Tenn.: American Association for State and Local History, 1977).

50. An excellent guide to insects and rodents, complete with line drawings of the major "villains," can be found in Thomas A. Parker, *Studies on Integrated Pest Management for Libraries and Archives* (Paris: UNESCO, 1988).

51. *Handle With Care: Fragile, A Guide to the Preservation of Archival Materials* (Ottawa: Minister of Supply and Services, 1977).

52. The other components of processing are discussed under "Box- and Folder-Level Arrangement" in the section on Arrangement and "Detailed Finding Aids and Container Aids" in the section on Description.

53. Nancy W. Gwinn, *Preservation Microfilming: A Guide for Librarians and Archivists* (Chicago: American Library Association, 1987); U. S. Library of Congress, *Specifications for Microfilming Manuscripts* (Washington, D. C.: Library of Congress, 1980); American National Standards Institute, *Specifications for Photographic Films for Archival Records, Silver Gelatin Type, on Cellulose Ester Base* (New York: ANSI, 1976 [PH1.28—1976]); *Residual Thiosulfate and Other Chemicals in Films, Plates and Papers* (New York: ANSI, 1985 [PH 4.8-1985]); *Practice for Storage of Processed Silver-Gelatin Microfilm* (New York: ANSI, 1970 [PH 5.4—1970]). Also refer to *RLG Preservation Manual* (Stanford, Calif.: Research Libraries Group, 1986); Helga Borck, "Preparing Material for Microfilming: A Bibliography," *Microform Review* 14 (1985): 241-43.

54. Larry Booth and Jane Booth, "Duplication of Cellulose Nitrate Negatives," *Picturescope* 30 (1982), 12-19; Weinstein and Booth, *Collection, Use, and Care of Historical Photographs,* 146-47.

55. Paul H. McCarthy, "Photofiching: A Catchy New Technique," *Conservation Administration News* 22 (July 1985): 1-2, 18-19.

56. Ritzenthaler, *Archives & Manuscripts: Conservation*; Carolyn Clark Morrow and Carole Dyal, *Conservation Treatment Procedures: Step by Step Procedures for Maintenance and Repair of Library Materials,* 2d ed. (Littleton, Colo.: Libraries Unlimited, 1986); Hedi Kyle, *Library Materials Preservation Manual* (Bronxville, N.Y.: Nicholas T. Smith, 1983).

57. George M. Cunha, "Mass Deacidification for Libraries: 1989 Update," *Library Technology Reports* 25:1 (January-February 1989).

58. Ritzenthaler, *Archives & Manuscripts: Conservation,* 78-80.

59. Detailed instructions can be found in Morrow and Dyal, *Conservation Treatment Procedures,* 117-22.

60. An excellent starting point is John P. Barton and Johanna G. Wellheiser, eds., *An Ounce of Preservation: A Handbook on Disaster Contingency Planning for Archives, Libraries*

and Records Centers (Toronto: Toronto Area Archivists, 1985). Also refer to the regularly updated work of Toby Murray, "Bibliography on Disasters, Disaster Preparedness and Disaster Recovery," available from the Oklahoma Department of Libraries, 200 North East 18th St., Oklahoma City, OK 73105.

61. William J. Maher, "The Use of User Studies," *Midwestern Archivist* 11 (1986): 15-16. For other definitions of "use," refer to Roy C. Turnbaugh, "Archival Mission and User Studies," *Midwestern Archivist* 11 (1986): 27-29; Lawrence Dowler, "The Role of Use in Defining Archival Practice and Principles," *American Archivist* 51 (1988): 78-80.

62. Elsie T. Freeman, "In the Eye of the Beholder: Archives Administration from the User's Point of View," *American Archivist* 47 (1984): 111-23; Bruce W. Dearstyne, "What Is the Use of Archives: A Challenge for the Profession," *American Archivist* 50 (1987): 76-87. This book's advocacy of use as a primary justification for academic archives needs to be balanced with Roy Turnbaugh's caution in "Archival Mission and User Studies" about creating unrealistic expectations of the level of use that might occur.

63. Underlying this emphasis on the significance of indirect use of archives is a belief that the outcomes of use are as important as the products (e.g., books, articles, and exhibits) on which archivists normally focus. Refer to Elsie T. Freeman, "Buying Quarter Inch Holes: Public Support Through Results," *Midwestern Archivist* 10 (1985): 89-97; Paul Conway, "Facts and Frameworks: An Approach to Studying the Users of Archives," *American Archivist* 49 (1986): 393-407.

64. For example, refer to Ching-chih Chen and Peter Hernon, *Information Seeking: Assessing and Anticipating User Needs* (New York: Neal-Schuman, 1982); or a general text on library reference service, such as Richard E. Bopp and Linda Smith, *Reference and Information Services: An Introduction* (Littleton, Colo.: Libraries Unlimited, 1991).

65. For an overview of some of these issues, refer to Linda J. Long, "Question Negotiation in the Archival Setting: The Use of Interpersonal Communication Techniques in the Reference Interview," *American Archivist* 52 (1989): 40-50.

66. The literature on research methods from an archival perspective is surprisingly thin. Two key discussions of the subject are Philip C. Brooks, *Research in Archives: The Use of Unpublished Primary Sources* (Chicago: University of Chicago Press, 1969); and William L. Joyce, "Archivists and Research Use," *American Archivist* 47 (1984): 124-33.

67. Maher, "Use of User Studies," 16-19. Paul Conway provides more elaborate models for studying users in "Research in Presidential Libraries," *Midwestern Archivist* 11 (1986): 35-56, and in "Facts and Frameworks," 393-407.

68. A general statement on the need for the accessibility of archives can be found in the "American Library Association-Society of American Archivists Joint Statement on Access to Original Research Materials in Libraries, Archives and Manuscript Repositories," *American Archivist* 42 (1979): 536-38; reprinted in Gary M. Peterson and Trudy Huskamp Peterson, *Archives & Manuscripts: Law* (Chicago: Society of American Archivists, 1985), 98.

69. Peterson and Peterson, *Archives & Manuscripts: Law*, 38-41.

70. Charles B. Elston, "University Student Records: Research Use, Privacy Rights and the Buckley Law," *Midwestern Archivist* 1:1 (1976): 16-32.

71. Peterson and Peterson, *Archives & Manuscripts: Law*, 44.

72. Unfortunately, a handful of court cases in the late 1980s regarding studies of literary figures have suggested that scholarly publishing may be restricted by copyright and privacy considerations.

73. Peterson and Peterson, *Archives & Manuscripts: Law*, 81-89. Also, refer to Jerome K. Miller, *Applying the New Copyright Law* (Chicago: American Library Association, 1979). For a comprehensive review of legal issues in copyright, refer to Harry G. Henn, *Copyright Law: A Practitioner's Guide*, 2d ed. (New York: Practising Law Institute, 1988).

74. Keyes D. Metcalf, *Planning Academic and Research Library Buildings,* 2d ed., Philip D. Leighton and David C. Weber, eds. (Chicago: American Library Association, 1986). Michel Duchein, *Archive Buildings and Equipment,* International Council on Archives ICA Handbook 1 (Munich: Verlag Dokumentation, 1977). Victor Gondos, *Reader for Archives and Records Center Buildings* (Ann Arbor, Mich.: Society of American Archivists, 1970).

75. Refer to the section on "Preservation" in this book and Duchein, *Archive Buildings,* 97-117; Mary Lynn Ritzenthaler, *Archives & Manuscripts: Conservation* (Chicago: Society of American Archivists, 1983), 30-37.

Special Records Problems

INTRODUCTION

Understanding the theoretical basis and technical nature of the core archival activities of appraisal, arrangement, description, preservation, and use enables the archivist to control vast portions of the documentation of colleges and universities, especially the conventional paper-based and textual office records that predominate at most institutions. The scope of archival responsibilities, however, cannot be limited to these kinds of records; it also must include all forms of documentation related to the institution. In particular, the archivist must know how to deal with such special formats as photographs, sound recordings, and computer files. Unfortunately, both the physical nature of these media and the inherent characteristics of the information recorded on them create many complex problems not solvable simply by following practices developed for conventional textual records. The principles and goals of the core archival functions will remain useful in managing these special record types, but additional attention is needed in several areas, especially physical protection, access, description, and custodianship.

To assist the academic archivist in these areas, the following sections examine five special record formats that must be considered for comprehensive coverage of the institution. These are dissertations and theses, photo-graphs, audiovisual materials, architectural records, and machine-readable records. Detailed technical discussions will not be attempted, but the sections will review major characteristics of each type of record, suggest the extent of the archivist's role in each area, and offer practical suggestions for incorporating these record formats into the archival program.

DISSERTATIONS AND THESES

At some point in their development, most college and university archives must consider whether they should assume, retain, or dispense with responsibility for han-dling their institution's theses and/or dissertations. Whether and how to handle dissertations and theses has long been a topic of discussion among college and univer-sity archivists.[1] Indeed, a 1975 resolution by the SAA's College and University Archives Committee defined the-ses and dissertations as records of the colleges and univer-sities where they are produced. The resolution also set forth basic preservation requirements and suggested that the institution's archives was an appropriate place to house the record copies of these documents.[2]

Based on policy statements and the commonness of the practice, one might think that archival responsibility for doctoral dissertations and master's theses is a foregone conclusion. Nevertheless, this book recommends that, if at all possible, dissertations and theses should not be the responsibility of the archives. Instead, the archivist should work to ensure that the campus library assumes responsibility for their proper preservation and accessibil-ity. This recommendation is based on the conviction that doctoral dissertations and master's theses are primarily library, not archival, materials, and that they are best handled by library procedures. This recommendation is also based on the recognition that procedures required for properly handling theses and dissertations entail far more than what most archives can afford to devote to such a limited part of their mission. If no other unit of the institution can or will take responsibility for the record or "archival" copy of these documents, the archivist must do so.[3] Generally, however, the archivist's responsibility should extend only so far as to ensure that the institution preserves these documents and makes them available through appropriate means, preferably library procedures. Therefore, this book recommends that the academic archivist avoid custody and management of theses and dissertations whenever possible. Because this position may be at odds with the practice of several institutions, its rationale merits explanation.

Archival or Library Materials?

Theses and dissertations have characteristics of both library and archival materials. The primary arguments for including dissertations and theses in archives emerge from the fact that they are records of the institution's degree-granting programs, as well as evidence of work conducted as part of two of an institution's primary missions: teaching and research. The cumulation of research conducted under the aegis of a department or faculty member can be of historical interest to scholars tracing the development of disciplines, and this is an appropriate, though uncommon, topic for archival research. In addition, since the institution needs to preserve record copies of these documents to provide evidence of completion of degree requirements, one might argue that they are vital records protecting institutional and individual rights and thus fulfilling a core responsibility. A third argument for placing theses and dissertations in the archives is that, as nearly unique items, they require security and preservation measures comparable to those for the rest of the archives.

On the other hand, libraries have long played a primary role in handling dissertations and theses, and there is ample justification for continuation of this practice. The subject content of dissertations and theses suggests that the need for library methodology for description, access, and preservation should override the security considerations that often have led to archival custody. Dissertations and theses contain discrete, synthesized treatments of highly disparate subjects, as do the monographs in the library's book holdings, and they are like library materials in terms of how the information in them is used.[4] Most researchers examine dissertations when seeking information on a narrow subject and will have little need or interest in understanding the relationship of one such work to the others generated by the same department or institution. By contrast, in archival research, the search for even a single document or fact is almost always conducted in the context of other documentation generated by the same institution.

Dissertations and theses conform to library materials also in that a principal preservation step is traditional library binding preceded by page-by-page collation. Because of the physical nature and the discrete focus and use of dissertations, they require standard library rather than archival methodology. They will also benefit more from library cataloging and bibliographic databases than archival description. In fact, the library profession has developed procedures for all aspects of handling dissertations and theses including cataloging, preservation, and creation of security and use copies.[5] Nevertheless, the library literature indicates broad variations in how institutions catalog and preserve these documents.[6] Unfortunately, many libraries have increasingly neglected dissertations as important holdings related to their core mission. The resulting reduction in acquisitions and cataloging, however, should be seen as a library, not an archival, problem.[7]

Another argument often made for placing theses and dissertations in the archives is that their security and preservation require archival facilities, but this is weak and potentially inimical to archival goals. Storage requirements alone should never dictate that documents be placed in archives, and the archives should not be the only campus information resource to provide secure storage. Both newer and older libraries include the appropriate space, and if they fail to provide for dissertations and theses, the practical issue of storage space is not sufficient justification for transferring them to the archives.

More importantly, the argument for archival custody based on security and preservation is flawed because it emphasizes physical characteristics at the expense of more important intellectual issues. It carries the unfortunate implication that the archives is a storage depot for problematic materials that other campus units have failed to learn how to handle. If extended beyond dissertations to include other problematic publications, such as politically and socially controversial magazines and journals, this practice could blur the focus and perception of the archives as a coherent program aimed at research on institutional history and subject areas emerging from the institution's strengths and character.

Conditions Necessitating Archival Accessioning

In view of these factors, college and university archivists should resist being assigned responsibility for dissertations and theses. If the archivist has inherited a program with this function, work in this area should focus on efforts to transfer the responsibility to the institution's library. The archivist should not ignore the fate of dissertations and theses entirely, but take steps to ensure that they are preserved properly somewhere else in the institution. Fortunately, many institutions have taken internal measures or entered cooperative agreements to preserve doctoral dissertations through microfilming programs. With such programs, especially that of University Microfilms International (UMI), the security and accessibility problems can be addressed quite systematically.[8] The preservation and accessibility offered by UMI (especially through *Dissertations Abstracts OnLine*) will be far superior to what most institutions will be able to attempt on their own. Unfortunately, the reluctance of some institutions to participate in UMI's program means they must take full responsibility for their own dissertations and theses. If no one at the archivist's institution has worked out such a cooperative arrangement or has microfilmed dissertations locally, the archivist may need to take a leading role in establishing procedures for campus or external units to assume ongoing responsibility for dissertations.

If the archives has the only space with the security and environmental controls needed for theses and dissertations, it may need to compromise and accept the documents until proper space can be provided in the library. This compromise should be limited to physical custody and retrieval; it should not include cataloging, acquisitions, or binding. If the institution compiles regular lists of dissertations by department, these should be collected by the archives to document faculty teaching and research interests and to support studies of the development of disciplines. When such lists are not available, the archivist should encourage the graduate college to develop them and the library to create such access points in its online or card catalog.

One instance in which archival accessioning of dissertations and theses might be considered is when dealing with limited bodies of such works generated by now-defunct predecessor and affiliate institutions. While library acquisition, cataloging, and preservation are preferable for such orphaned works, it may be far more difficult for the archivist to persuade the campus library to take responsibility for these products of bygone enterprises. This also applies to documents from preparatory and other specialized schools that often were sponsored by private and public colleges and universities in their earlier years. If the volume of these works is high, the archives may need to develop an appraisal policy for the selected preservation of such works. A similar approach might be useful in dealing with current bodies of undergraduate honors theses when the institution's library is not able to acquire, catalog, and preserve these items. At smaller colleges or very prestigious institutions, the archives might consider retention of all undergraduate theses in the archives. In these cases, archival control can be limited easily to custodianship and preparation of a chronological checklist of titles and authors held.

Handling Procedures

If the failure of the library to execute its responsibility makes it necessary for the archives to handle dissertations and theses, the archivist must use the same procedures as librarians are required to follow. Therefore, the archives will need to ensure that campus-wide standards are established to address paper quality, number and types of copies, ink, typing, corrections, illustrations, and binding.[9] Once the thesis or dissertation is received, it should be examined page by page for completeness and legibility and missing and defective pages should be replaced. For full library accessibility, the items should be cataloged into the library's online or card catalog, and appropriate institutional and subject access points should be provided.[10] A security microfilm or circulating paper copy should be made, and the record master (hard copy or film) should be placed in a secure, noncirculating area. Given the number of tasks necessary for proper handling of theses, it is clear that assigning responsibility for theses to the archives will require allocation of additional staff, perhaps at least one full-time person. Support services, such as microfilming and remote storage of negatives, should also be provided.

Despite this recommendation to avoid dissertations and theses, the archives should acquire reference copies of dissertations and theses (from any institution) that focus on the history of the parent institution or on subject emphases in the manuscript collections. The archivist should also attempt to acquire copies of dissertations as well as other published works based heavily on research in the archives. Finally, the archivist may also consider soliciting background material and research notes used by these authors if the subject and quality of treatment are centrally related to the archives' mission and their research cannot be easily replicated.

PHOTOGRAPHS

Photographs and iconographic materials can be found in all types of archives, and they form an important element in the documentary record of colleges and universities. Despite the simplicity of the imperative that academic archives should include photographs, this is a complex and challenging area of archival work. Photos present special problems in the management of any archives because of their physical properties and the nature and format of their informational content. Together, these factors create a broad range of difficulties not encountered with conventional types of documents. Thus, a normative approach is not appropriate, even if it allows for local variations. Instead, the care of photographic materials should be dictated by the nature of the holdings, level of user demand, and availability of resources. Moreover, even the smallest repositories contain such a variety of photographic documents that the methods suitable for one part of their holdings may need to be vastly different from those for other parts.

The literature on photographic collections is extensive and detailed, but it often provides little help in developing realistic applications for smaller archival programs. Once one has become familiar with the technical basics, a more useful approach will be to review the practices of other repositories to see what approaches can be adapted to one's own institution. Of interest will be the scope of holdings; the relationship of available resources to level of description, extent of physical care, and use; and how these vary with the type of material. This book can only touch the surface of the many administrative and technical issues involved in handling photographic and iconographic materials; archivists needing specific guidance are well served by general texts, handbooks, and journal articles.[11] While these can provide more detailed coverage than possible here, it is appropriate to discuss photographs in the context of college and university archives to explain how these visual materials fit into the overall program the manual outlines.

For this discussion, photographs and iconographic materials will be defined to include all images utilizing a photochemical, mechanical, or manual process to record a single pictorial image. This includes photographic prints, negatives, and transparencies (regardless of process) as well as postcards, engravings, paintings, line drawings, pencil sketches, and any other process used to record a still image on a physical medium. It does not include moving images, such as films and videotapes, or nonpictorial images, such as architectural drawings, which are covered in separate sections. The emphasis here will be on photographs.[12]

Because photographs and other graphic images depend on a mixture of chemical and physical processes to record an image, and because there are so many varieties of such processes, each with different technical demands, their preservation, storage, and handling are very complex. Their informational content is no less complex because each image can contain many layers of meaning, most of which are not apparent on casual inspection. These physical and informational characteristics raise substantial problems for the archival handling of photographs; they are also the reasons these images are such rich and important documentary sources.

Collection Scope, Provenance, and Appraisal

The first element in the archives' iconographic image program should be a recognition that these documents are an essential part of the record of the institution, and that the archives should give them the same level of attention it affords to administrative correspondence, official publications, or faculty papers. Second, photographs should be seen as more than just illustrative material for enlivening displays and publications. This function is important, but photos are also critical sources of information about the past and, like so much of archival documentation, can support research in areas never envisioned by the photographer and not evident from the apparent subject of the photograph. Thus, photographs of early campus buildings

under construction might be useful for researching structural elements of the building, the introduction of mecha-
nized equipment, or worker-foreman relations. For
example, at the University of Illinois at Urbana-Champaign, a photo of post-World War II temporary housing
was useful to 1980s researchers needing historical evidence of airborne pollution from the burning of high-sulfur
coal (at a power plant visible in the background) as they
considered the environmental impact of reconverting the
plant to coal.[13]

While such uses of photographs are important, they
cannot be anticipated and should not dictate either acquisitions policy or descriptive practices. Instead, the scope
of holdings should be based on the repository's overall
documentation policy. At a minimum, college or university
archives should cover the following kinds of images: buildings and grounds, including exteriors, interiors, statuary,
plaques, and memorials; portraits and informal group
photos of faculty, administrators, and students; student
activities and organizations; classroom and laboratory
instruction; library usage; research; other campus service
and program activities (e.g., conferences, seminars, and
institutes); aspects of student life (e.g., moving into dormitories, registration, parties); campus events (both scheduled ones, such as commencement, and irregular ones,
such as demonstrations); and athletic events. The location, research, and service foci of the institution are likely
to suggest additional areas so that the impact of the
institution on its neighbors and its constituencies can be
assessed.

The age of the institution and the breadth of its programs are major influences on the number of photographs
generated, as well as their survival, but many other factors, such as the architectural interest of the campus or
the social status of students and faculty, may have affected
the extent to which the campus has been photographed.
Thus, the size of the archives' iconographic holdings may
bear little relationship to the volume of written records
that have survived.

In managing a photo collection, it is important for the archivist to recognize that it is neither possible nor desirable to document all buildings, events, activities, and athletic contests for all moments in time. In fact, what will accumulate may seem to be little more than a sampling with quite uneven coverage. This is true not only because of the usual vagaries in preserving material before it comes to the archives, but also because of the ease of photographing some items (e.g., buildings and regular events, such as intercollegiate football games) and the difficulty of capturing other images (such as interiors of student rooming houses, and student or faculty social life). It is precisely to cover these less formal and "off-beat" activities and locales that the archives should actively collect student scrapbooks and amateur photographers' files. A useful solicitation technique is to include such shots in exhibits and publications to draw attention to their archival value and to request that persons with similar photos consider donating them to the archives.

In most instances, the archivist can rely on institutional sources for a large part of the photograph collection. Campus newspapers, public relations offices, and alumni offices are prime sources, but local newspapers may also be able to donate or copy their files of campus-related photographs. Faculty, student, and local photographers, whether hobbyists or professionals, are frequent sources of photos, often providing more personal or creative insights than found in images from official photographers. In some cases, the archivist may want to acquire a camera or contract with an experienced photographer to ensure documentation of certain events, such as the construction or restoration of major buildings, demonstrations, or activities not normally well represented in the photo files that are regularly transferred to the archives.

Since the first focus of attention in an academic archives should be the parent institution and its programs, the scope of the photograph collection is relatively easy to define, and it can provide guidance in applying archival techniques, especially in the areas of acquisition, selection, and appraisal. Relying on the parent institution as

the source for photos may solve many methodological
problems, but the archivist should not ignore the issues
posed by photos in personal papers and manuscript collections. Obviously, any image related to the institutional
focus of the archives can be either removed and placed in
the repository's main photographic file, with appropriate
separation records, or cross-referenced in the main file.
However, personal papers and manuscript collections
often contain large numbers of noninstitutionally related
subjects and many unidentified or inadequately identified
images. If these problems are combined, as they often are,
there is little the archivist can do except maintain the
images intact and hope a future researcher or curator will
find them useful.

When working with photos in personal papers, maintaining provenance can be an important issue. If the
papers contain well-identified images on noninstitutional
subjects, the archivist needs to decide whether the group
of photographs should be merged into a larger body of
images, or a centralized index to photographs should be
developed, or the images are best controlled through the
regular finding aids for each collection. The approach
should be determined by available resources, the quality
of the photos, the closeness of the subject matter to the
central focus of the manuscript collection, and anticipated
use. In general, it is best to retain the photos with the
manuscript collection unless they relate to major existing
photographic collections or present unusual preservation
problems.

Resolving these problems can be quite intricate because many student scrapbooks and faculty papers contain a great mixture of images. A quick appraisal of the
uniqueness and visual quality of the images often will
reveal that the institutionally significant photographs are
few enough that they can be handled by cross-references.
The other images may be handled best by the collection-
level finding aids, which note the presence of these documents and the general subjects covered, just as for other
components of a manuscript collection.

Appraisal is an important, but often neglected, aspect of managing photographic materials. Images are often considered to be so inherently unique as to make retention automatic, but the bulk of some collections and the care needed for others suggest that assessment of the value of photos must be part of their archival control. However, unlike traditional university records and papers, for which appraisal can be focused on series-level evaluations, appraisal of photographs must sometimes be conducted at the item level. The greatest appraisal challenges may be found in the large photographic files from campus media offices, local photographers, or newspapers. If the originating office has already reviewed all negatives from its photographers and retained only those it found useful for its own needs, the archivist will generally receive a coherent and manageable body of images. In recent years, however, as photographers have moved to 35mm film, and thus strips of smaller negatives, and as personnel changes have reduced administrative support for identification and indexing, photo files from campus news offices have become more difficult for archivists to access and control. Similar problems confront those archivists who must deal with photo files from student newspapers and publications, where staff support and continuity are even more problematic.

Perhaps the best long-range solution is for the archivist to approach the originating office and request either selecting, copying, and indexing of the best image(s) on major subjects, or greater attention to identifying and indexing all negatives. Since the creation of a balanced historical record is not likely to be a priority for these offices, the archivist's appeal may not be heeded. In these cases, the archivist will be left with the burden of work in assessing, arranging, and describing the photos. Success in this work will depend on the initial recognition that the archivist always has the option *not* to improve on the physical condition or accessibility of the items. This can be a hard choice for archivists who are so accustomed to preservation and access, but it can be defended by compar-

ing the informational value of the photos to the extent of
resources needed to care for them.

Arrangement and Description

As already suggested, there are two major alternatives
for the arrangement of institutionally focused photographs. First, the archivist can maintain each body of
photos received as a separate accession and can illustrate
provenance by assigning the material an appropriate record group, subgroup, and series number, as is done for
paper records. Thus, all photos from the campus news
bureau would be classified or grouped with all of its correspondence files and publications but separate from very
similar photo files from the alumni office. This approach
requires a centralized subject index so that reference
inquiries can be directed to all record series with relevant
photographs. An alternative is to establish a single photographic subject-reference file, often around a core series
from an office such as public relations. Regardless of
source, photographs would be placed in this single file
after provenance and accession information had been
marked on the verso of each print. This approach would
require careful accession and separation records so that
the original body of material could be reassembled if
necessary for research use.

Many archivists may find that a combination of the
two approaches is best. Thus, a large subject-reference file
of photographic prints can be maintained as part of the
record group for campus public relations, and new photos
can be interfiled when received from this or other sources.
Larger groups of institutionally related photographs received from individuals, especially those collections reflecting a distinct personal vision of the institution, may
be maintained as separate record series but arranged in a
parallel fashion. Collections of photographs with no institutional focus should be maintained as individual accessions unless the repository's manuscripts-collecting focus
suggests the need for special photo reference files for such
subjects as local history or railroading. In all cases, the

archivist should remove all negatives for which reference prints exist, and the negatives should be assigned a unique serial number and placed in a separate series and location suited for negative storage.

Admittedly these recommendations conflict with strict rules of provenance and *respect des fonds*. While archivists should be loath to dispense with provenance, there are practical reasons to modify the rules for photographs. Access systems may need to take precedence over strict arrangement by provenance because of the demands posed by photographs' physical form and the need for retrieval of discrete images. Subject grouping of photos can also be defended on theoretical grounds, since photos are often created and used as discrete items and since their connection to their creating office generally has far less value as evidence than do correspondence files.

A major justification for establishing a single subject file of reference prints is that it permits retrieval of images without necessitating a separate subject index for each photograph. A number of archives and manuscript repositories, as well as originating offices, have attempted to create detailed subject indices to photographic holdings by means of card files, microcomputer databases, and contact sheet images. This kind of index, with the possibility of multiple access points for each photograph, can greatly facilitate the use of photos, but it is not a realistic option for most repositories with active and sizable collections of institutional photographs. Unfortunately, such ambitious indexing projects too often can be extended only to part of the holdings, leaving other parts with little or no access. A specialized collection of photographs on a particular subject area (e.g., a reference collection of architectural photographs for one city) may be suitable for a subject index. However, this is not a viable approach for the generalized photograph holdings that are needed in an academic archives. To be done properly, an index would have to offer multiple subject terms as access points, a procedure that can be prohibitively expensive to develop.[14]

This recommendation is not simply a matter of economy and time, but is based on a recognition of the complexity of information contained in photos, researchers' methods of approaching that information, and the way researchers use the images for evidence and illustration. Moreover, the factors that contribute to why a user chooses a particular image are so unpredictable (such as age, angle of view, time of day, quality of composition, clarity, presence or absence of people) that no indexing system could possibly satisfy these needs. In addition, no matter how detailed the indexing and cataloging information is, the user will want to examine the image itself, rather than an index card or computer screen. The time required for comprehensive indexing of a few photos could be devoted more productively to approaches that focus on group techniques for extensive photographic files.

Many repositories have found that the most effective way to handle large bodies of photographs is to file the photograph in a classified "self-indexing" subject file of reference points (with negatives numbered serially and filed separately). In such a system, the archivist needs to develop and regularly revise an overall subject classification scheme to cover institutional photographs. Such a system can be based on provenance, often following the archives' general classification guide supplemented by generic headings for common types of images. This method of arrangement will reduce access problems by grouping together the images on related institutional activities, just as archival arrangement keeps together the records of one office. Major headings for a photographic subject-classification system might include:

> Administrative and service activities
> Alumni
> Athletics
> Buildings
> Campus views and grounds
> Colleges, institutions, schools, or other organizational
>   units
> Dormitories and housing

Events (commencement, homecoming, etc.)
Faculty and staff
Student activities and organizations
Students

Additional and subordinate headings may be suggested by each institution's history. A college that has moved
its campus may include a major subject heading for images
of the old campus, site selection, and moving. Each repository will need to establish appropriate subheadings
within the major classification areas (e.g., views of buildings can be arranged alphabetically, then by exteriors and
interiors, then chronologically). The headings for colleges
and schools might be subdivided by department, and photos for each department might be placed in parallel sequences, such as classrooms, laboratories, departmental
meetings, and gatherings. Faculty, staff, and student photos can be divided into sequences for groups (filed chronologically) and individuals (filed alphabetically).

There are limitations to such a self-indexing subject
classification. It requires that users handle prints, thus
creating extra wear and inevitable misfiling. Ideally, this
system should be used only if archival-quality negatives
have been produced before any print is placed in the
reference file. Misfiling can be controlled by careful read-
ing-room supervision and diligent marking of classification information on the verso of each print. A more
fundamental limitation is that in a self-indexing system,
each image can be placed in only one subject classification
and there are no other access points. For instance, the
archivist will have to select the one and only place to file
a laboratory scene in an 1890s building among several
topics of interest in the photo (e.g., the interior of the
building, the college and department illustrated, or the
persons in the photo). The filing of an exterior view showing features of two buildings presents a similar dilemma
for providing access to both buildings. A carefully developed set of rules for classifying such photos can provide
consistency in ambiguous cases and thereby help researchers find appropriate sources. Where the filing deci-

sions for important images are not clear, cross-reference sheets, or even duplicate photos or photocopies, can be employed. Given the time and expense involved in both, however, these should be used sparingly and not as a substitute for the willingness and ability to make intelligent classification decisions.

Many other alternatives exist for subject access to photographs. A summary card index or computer file can provide pointers to major groupings of photographs that are held in separate collections, each of which, in turn, is self-indexing. A selected group of images can be copied and placed in albums, binders, slide carousels, or videotapes for highly popular subjects. Each approach has its merits, and most archives will find that the scope of their holdings and level of use will suggest simultaneous applications of several strategies.

Preservation

Archivists face considerable problems in the physical preservation of photographs. Each type of image (negative, print, transparency) and each physical and chemical process or material (e.g., albumen print, glass or nitrate negative, dry-mounted print on acidic board) requires a different kind of storage environment and restoration treatment. Given the breadth and complexity of photographic preservation, the archivist is better served by the excellent literature than by any summary that could be presented here. For large collections, the archivist may be able to accomplish only the most rudimentary steps in preservation, but these can be major strides in protecting the items. First, the negatives and prints should be stored separately. Second, closeable acid-free boxes and folders (or negative envelopes) should be used to shield the items from light and dirt. Third, nitrate and other unstable negatives should be recopied onto safety film.[15] Finally, the archivist should take measures to reduce excess light, heat, and moisture in the storage environment because photos are particularly susceptible to damage from these conditions.

More advanced preservation techniques for the most important parts of the photo collections include making reference prints for negatives lacking prints and making negatives for prints lacking negatives, restoring and cleaning individual prints and negatives, creating refrigerated storage for color negatives, and developing a collection of service negatives for images that are copied frequently. Additional preservation within the reach of the average repository will include removal of harmful enclosures (e.g., glassine or kraft envelopes, "magnetic" or polyvinylchloride album pages) and use of archival-quality supplies (e.g., polyester sleeves, acid-free paper). Once photographs have been stored in protective enclosures and boxes, the most important preservation step is to protect them during use. Considering the habits of many photographic users, such as last-minute scrambling to illustrate a completed text, use procedures can be the most important aspect of archival preservation.

Use of Photographs

Foremost in the successful administration of photographic collections will be specialized policies and procedures to address issues posed by the volume and nature of use and by the physical and informational content problems of photographs. The policy should outline handling practices to protect the original prints, procedures for obtaining copies, and the user's responsibility for securing copyright and reproduction permissions. Whenever possible, users should be given access only to reference prints and only to one box or folder at a time. Archivists should also prohibit anyone from charging out photos, unless the individual is a campus staff member working with previously arranged copy services. The archives should be able to provide users with a reasonably convenient means to reproduce photographs, even though few archives are equipped to produce copies on order for users. One option is to contract with the library or campus photographic services bureau or a local commercial studio to accept photos from the archives for reproduction on behalf of researchers. Alternatively, if the archives acquires a copy stand, it can accommodate researchers who wish to copy photos with their own equipment. Regardless of approach, the following principles should apply: the user is responsible for securing all copyright and reproduction permissions; the photos should not leave the archives except in the custody of archives staff; the user should be responsible for all reproduction costs, including the making of an archival-quality negative if one is not currently available; and the archives must always be given credit in any publication or public presentation using the images.

Often the most challenging problems in administering use of photographic collections will occur with projects conducted by campus offices that prepare institutional publicity materials. Historical photographs are excellent and popular illustrations for fund-raising, press releases, memorials, in-house and alumni magazines and newspapers, and exhibits or audiovisual presentations at meetings, banquets, and reunions. While the archives should support such use, three significant problems are common in such encounters: expectations that the archivist can devote extensive time to the projects, generally very short production schedules with little time for copying images, and expectations that the archives will forego its usual policies regarding noncirculation of images to facilitate production. These projects can create considerable pressure on the archivist to do whatever is necessary to expedite the project. However, the archivist should not lightly waive the repository's photographic use policy because doing so will only invite future excessive demands from publicity offices. Furthermore, the archivist should limit reference time to providing an overview of the collection and orientation to the subject matter. Original photos should be charged out only to the office that originally deposited the images, and they should never be sent to printers unless they are accompanied by a campus employee and returned within 24 to 48 hours. The archivist, however, might temper his or her reluctance to participate in such projects if they present opportunities to solve problems in the photo collection, such as obtaining wide circulation of a photograph needing identification or acquiring negatives for images where only prints exist. In deciding on how much time to allocate to such projects, the archivist must balance the intensive care needs of the users and particular areas of the collection against the general need for uniform control and preservation of the entire photographic collection.

If there are frequent and numerous inquiries for photos of major buildings, prominent faculty, and popular campus events, the archives should consider assembling a reference file of popular photographs. This file could consist of duplicates or fresh copies of a selection of the best images of the most popular campus subjects, placed in ready reference folders or binders. Such a file can reduce dramatically the wear on popular images in the main photo file, and it can enable the archivist to limit use of the full file to only those whose needs cannot be met by the images in the ready reference file.

Even this brief review of appraisal, arrangement, description, and preservation issues posed by photographs suggests that the problems are not only quite vexing, but also not amenable to formulaic approaches. Every academic archives will have to develop policies and procedures based on available resources and users' interests to ensure the availability of visual documentation. As in many other areas of academic archives, the major challenge may be to avoid becoming discouraged at how much needs to be done if one were to follow all the advice obtained from technical literature and specialists. Instead, the archivist should confidently make choices to balance program resources with the needs of photographic materials and their value in documenting the institution.

AUDIOVISUAL MATERIALS

A necessary part of most college and university archives, but one requiring special skills and facilities, is the acquisition, preservation, and use of audiovisual materials including sound recordings, moving images, and combinations of still images with other media to constitute multimedia presentations. Most archives encounter a variety of these materials even if they are not a major collecting focus or a sizable portion of the holdings. An inescapable feature of audiovisual records is the proliferation of physical formats, each dependent on a different type of machinery to record and retrieve the information. Thus, sound recordings may be on cylinders or discs (acoustic, electric, or optical) or on magnetic media (open reel, cassette, cartridge, wire). Moving images may be on film, videotape, or videodisc or may consist of a group of fixed images assembled to be presented in sequence, as with a multiple-projector slide show.

Given the physical nature of, and the information on, these materials, the lines between audiovisual and other non-textual, photographic, and machine-readable records often blur. Regardless of physical format, there are two common elements of audiovisual materials: the information they contain is of an aural or visual nature (or both); and the intervention of machinery is necessary to examine the documents and retrieve that information. The physical formats of audiovisual materials, and thus the problems they pose for the archivist, are too diverse for in-depth coverage in this book. Rather, the purpose of this section is to provide guidelines on how they should be incorporated into academic archives and integrated with other archival materials and control practices.[16]

Collection Scope and Appraisal

The most fundamental principle to guide the archivist in working with these problematic materials is that audiovisual materials are documents like any others. They can and should be subjected to the same general principles and procedures as the rest of the archives. Audiovisual materials are important parts of the record of the institution, people, and subjects for which the archives is responsible, and they should be part of the archives' basic documentation policy. Thus, the archivist should not hesitate to acquire motion pictures of varsity athletic events just because the format poses unfamiliar problems, nor should the archivist retain all such films just because they are complete copies of an event in the institution's past. In other words, the archivist should approach all sound recordings, motion pictures, videotapes, and filmstrips with the same basic theoretical considerations and practical techniques as would be used for textual materials.

Audiovisual materials differ from the rest of the archives, and thus require specialized attention, because their physical nature makes it very difficult to apply standard archival principles and practices. Appraisal can follow the steps outlined in this book and other archival literature, but completing the process will be far more cumbersome because audiovisual materials are not legible or intelligible to the naked eye. Thus, the quick scanning or systematic reading used when appraising a correspondence file becomes more time-consuming and often impossible when tape recordings, for instance, are being considered. Similarly, before one decides to dispose of a tape recording, it may be necessary to listen to the entire reel to ensure that none of the events on it merits retention and that the events listed on the label match those on the tape. Checking for duplicates also can be quite difficult, especially with motion pictures.

Standard archival techniques can be quite useful in appraising audiovisual materials, but because audiovisual materials often lack detailed or even adequate descriptions when they first come to the archivist's attention, appraisal often cannot be done until after accessioning. Indeed, appraisal sometimes is possible only after most of the processing has been completed. Nevertheless, once a brief description of the contents of the recordings is available, the archivist should assess the significance of the subject matter for research and determine how the document's age, physical condition, and image quality will affect the future accessibility of the information. For example, if the material is deteriorating rapidly, this preliminary review should lead the archivist either to immediate recopying (if the event is very important) or immediate disposal (if the event is routine or only of passing interest).

A specialized concern will be whether the equipment needed to use the material is readily available and if not,
whether there are economical means of transferring the
material to more accessible format for preservation and
use.

A key consideration is that not all audiovisual material
merits long-term retention, and there is no reason that
their special format should dictate their retention. The
archivist must be rigorous in assessing the significance of
the recorded event and the relationship of the audiovisual
material to other documentation of the same event. Obvious targets for close appraisal and possible sampling include accessions with large numbers of sound recordings
of guest lecturers or commencement speakers, films of
football or basketball games, or annual slide-tape promotional productions prepared for alumni gatherings. At the
other extreme, obvious examples of items for retention
would be films of the student union and student activities
in the 1920s, recordings of speeches by key academicians
and public figures on substantive rather than ceremonial
subjects, and films of student demonstrations and unique
events.[17]

Arrangement and Description

Both the physical and the intellectual nature of most
audiovisual materials dictate that arrangement and description be considered as an integral process. This is
because the physical nature of sound and video recordings
may require their storage separate from the rest of the
records of the creating office. In addition, these documents
are often the result of extensive conceptual work by individual or corporate authors meriting item-level control
rather than the aggregate description that would be used
for other records from the same offices. If arrangement
and description can be conducted in tandem, with each
process compensating for what the other cannot accomplish, both the greatest efficiency in managing the materials and maximum accessibility to users will be ensured.

In general, the arrangement of audiovisual materials should follow the basic principles of provenance as used for the rest of the archives. They should be placed in record groups reflecting their office of origin, and the original order should be maintained whenever possible. Given the physical nature of the material, exceptions will be necessary, but the overall approach is best understood when one examines how audiovisual materials come to be placed in archives. They are often transferred as large groups of items in the same format, frequently from offices with an institutional mandate to produce these materials. Deciding on the appropriate record group and subgroup to reflect the office of origin of such large series can be very simple. Common sources include campus radio stations, lecture bureaus, public relations offices, athletic publicity offices, and alumni affairs offices. While the bulk of such accessions may present greater appraisal problems than isolated recordings given to the archives, they frequently come with a rudimentary arrangement and indexing system. Far less effort will be needed to decide the proper record group/subgroup for a run of 38 football game films than to decide the best place for a single audiocassette of one lecture by a visiting dignitary with no clear connection to the campus. The average archives may need a dozen or so series for these larger files, but a single artificial file for each type of material (e.g., Campus Sound Recordings or Campus Motion Pictures) may be used when the production of audiovisual materials has been uncoordinated and poorly controlled by the institution. If such an artificial series is created, its internal arrangement will need to be established by the archivist.

Often, resolving arrangement problems may require item-level description to maintain a record of provenance and provide accessibility. This will be especially true if a central "artificial" file has been created. It can also be a means to address the fact that audiovisual records often resemble library monographic materials in that each item is a single and self-conscious representation of an event or an idea. Thus, item-level description and control may be more necessary and the relation of one item to the next may have far less evidential significance than with textual documents in office files. In these instances, a chronological or serial arrangement will offer the simplest means of control, provided that a separate subject index or computer searching capability is provided. In other cases, the audiovisual documents may resemble library serials in that they are part of a regular series (e.g., football game films, Wednesday lecture-series tapes, or campus radio-station feature programs) and that series may be a very logical record series. Regardless of the arrangement, it will normally be necessary to use a simple local indexing system to provide access by subject, author/speaker, and type of event.

Another arrangement problem is that audiovisual materials frequently appear within textual record series and manuscript collections. Typically, there will be a few isolated tape recordings, films, or slide shows filed with a much larger and often related body of professional correspondence, research notes, and teaching materials. In most cases, audiovisual records should be maintained in the series or collection with cross-references in a repository-wide finding aid or subject index when the materials cover topics of general campus interest. If the materials present particular preservation problems, such as the deterioration of shellac disks or embrittlement of film, the items should be stored separately after completing a separation sheet and listing the items on the series or collection finding aid.

Faculty papers and other manuscript collections sometimes contain extensive audiovisual materials as a form of research notes; e.g., an anthropologist's papers may contain rare recordings of Native American languages and dialects or unique films of ceremonies. Audiovisual materials on such highly specialized subjects will be controlled better as part of the individual collection than through a centralized finding aid or index. Thus, it is better to retain them within the collection than to move them to a repository-wide audiovisual series.

The most difficult arrangement and description problems occur with those isolated accessions of audiovisual records that are characterized best as odds and ends. An archives will not exist for long before campus employees, the public, and alumni send tapes, disks, films, and video-cassettes they have discovered, preserved, or produced and which appear to relate to the campus' history. Often these accessions can be extremely valuable additions to the archives, filling important gaps in holdings, but it can be difficult to find the most appropriate record group and subgroups. They will be especially problematic if the archivist attempts to establish distinct record series for each accession. Such accessions should become separate record series only if the item(s) are a consciously compiled group of materials conceived as a unit to accomplish a function beyond recording a single event (e.g., a group of slide shows and videotapes used to support a major fundraising drive). Sometimes these small accessions are closely related to existing documentation, especially publications, and can be held with those records. In most instances, however, they will be isolated in their subject and documentary focus (e.g., a recording of a pep rally before a 1958 NCAA basketball championship game or a motion picture of the burning of Old Main taken by a local photographer). In these cases, the items may be best controlled in a centralized, "artificial" record series based on format (e.g., Campus Motion Pictures) with appropriate provenance notes and cross-references in the subject index or the finding aids used to control access to that series.

To a great extent, guidelines for describing audiovisual materials will emerge as each archives addresses the arrangement issues described above in the context of the repository's general descriptive practices and goals for user access. Nevertheless, description of audiovisual materials is tedious and time-consuming because it requires listening to, or viewing of, substantial parts of each item. Moreover, the summary level of descriptive control that is quite useful for other archival and manuscript materials is often inadequate for audiovisual documents because each item may represent a discrete event that cannot be traced easily through generalized description. In addition, since the use of such documents often focuses on a specific event, the finding aid, whether container list, card index, or computer database, should identify each physical item. When more than one event is recorded on a single physical piece, such as a tape containing a lecture and an interview of a prominent environmentalist, the finding aid will need to provide access to each event. In the case of large series of homogeneous material, such as films of football games or commencement exercises, a simple typewritten list or database with one line per item or event will suffice.

Mature archives may also need a centralized finding aid that provides access to all sound recordings and visual materials located in series and collections throughout the repository. In some cases, this specialized index might be merged with the finding aid for a centralized artificial file of materials (e.g., Campus Sound Recordings). This finding aid should provide a number of access points: event, date, personal names of speaker or key participants, subjects, recording format, and physical and series location. A sample card is shown in Figure 6.

This kind of finding aid may be far more detailed and complex than those used in other areas of the archives, and could be seen as appropriate for library cataloging. A repository with sufficient resources, resident library cataloging expertise, and nationally significant audiovisual records should consider such an item-level approach utilizing the appropriate cataloging rules and MARC format (Visual Materials, Music/Sound Recordings, or even Archives and Manuscripts). Most college and university archives, however, will find that a simple local system will suffice for access and control and be the most that their resources permit. The local system will have to include a minimal set of rules to provide consistency and permit work by less experienced staff while also providing enough flexibility for variations in description depending on significance and time available.

Preservation and Use

Audiovisual materials pose many complex preservation problems that are not only beyond this book's level of

Audio / Video Summary Index Record

Record Series Number 13/5/18   Box or Recording No. 1588–1590

Event Benjamin Franklin Awards Dinner   Date 6/15/55

Speaker(s)   Morey, Lloyd
             Nevins, Allan
             Nickels, William H.
             Pearson, Leon

Subjects   Freedom of the press
          International relations
          Magazine publishing
          Race relations
          School desegregation

Recording Format (X audio ___ video) (___ tape X disc ___ film) Other format info. 33 1/3 rpm

Length 58:32:16 (hr: min: sec)

Figure 6. Audio / Video Summary Index Record

coverage but also far greater than can be addressed by most academic archives' facilities, staff, equipment, and budgets. Nevertheless, the archivist should be aware of the problems posed by each type of material and what basic steps can be taken for minimal protection during storage and use.[18] The most fundamental problem stems from the fact that audiovisual materials require the intervention of specialized machinery before they can be used. The machinery not only abrades the material during each playback, but, more importantly, often becomes obsolete in a very short period of time. Even more problematic is that the formats for encoding and playing back audiovisual material become superseded with alarming frequency. Thus, the archivist's first concern should be whether the equipment needed to use the material will continue to be available and repairable for the indefinite future. For example, when a wire recording or a 2-inch quadraplex videotape is accessioned, the archivist will need access to equipment for listening or viewing. If the equipment is not readily available in the archives and the format of the record is likely to become obsolete, the archivist should attempt to have the item transferred to a format that has archival or broadcast quality and shows some promise of future availability. For example, significant audiocassettes should be copied onto archival-grade open-reel archival tape at 7-1/2 inches per second, and VHS videocassettes should be dubbed onto broadcast grade U-matic format 3/4-inch videotape. Given the changes in recording technology, especially in video equipment, the archivist should avoid storage media that have not been in wide use for a long period of time, no matter how promising or currently popular they are. Copying to a new format as old ones become obsolete also has limitations. It is expensive, requires long-range allocation of resources for regular dubbing, and often involves image degradation with each generation. If playback equipment can be acquired to deal with the formats most commonly accessioned, then reformatting may not be necessary. One means, albeit an expensive one, of insulating the archives from format changes inherent in much of the mass-market equipment is to purchase two or three of the best recording and playback devices for the formats the archives chooses as standards. A major consideration should be to select brands that have a history of parts and service availability long after the particular model is out of production.

There are other major preservation challenges for audiovisual materials. All the materials are dependent on the plastics used in recording media. Not only is the quality of plastic highly variable and hard to assess without sophisticated equipment, but the plastic base is more subject to irreversible damage from heat, moisture, and common chemicals (e.g., human finger oils) than paper-based media. In addition, these materials have preservation demands that are specific to each medium. Thus, all magnetic media should be kept away from magnetic fields, such as telephones, transformers, and motors. Tape recordings should be transferred to unspliced archival-quality tape (e.g., open-reel tape of 1.5 mil polyester base with low read-through and recorded at 7-1/2 inches per second). Ideally, magnetic recordings should be played through annually to limit the effects of magnetic image read-through and stiffening of the tape itself, and they should be returned to storage wound "tails out" after a "real-time," not fast-forward or rewind, playing. Disc sound recordings and motion picture films should be cleaned and lubricated before storage and use.[19]

For large collections, this level of maintenance is likely to require both more equipment and more staff than most academic archives can afford. The preservation needs of audiovisual materials can be so extensive that the best that most archives can do is to store the materials in boxes away from heat, light, chemical, and electromagnetic hazards and to protect them from undue abrasion and accidental erasure during use. If at all possible, they should be stored in a temperature- and humidity-controlled area. Additional preservation work may have to be limited to on-demand maintenance and repairs when the material is used, regular cleaning of playback equipment, and strict handling procedures.

The factors affecting use of audiovisual materials are not significantly different in principle from those governing use of the balance of the archives, but format and preservation considerations can make service more complex. The archives needs equipment capable of playing back all the formats it holds or access to such equipment elsewhere in the institution. Relying on a campus audiovisual center for projection may solve costly equipment problems, but it also requires special procedures and staff time for ensuring that charged-out materials are handled properly and returned. Regardless of where materials are used, precautions are needed to prevent accidental erasure (e.g., by defeating the recording function on equipment) and breakage. If the users require copies of the recordings, arrangements for dubbing will be necessary, and staff will need to apprise users of the copyright limitations on subsequent broadcast or performance of the materials.

Finally, the nature of audio and visual information engenders several difficult use problems: searches for short sound or video "bites" on narrow topics; very short lead times, especially in serving broadcast media and campus publicity offices; and the need to copy recordings to permit access by off-site users. To meet these user demands, staff resources may be strained, and the use can hinder the balanced development of the archival program. Consequently, the archives should consider defining its goals and levels of service for those requesting audiovisual recordings. For example, the archives may need to institute a policy of requiring at least two weeks to respond to any external request for videotape copies of films. Similarly, the archives' policy may need to limit the time staff will spend searching for footage on a specific topic. Such limits are necessary for sound program management, but they are best developed as responses to actual experience in providing access to the collection.

ARCHITECTURAL RECORDS

As intermediaries who assist present generations to examine links with the past, academic archivists need to recognize the importance of architectural records to their mission. These records vividly exemplify the usefulness of archives for current administrative needs while also illustrating the relevance of documents to highly visible phys-. ical entities. The centrality of campus architectural records should be apparent even to the novice archivist, but equally obvious should be the many methodological problems that emerge from the physical format, informational content, and common uses of these records. An adequate but not abundant literature on architectural records addresses many of these methodological issues. It should be consulted when technical information is needed, but it can be frustrating for the academic archivist since it is written from the perspective of repositories specializing in such records.[20] This book, therefore, will focus on helping archivists understand how to incorporate architectural records into the overall documentary responsibilities of the repository.

The term *architectural records* is problematic for the institutional archivist because many kinds of records can be used to examine architectural questions. For example, an 1870 register of warrants can be invaluable to an architectural historian because it provides clear documentation of who performed design, masonry, or landscape work on the college's first dormitory. Archivists concerned with adequately documenting their college and serving researchers should adopt a broad definition of architectural records as including any document reflecting on the built or manipulated environment.[21] As a practical matter, however, the term *architectural record* is commonly reserved for documents relying on pictorial, graphic, and mathematical, rather than textual, means to record the concept, design, and construction of a building, structure, or other physical feature (e.g., landscape design) that has been altered from its natural condition by human intervention.

The major categories of architectural records include program and design statements, renderings and drawings, construction specifications, insurance records, three-dimensional models, photographs, and machine-readable files in computer-assisted design systems.[22] Most of these materials present archival problems because of the nature of the physical medium, size, limited reproducibility, and detailed technical content, and because of the highly specific level of recall often required by researchers. The literature on architectural records can be used to understand the technical composition and function of these records, but the emphasis here will be on the extent of the academic archivist's responsibility for architectural records and on procedures to facilitate a minimal level of control when state-of-the-art techniques are out of reach.

Collection Scope and Appraisal

The architectural-record holdings of academic archives should include information on all campus buildings. For minor temporary and generic buildings, such as barracks housing, sheds, storage buildings, and garages, the holdings can be limited to a few summary records such as a photograph, site plan, floor plan, elevation, and section. For more important buildings, such as classrooms, laboratories, student union, dormitories, and administration buildings, the archives should include much more extensive documentation. For these buildings as well as for overall campus plans and major landscape plans, the archives should contain program statements, design drawings, presentation drawings, working and as-built drawings, shop drawings for major architectural features and decoration, building specifications, and photographs.

The depth of documentation retained should vary with the significance of the building or place. Factors contributing to significance include the building's or site's:

1. Relationship to major institutional functions, colleges, or departments, such as classroom buildings, libraries, student unions, and faculty clubs.

2. Longevity, such as an early campus clock tower and carillon (even if now demolished), the recently renovated and converted campus chapel, and the aging auditorium that has been the center of a controversy between campus preservationists and space efficiency experts.

3. Associations with noted architects, designers, or engineers, such as an auditorium designed by Frank Lloyd Wright.

4. Innovations or good examples of a particular architectural style, such as a prototypical round barn.

5. Association with major campus events, historical figures, or controversies, such as the first president's house or a science lab that became the site of major demonstrations against the Vietnam War.

When there are similar records in different formats for a particular building or site, the archivist should favor those that are superior as evidence or artifacts, such as ink on linen or pencil on tracing paper rather than blueprints, diazo prints, or photostats. However, the archivist will often need to settle for the form available and retain less permanent copies as well to facilitate research access and reduce the risk of damage to fragile originals.

Source and Custodianship

To secure adequate architectural documentation, the archivist will need to establish close relations with those units responsible for planning, constructing, and maintaining buildings and grounds. The major sources for architectural records will be the offices of the campus architect, capital programs, buildings and grounds, and physical plant. Most institutions centralize the responsibility for drawings and specifications of completed structures, but documents related to early planning and review may be held by offices of major campus administrators such as Provost and Vice President. Additional sources for drawings and specifications will be the offices of the colleges, departments, and other units that are the primary occupants of a building. For example, the student union office may hold the set of drawings provided to its director at the time of its construction. In many cases, these are only copies of the drawings in the campus architect's office, but they may also be the first or only sets available to the archives.

Custodianship, normally a simple matter for other kinds of records, can be a major problem in dealing with architectural records. The archives' holdings should encompass all campus buildings, but in many cases the units responsible for building maintenance must retain complete sets of drawings and specifications to be able to do their work. If the archives were to try to gain custody of all such records, it might encounter not only strong resistance from maintenance personnel, but also heavy and complex user demands from those maintaining the buildings. Therefore, a key step will be to develop understandings with the offices that hold those working records. To accomplish this, it will be essential for the archivist to

1. Examine the records' storage environment and handling practices to make sure that the originals are maintained in conditions that will not reduce their longevity.

2. Assess the offices' procedures for making their records accessible to in-depth researchers.

3. Determine whether the offices need to make extra copies for the archives of those architectural records related to popular research topics.

For example, the archives might obtain copies of elevations, floor plans, and structural details of any landmark buildings, as well as floor plans, possibly in reduced size, for all campus buildings, but the extent of such copying should be based on the archives' experience with research inquiries. If the archivist cannot secure cooperation in pursuing these three basic activities, the campus administration should be lobbied to provide the archives with custodianship of the drawings as well as the space, facilities, and staff needed to ensure their preservation and accessibility.

Arrangement and Description

The arrangement and description of architectural records in academic archives presents special problems, but they are not extraordinarily complex unless the archivist attempts highly detailed control. At the record-series level, the arrangement of architectural records should follow the usual lines of provenance to reflect the records' office of origin. Within the record group and subgroup for the office of campus architect, physical plant, or capital programs, two or three series should suffice for the bulk of campus-related architectural records. Separate series might be created for each physical format, such as program statements, specifications, and plans. Other categories of architectural documentation, such as photographs or minutes of building planning committees, should be kept with broader record series of campus photographs or office records rather than as special series of architectural photos or minutes. When architectural records are obtained from the departments or colleges that occupy a building rather than from an architect's office, the archivist will need to determine whether the departmental files are unaltered copies of documents also held by the central office. If there are few significant alterations, the departmental copies may be filed in the archives' series for the architect office's records or discarded as duplicates. If, however, they contain many departmental or college annotations and the annotations concern important design or structural changes, the archivist will need to retain them in the department's record group and subgroup.

Within each series of architectural records, arrangement by project will be most effective and true to original order. Generally, this will be an alphabetical sequence of the names of buildings or places. Within each project, records should follow their original order which will usually be chronological, and thereunder it will be according to a standardized sequence used by architects to organize their drawings (i.e., site plans followed by floor plans, roof plans, elevations, sections, architectural details, and details for structure plumbing, heating, ventilation, and electrical wiring). While the conceptual and descriptive arrangement of architectural plans may follow this sequence, their physical properties, especially if oversize or microreproductions, may dictate shelving by size and format. Thus, if plans for the Student Health Center are retained in both blueprint and microfilm formats, they will need to be stored separately, and finding aids and cross-reference sheets will be needed to draw the material together.

Description of architectural records should not be difficult, but a greater level of detail may be necessary than is used elsewhere in the archives. At the series level, the description can and should be kept quite short. A few lines providing inclusive dates, types of records, formats, and scope of buildings and places covered should suffice for the summary description of the main series of drawings and specifications. The detailed finding aids for each series normally should be limited to a container list of the buildings or projects for which records are held, with span dates for the documents relating to each building. The archivist should avoid further detail such as itemizing the kinds of plans and number of sheets, or stating scale and technical details. Only in the case of rare and artistically valuable drawings, such as a hand-colored presentation drawing or an artist's rendering submitted for a design competition, should the archivist attempt item-level listings of architectural records.

In addition to series-level and building or project inventories, archivists will need to consider descriptive access for architectural records by means of repository-wide indices and specialized finding aids. A repository-wide subject index, whether accomplished manually, via local computer, or MARC-AMC entries, will be especially important for ensuring the accessibility of architectural records found in departmental and college files. A procedure for cross-indexing also will enable the archivist to link formal architectural records (e.g., blueprints) to related textual records (e.g., the correspondence and reports of the psychology department's building planning committee). In addition, or as a low-cost substitute, it may be useful to create a single, specialized finding aid for all architectural records in the archives. This finding aid should be arranged by building or project name and should index such key access points as date of construction, architect's name, and storage location. By means of simple word processing documents, the archivist can produce a reference tool that can be the first step in answering most architectural inquiries.

Preservation and Use

Where and how to house architectural records will be as key an issue in preservation as it is in arrangement. The best that many academic archives will be able to do for most of their non-textual architectural records is to place them in containers or cabinets that protect them from light, dust, heat, humidity, and physical stress such as abrasion and tears. This is only a partial solution since each physical format presents different preservation problems. For example, the linen-cloth backing used on nineteenth- and early twentieth-century drawings is susceptible to insect damage or to mold if humidity is high. Similarly, many of the inks, charcoals, and colors used for hand drawings or presentation drawings are water soluble and susceptible to damage through abrasion or through static charges that can occur with Mylar encapsulation.

Most academic archivists, however, will not be fortunate enough to be able to work on such problems. Instead, they should concentrate on obtaining horizontal plan cases with large (e.g., 36" x 48" x 2") steel drawers to hold the plans and drawings. Drawings should be placed in acid-neutral file folders, and valuable original drawings should be interleaved with archival-grade paper for added buffering. The number of drawings and sheets per folder should be varied according to their value, physical condition, and likely use, with the most valuable being interleaved with no more than ten to a folder. With small sets of drawings, a separate folder should be used for each building or project.

When horizontal plan cases are not available, vertical suspension cabinets may be substituted if they are of the pin-and-post rather than pocket type. These units require less floor space than flat files and are sometimes donated to the archives along with drawings. Smaller drawings might be placed in the oversize flat-file boxes available from major archival suppliers, but these boxes generally do not exceed 24.5" x 20.5" x 1.5." When plan-file cabinets and boxes are not available for all drawings, the archivist may have little choice but to store them rolled, often on open shelving, in which case a few precautions can make this compromise more acceptable. Large sets of drawings can be rolled and wrapped with acid-neutral paper (map folders cut to size work quite well) and tied firmly, but not tightly, with acid-neutral string or ribbon. When rolling individual drawings or small sets, a cardboard tube (covered with acid-neutral paper) should be used as a core to provide strength. Each roll should be clearly labeled on the end with a tag attached to the wrapping tie, to minimize handling during retrievals. The rolls should be stored horizontally, not vertically, on shelving and kept away from light and sources of dust. Additional preservation and conservation measures, while desirable, may need to be deferred until more resources are available or the need becomes overwhelming.

The reference use of architectural records, especially plans, will present several challenges to their preservation. First, care is needed to ensure that drawings are not damaged as they are moved from storage to reading areas and that researchers do not damage the documents during handling. The archives will need adequately sized tables available away from the hazards of light and dirt. Protection during use will also require policies and procedures to govern copying of plans. Tracing over drawings generally should be avoided unless the user is trained in non-damaging techniques and is meticulous in handling the documents. Instead, the archives should provide arrangements for drawings being taken to campus or commercial blueprint shops for inexpensive duplication for users. The archives will also need a policy indicating when copying cannot be done because of the poor physical condition of the drawings, limited staff time, or size of copy request.

Beyond these physical aspects of use, the archivist needs to be proficient in locating many types of documentation throughout the archives to answer architecturally related questions. The archivist often may need to educate users, especially students, about the breadth of documentation of buildings beyond the familiar drawings and blueprints. In response to requests for architectural records, the archivist frequently may need to retrieve highly detailed pieces of information from photographs, office files, accounting ledgers, campus publications, and even personal papers, correspondence, or diaries. Where student or novice inquiries for architectural information are common, such as in universities with schools of architecture, the archivist would be well-advised to develop special handouts or guides to introduce architectural documentation and explain handling policies and procedures. If the archives' architectural records are underutilized, the archivist should consider a range of outreach activities, such as exhibits, lectures to classes and campus administrative groups, and contacts with news media and local architectural historians, to promote interest in these records. Architectural records should not be overlooked. They provide an excellent opportunity for the archivist to demonstrate the ability of documents to explain the past and the present in very tangible ways.

Glossary of Architectual Terms [23]

ARCHITECTURAL DRAWING. A drawing depicting the precise concepts and measurements needed for the design and construction of specific structures.

BLUEPRINT. A reproduction of a drawing by a contact printing process on light-sensitive paper, producing a negative image of white lines on a blue background.

DESIGN DRAWING. An unmeasured freehand drawing showing the basic form and nature of a building, including its general ground plans and outside elevations. Examples include preliminary sketches, perspective drawings, and presentation renderings.

DETAIL DRAWING. An enlarged drawing of specific parts of buildings or special features of construction such as windows or cabinets.

DIAZOTYPE. An inexpensive copying processes, which can be produced in several colors, of which blue is the most popular (called bluelines).

DRAFTING CLOTH (commonly called LINEN). A linen or cotton fabric on which permanent tracings are made.

ELEVATION DRAWING. A drawing showing the vertical elements of a building, either exterior or interior.

FLOOR PLAN. A drawing of a horizontal section taken above a floor to show, diagrammatically, the enclosing walls of a building, its doors and windows, and the arrangement of its interior spaces.

LANDSCAPE DRAWING. A vertical view that illustrates the position of trees, shrubbery, and other landscape features.

LANDSCAPE PLAN. A horizontal view of the position of trees, shrubbery, and other landscape features.

LINE DRAWING. A drawing of lines, dots, and solid masses, as distinguished from the tonal variations of a watercoloring.

MODEL. A three-dimensional representation of a finished building or group of buildings at a reduced scale.

PERSPECTIVE DRAWING. A graphic representation of a project or part thereof as it would appear three-dimensionally.

PLAN. A horizontal view of a building and surrounding landscape. Also may refer to specific plans: foundation plans, roof plans, framing plans, etc.

PROGRAM STATEMENT. A textual document used in the early planning of a building to describe the occupants' conditions and objectives, the building's purposes, and the kinds of space and equipment required.

RENDERING. A drawing in perspective, and frequently in color, of a building on its site, generally prepared for presentation and publicity purposes.

SECTION. A representation of a building or portion thereof to show the internal structure as it would appear if cut by an imaginary plane.

SHOP DRAWING. A detailed drawing of a part of a building prepared by contractors or subcontractors to show embellishments, interior designs, and equipment.

SITE PLAN. A map of a small area showing the structural outline of one or more buildings in relation to the surrounding terrain and landscape.

SPECIFICATIONS. A part of the contract documents consisting of written technical descriptions of materials, equipment, construction standards, and workmanship.

STANDARD DRAWING. A drawing of a standard detail used in several places in a structure.

MACHINE-READABLE RECORDS

Since the beginnings of written information, the recording technologies themselves, whether they involved clay tablets, papyrus, parchment, or wood-pulp paper, have played a significant role in how archivists select, preserve, and make information accessible. Increased technological capabilities have made the recording and storage of large amounts of information more efficient, but each new technology has added as many problems as it has solved. For the foreseeable future, these problems will continue to be most troubling for those records requiring the intervention of a computer for their examination and use. These machine-readable or electronic records use mechanical (e.g., punched cards), magnetic (e.g., computer tape), or optical (e.g., laser disks) technology to record information in a form that can be stored and subsequently processed electronically by a computer. Although their machine dependence makes them similar to audiovisual materials, electronic or machine-readable records are different because they contain vast amounts of textual information in coded form and because the storage and processing devices allow the rapid manipulation, alteration, and rearrangement of the information itself.

These records pose particular challenges for academic archivists because they account for large quantities of information relevant to the archives' documentary mission, and because increasingly they contain data that are unavailable in any other form. Electronic records pose problems especially for appraisal, preservation, and use, and they require specialized techniques quite unlike those needed for managing the more traditional textual paper or even photographic records. Fortunately, once the nature of electronic records and their centrality to archival responsibilities is understood, archival solutions can be found by combining specialized techniques with traditional archival principles.[24]

The varieties of machine-readable records can be quite bewildering, but they are all based on the use of a machine both to record and to read information on a physical device. For the vast majority of electronic records, information is recorded in a digital format. Data are represented by a system based on binary numbers (*bits*), each of which acts as a simple on/off switch for the flow of electricity. Several bits (usually eight) are combined to form a *byte* or code to record an alphabetic, numeric, or symbolic character. Just as with conventional numerals and letters, these bytes can be further combined to represent numbers and words and thereby permit the encoding of information. These numbers and words can be assembled into languages, and those languages into programs, or sequences of instructions, enabling a data-processing device (i.e., a computer) both to store and to manipulate coded information. The machine instructions, generally called software, can be divided into two categories based on their function. Systems software controls the computer hardware operations, especially storage (or memory), computation (or processing), and use of input and output devices. Applications software is the detailed set of instructions for using the hardware's processing power to accomplish specific tasks, especially storage, manipulation, and retrieval of data. The sequence of software languages (machine, assembly, and higher-level or compiler languages) enables individuals to use computers without any specialized knowledge of internal codes or operating systems.

All computers function along these lines, but the operating systems and applications software will not always be transferable from one computer to another. Unless special steps are taken, the retrievability and use of information is totally dependent on the availability of the same configuration of hardware and software as used to record the information initially. Therefore, archivists need to work with system designers to develop methods of encoding data that will be as independent of hardware and software as possible. Failing that, they should plan regular conversion of data and programs to maintain compatibility with new hardware and software. Otherwise, whether the medium is punched cards, optical characters, magnetic tape, or rigid or floppy disks, machine-readable records that lack matching hardware and software configurations will be unreadable and useless except as artifacts, paperweights, and doorstops.

Types of Electronic Records

Hardware and software issues often seem to dominate the archivist's consideration of machine-readable records, but the primary question always should be the informational content of the records themselves. Because the substance of the records should determine whether the archivist needs to delve into complex hardware and software issues, it is appropriate to begin by focusing on the kinds of uses to which electronic records have been put at colleges and universities. The early uses of automated records have been for large databases on mainframe computers recording relatively short pieces of information about persons or transactions. In central administration, uses of machine-readable records have included budgeting, accounting, financial transactions, inventories of equipment, property, and space. In academic administration, applications have included course enrollments, course evaluations, registration, financial aid, and grades. In the area of administrative support, applications have included listings of personnel, compilations of address directories, analyses of staff time and productivity, and development of specialized databases to support administrative research. Other traditional and mainframe-based applications include support of auxiliary services, such as ticketing for athletic and cultural events, parking regulation, dormitory assignment, library catalogs, and electronic mail and bulletin boards.

With advances in mini- and microcomputer capabilities, especially in the 1980s, there has been a tremendous expansion in the kinds and numbers of computer-based records at colleges and universities. While the overall use of microcomputers has paralleled the development of mainframe applications for databases, finances, and statistics, two recent trends have had particularly important implications for archivists: the growth of word processing and other text-based capabilities, and the tremendous increases in decentralized computing made possible by the low-cost of powerful microcomputers. In combination with the growing complexity of mainframe databases, the two trends of text-based systems and decentralization have intensified the very substantial challenges to the archivist's ability to document the college or university. With more text-based information being processed by computers, there is greater likelihood that the textual documentation that has traditionally formed the core of academic archives may be available only through machine-readable files. If the texts are relatively static, e.g., one-time letters and reports, a reasonable solution is to have them printed out and retained on paper. Where the texts themselves are constantly evolving online (e.g., electronic mail and conferences), special procedures should be implemented early in these records' "life cycle." Furthermore, the decentralization of computing has made it more difficult to establish control over machine-readable files than when such data were held only by one or two campus computing centers. Finally, when the dynamics that are permitted by decentralized access are combined with increased use of integrated microcomputer/mainframe databases across campus, it is clear that timely confronting of electronic records issues is crucial to the future of academic archives.

The files of faculty members about their research and creative activity are part of machine-readable information systems at colleges and universities both on traditional mainframe and newer microcomputer systems. These may include highly structured statistical files containing survey response or experimental data, word processing and database files of text and research notes, or computer-based artistic works. As part of a program to collect and preserve faculty papers, the archives will need to consider which faculty machine-readable files should be acquired and how they can be made available. These questions will be easier to answer for the larger, structured data files, especially those using mainframes and standard statistical packages; it will be harder for smaller, one-time files of microcomputer-based text, graphics, or sound. Unfortunately, since the significance of the material and its potential archival value are unlikely to parallel its manageability, the archivist cannot take a minimalist role, but must be active in identifying those faculty whose electronic records have long-term research value.

Impact of Recent Changes

The 1960s and 1970s witnessed rapid progress in the development and application of computer information systems, but changes in the 1980s have been particularly momentous for archivists. The advances in programs, storage, memory, and printing devices have placed sophisticated computing capacity within reach of many of those who create the documentary record of colleges and universities. These changes have had three major effects on the records available for academic archives. First, far more campus administrators, staff, and faculty are creating machine-readable records than ever before. Second, machine-readable records are being used for conducting administrative functions that were previously managed with manual records or for recording information about functions that were previously undocumented. Third, the variety of information formats, computer software, hardware, and storage devices has burgeoned, and there seems to be an accelerating rate of obsolescence. What is most important about these trends is that in taking advantage of technological possibilities and responding to individual needs, academic computing has become very diffuse and therefore resistant to the kinds of central control that normally facilitate an archivist's work. The autonomy of campus computer users as well as hardware and software changes require the archivist to take an active stance in raising archival issues in the minds of those who use automated techniques to handle campus information.

These problems are formidable for academic archivists, especially since there is already such a shortage of resources to handle current paper-based, photographic, and audiovisual holdings. Unfortunately, the history of machine-readable records suggests that many problems need to be addressed promptly to capture and preserve machine-readable data during their inherently short life span instead of waiting until more ample time or money seems to be available. Strategies for solving these problems will involve more specialized knowledge and techniques than can be presented in this book. Furthermore, because rapid changes in technology would render such guidance quickly out of date, the following discussion will be limited to an overview of the relationship of basic archival processes to machine-readable records while emphasizing the need to adopt alternative techniques when dealing with many aspects of these materials.

Archival Processes and Machine-Readable Records

The most fundamental archival consideration is that machine-readable data are records as much as any paper file of correspondence or case documents. Therefore, they should be subject to the same campus policies as apply to all other records. In particular, the archivist must take an interest in machine-readable records and convince campus officers that the archives should be given both the authority and resources to ensure that machine-readable records are not destroyed or erased without prior archival review of the record system.

All of the core archival functions must be completed for machine-readable records, but each may be complicated by the nature of the records. Detailed instructions can be found in the literature for machine-readable records, but the following explains the academic archivist's responsibilities:

1. Appraisal is critical. Many machine-readable data are of only transitory value, but a small quantity are permanently valuable and may be unavailable (or at least far less accessible) from any other institutional records. Because changes in hardware and software threaten the future usability of machine-readable records, appraisal should be conducted as early in the life of records systems as possible. Ideally, appraisal and authorization of retention or disposal (normally by erasure) should be part of the very creation and design of systems.[25]

Appraisal will be more difficult and time-consuming because machine-readable records are not eye-legible. Furthermore, because selective retention through use of the computer's processing ability to delete data fields without archival value is an option, appraisal often needs to focus on very minute facets of the information system. An additional issue will be the need to assess both the authenticity of the data and the accuracy of its entry by applying skills akin to those used for the venerable archival science of diplomatics.[26]

2. Accessioning normally is not a major issue, but with machine-readable records, the archivist may need to allow others to assume custody of records. This is particularly true of large mainframe databases that require special storage conditions as well as specialized hardware for operations. In these cases, records schedules and system documentation may call for archival tapes to be prepared on a regular basis along with descriptions for the archives' finding aids, but the tapes may well be scheduled to remain at the computer center.

3. Arrangement at the record-group and subgroup level should present few problems for files that are generated by one office only. For instance, student academic records held by the registrar could be placed in the segment of the classification system used for other records of that office. However, other computer databases, even those for core functions such as campus finances, may be comprised of information contributed by several different departments. For example, an alumni and foundation information system may contain biographical data from the alumni association on its members combined with information from the development office regarding the demographic, economic status, and giving patterns of alumni and non-alumni donors. For such files, traditional archival arrangement by office of origin is inadequate, and the archivist will need to illustrate provenance through descriptive records and system documentation. Similar problems may occur with small or specialized databases maintained by departments but based on downloading of data from the campus' large systems (e.g., a tracking file for honors students built with data from the registrar's records system).

Within individual records systems and files, the actual arrangement of data is unimportant—unlike paper file drawers and folders the computer can reorder data and access different sequences on demand. However, the quality of the documentation and access system design will be critical to ensure that the nature of the data fields is clearly outlined and that the system will permit sorting and searching of all important data elements.

4. Description should generally focus far less on the specific informational content of particular records and far more on the overall design and purposes of the records system. Thus, descriptions of machine-readable records should focus on field definitions and file structure. Descriptive control of records also will require the creation and preservation of system documentation that is technically precise about hardware (e.g., tape size and density) and software (e.g., program and version used to record and analyze data) even when data have been manipulated to be as independent of hardware and software as possible. As with appraisal, description will be more difficult and accuracy more critical because the records will not be legible without the right hardware and software.[27]

5. Preservation is an important problem with machine-readable records because they generally consist of magnetic signals on plastic media. Such media have not been found to have archival permanence, but the data can be recopied at regular intervals without fear of degradation (as would occur with analog recordings or photographs) if careful verification procedures are followed. Still, the storage media must be retained in strictly controlled environments free from dust, magnetic fields, and excessive heat and humidity. Furthermore, archivists should be cautioned that the kinds of data-processing activities commonly called "archiving" and "archival" often fall far short of the standards needed for truly archival preservation. The most important preservation threat may be the rapid obsolescence of computer hardware and software. Future usefulness of the records will require ongoing attentiveness to ensure that data are transferred and/or translated as hardware and software are updated.[28]

6. Use will require different approaches from those needed for paper records. On one hand, most machine-readable records can be searched and copied speedily for users. On the other hand, examination of the records is unlikely to occur in a supervised archives search room. Special system precautions will be needed to ensure that users cannot alter data in master files and that personal or confidential information is not revealed except to those with special permission. Overall, provid-

ing for use of machine-readable records will require collaboration of the archivist and the computer center long before the first user arrives to examine the files.

If one looks at the relationship between conventional archival processes and machine-readable records, it becomes clear that the archivist need not abandon archival principles when confronting such records. Instead, it will be necessary to adapt specialized techniques and practices that are not necessary or applicable for the rest of the archives' holdings.

Strategies and Tactics

Several strategies and tactics can help ensure success in handling machine-readable records. First, the campus records policy prepared by the archives should incorporate machine-readable materials in its definition of records and statement of the archives' authority. Records disposition schedules, such as those described in the section on records management, can be very useful for larger files. Schedules can ensure that the informational content of a machine-readable system is systemically assessed by the same appraisal criteria as for the rest of the archives so that data with potential for long-term use are transferred for preservation; the balance of unimportant data is erased on a scheduled basis. To achieve this level of control, the archivist will need both the authority and the opportunity to be consulted during the planning stages of computer-based information systems.[29]

Unfortunately, these approaches will not ensure the archives' involvement in all significant campus systems, especially smaller department-based ones that are hard to control through centralized directives. When the archivist encounters such small and independent systems, a records management approach of scheduling the information they contain may provide the best hope for archival control. By focusing on retention and disposal plans for information rather than on hardware and software, the archivist will be in a stronger position to educate the system creators and users in their responsibility for ensuring the preservation of information of enduring value.

After all is said and done, however, the archivist needs to remember that not all machine-readable records merit retention and that alternative formats, such as printouts or computer-output microforms, often are very adequate substitutes for electronic files. The scheduled transfer of printed summary and analytical reports may offer a better way to gain control of such information. In other cases, the archives may be aided by campus-wide directives issued by a chancellor or dean reminding offices that records held only on active computer systems are not sufficient as long-term documentation of current operations and that each office needs to provide for permanent retention of its data unless otherwise authorized by the archives. Although directives alone cannot solve electronic records problems, they can provide the archivist with a critical basis for working with offices to ensure future accessibility of electronic data.

Clearly, the broadening uses of machine-readable records on campuses makes it imperative that archival issues be addressed in the design and use of such systems. Given the rapidly changing technology, few except the archivist will be concerned about the longevity of computer-based information. This is why it is critical for the archivist to stay abreast of technical issues and to initiate contacts with campus offices so that the interests of future researchers in the data of the past are not sacrificed to the current needs of personnel operating "futuristic" computer systems.

Notes

1. For example, refer to Andrew H. Horn, "The Thesis Problem," *American Archivist* 15 (1952): 321-31.

2. Society of American Archivists, College and University Archives Committee, "Resolution on Theses and Dissertations," 30 September 1975, reprinted in *College and University Archives: Selected Readings* (Chicago: Society of American Archivists, 1979), 175.

3. This may also be necessary for undergraduate honors theses, because they often are less well covered by institutional and library policy.

4. It can be argued that the lack of refinement common in dissertations and theses places them in a substantially different class as non-book material. For example, refer to Robert Plant Armstrong, "The Qualities of a Book, the Wants of a Dissertation," *Scholarly Publishing* 3 (1972): 99-109. While there is truth in such negative judgments of the quality of dissertations, the library cataloging rational that these works are discrete intellectual statements is a substantive basis for handling them as library rather than archival materials.

5. Jane Boyd and Don Etherington, *Preparation of Archival Copies of Theses and Dissertations* (Chicago: American Library Association, 1986).

6. Kelly Patterson, Carol White, and Martha Whittaker, "Thesis Handling in University Libraries," *Library Resources & Technical Services* 21 (1977): 274-85. George Harris and Robert Huffman, "Cataloging of Theses: A Survey," *Cataloging & Classification Quarterly* 5 (Summer 1985): 1-11.

7. A criticism of the two shibboleths that dissertations are never read and that the "best" ones are eventually published can be found in Manuel D. Lopez, "Dissertations: A Need for New Approaches to Acquisition," *Journal of Academic Librarianship* 14 (1988): 297-301.

8. For an outline of University Microfilm International's procedures for subject access and guidelines for obtaining copies of dissertations, refer to the 1961-1972, 1973-82 and annual supplement volumes of its *Comprehensive Dissertation Index*. Detailed information on content of dissertations and microform availablility can be found in *Dissertations Abstracts International*. Also refer to *Masters Abstracts* and *Masters Abstracts International* (Ann Arbor, Mich.: University Microfilms, 1962-).

9. Boyd and Etherington, *Preparation of Theses and Dissertations*.

10. Refer to Michael Gorman and Paul W. Winkler, eds., *Anglo-American Cataloging Rules,* 2d ed., 1988 revision (Chi-

cago: American Library Association, 1988), chapter 4; Harris and Huffman, "Cataloging of Theses," 3-4.

11. Two texts should be on every archivist's bookshelf: Mary Lynn Ritzenthaler, Gerald J. Munoff, and Margery S. Long, *Archives & Manuscripts: Administration of Photographic Collections* (Chicago: Society of American Archivists, 1984); and Robert A. Weinstein and Larry Booth, *Collection, Use and Care of Historical Photographs* (Nashville, Tenn.: American Association for State and Local History, 1977). The less well-analyzed area of paintings, drawings, and other "artistic" images can be approached through Hugh Taylor's "Documentary Art and the Role of the Archivist," *American Archivist* 42 (1979): 417-28. To keep abreast of technical developments, the archivist should regularly review periodicals such as *Picturescope,* the quarterly bulletin of the Picture Division of the Special Libraries Association, and *Photograph Conservation,* from the Graphic Arts Research Center at the Rochester Institute of Technology.

12. Paintings, drawings, and engravings are less common in most academic archives and present a complex range of physical preservation problems that are beyond the scope of this book. For purposes of research access and use, they may be controlled in many of the same ways as photographs—especially if a quality photograph of the original can be made for the appropriate reference and negative files. The preservation and storage demands of each medium can be quite specialized, and these are best addressed on an *ad hoc* basis or through local museum professionals.

13. For a discussion of the multiple dimensions of photographs as sources of information, refer to John Tagg, *Burden of Representation* (Amherst, Mass.: University of Massachusetts Press, 1988), especially chapter 5, "God's Sanitary Law: Slum Clearance and Photography," 117-52. For a historian's perspective, refer to Walter Rundell, "Photographs as Historical Evidence: Early Texas Oil," *American Archivist* 41 (1978): 373-91.

14. A successful, highly detailed indexing and access system has been developed by the National Air and Space Museum archives using laser optical-disk technology, but it is more labor-

and equipment-intensive than could be supported by most academic archives.

15. If it is not possible to recopy the nitrates, they should be removed from the rest of the photographs and stored separately in a cool, preferably refrigerated, environment.

16. An interesting discussion of the documentary context of audio recordings, as well as practical guidance in handling these materials, can be found in Frederick J. Stielow, *Management of Oral History Sound Archives* (Westport, Conn.: Greenwood Press, 1986), especially chapter 2, "Toward a Theory of Sound Archives."

17. For more detailed guidance on appraisal of audiovisual records, refer to Sam Kula, *The Archival Appraisal of Moving Images: A RAMP Study with Guidelines* (Paris: UNESCO, 1983); and Helen P. Harrison, *The Archival Appraisal of Sound Recordings and Related Materials: A RAMP Study with Guidelines* (Paris: UNESCO, 1987).

18. For detailed technical information on audio materials, refer to Jerry McWilliams, *Preservation and Restoration of Sound Recordings* (Nashville, Tenn.: American Association for State and Local History, 1979). For motion pictures, refer to Craig Jones, *16mm Motion Picture Film Maintenance Manual*, Consortium of University Film Centers, Monograph Series 1 (Dubuque, Iowa: Kendall Hunt); and Richard Noble, "Archival Preservation of Motion Pictures," American Association for State and Local History, *Technical Leaflet* 126, published in *History News* 35 (April 1980): 23-30.

19. McWilliams, *Preservation and Restoration of Sound Recordings,* 43-64; "Care and Preservation of Sound Recordings," *Conservation Administration News* 23 (October 1985): 4-5, 24; Jones, *16mm Motion Picture Film Maintenance Manual,* 17-20; "Film/Videotape Factsheet," *Conservation Administration News* 22 (July 1985): 6, 21.

20. Ralph E. Ehrenberg, *Archives & Manuscripts: Maps and Architectural Drawings* (Chicago: Society of American Archivists, 1982); Alan K. Lathrop, "The Provenance and Preservation of Architectural Records," *American Archivist* 43 (1980):

325-38; and *Managing Cartographic, Aerial Photographic, Architectural, and Engineering Records,* Instruction Guide Series (Washington, D. C.: National Archives and Records Administration, 1989).

21. In her analysis of the documentation of higher education, Helen Samuels describes the great breadth of records that document the campus as a built environment. Refer to the chapter on "Physical Plant" in the "Sustain" section of Helen Samuels, *Varsity Letters: Documenting Modern Colleges and Universities* (Chicago: Society of American Archivists, forthcoming).

22. Summary definitions of major types of architectural records may be found at the end of this section.

23. These definitions are based on Cyril M. Harris, ed., *Dictionary of Architecture and Construction* (New York: McGraw-Hill Company, 1975); and Henry H. Saylor, ed., *Dictionary of Architecture* (New York: John Wiley & Sons, Inc., 1963) as well as on the publications of Ralph Ehrenberg, Alan Lathrop, and the National Archives cited previously.

24. For a detailed introduction to machine-readable records refer to Margaret L. Hedstrom, *Archives & Manuscripts: Machine-Readable Records* (Chicago: Society of American Archivists, 1984); or Charles M. Dollar, *Electronic Records Management and Archives in International Organizations: A RAMP Study with Guidelines* (Paris: UNESCO, 1986).

25. The techniques for appraising mainframe-based records are an excellent basis for understanding the complexity of appraisal of all electronic records. These techniques are well-described in Charles M. Dollar, "Appraising Machine-Readable Records," *American Archivist* 41 (1978): 423-30.

26. Diplomatics is the critical study of documents to determine their authenticity by examining their creation, composition, and transmission. Its establishment is most closely associated with Jean Mabillon (1632-1707), but authentication is a core part of all archival work. Cf., Luciana Duranti, "Diplomatics: New Uses for an Old Science," *Archivaria* 28 (Summer 1989): 7-29.

27. Hedstrom, *Archives & Manuscripts,* 53-58, provides an excellent explanation of the steps needed for the description and documentation of electronic records.

28. For details on the durability of, and care for, electronic records, refer to Sidney B. Geller, *Care and Handling of Computer Storage Media,* NBS SP 500-101 (Washington, D. C.: National Bureau of Standards, 1983).

29. Academic archives looking for assistance in informing campus offices of the archival implications of their machine-readable records will find an excellent model for a campus handbook in Information Resources Management Service, General Services Administration, *Electronic Recordkeeping* (Washington, D. C.: U. S. Government Printing Office, 1989).

Special Challenges and Opportunities in Academic Archives

INTRODUCTION

Excellence in managing an academic archives requires more than combining knowledge of archival theory with the resources to put it into practice. It also requires the ability to respond to the special opportunities and challenges that arise in daily operations. By being situated within a college or university, the academic archivist will face problems and opportunities that emerge from the very core characteristics of institutions of higher education. The archivist needs to know how to adjust archival practice to resolve these problems and take advantage of the opportunities. Six areas are particularly important and can exemplify how to respond to other special challenges that may arise. These areas are maintaining a classification system in the midst of institutional change, managing the documents of student and faculty organizations, managing students as staff, serving students as users, managing artifacts, and coping with the historical consciousness endemic to colleges and universities.

Sensitivity and skill in these areas will make the difference between an adequate and an exemplary archival program. The problems and opportunities in each illustrate how real-world situations challenge the adequacy of textbook descriptions of archival practice. The successful academic archivist will need to manage each area with a combination of pragmatism, adherence to archival principles, and awareness of the overall purposes of archival work. Great variations will be necessary to deal with local conditions, but the following sections provide a starting point and place these challenges in the context of the overall balancing act that the academic archivist must master.

INSTITUTIONAL CHANGE AND ARCHIVAL CLASSIFICATION SYSTEMS

One of the more frustrating problems faced by academic archivists is how to maintain a provenance-based classification system in the midst of constantly changing and often confusing lines of authority in colleges and universities. No sooner does the archivist complete work on a classification guide than the campus undergoes minor or major organizational changes, and the outline of record groups and subgroups is obsolete. For example, an archivist establishing a new program in the mid-1970s might have created a record group for the Dean of Students, with appropriate subgroups for Student Affairs, Housing, and Financial Aid. A few years later, the "easing out" of a Dean of Students leads to a major reorganization that retitles the position "Vice-Chancellor for Student Affairs," elevates Housing to the status of an independent division reporting to a Vice-Chancellor for Administrative Affairs, and transfers the Financial Aid function to the Admissions Office. Similar problems occur as academic colleges are redefined, merged, or divided, and departments are moved from one college to another. The archives may be left with a classification scheme that no longer reflects the institutional structure and is of little help in illustrating the provenance of accessions to reflect their source and relationship to other materials in the archives.

Similar problems occur if one tries to reconcile an archival classification system with the many layers of institutional hierarchy. If each segment of the classification system were used for only a single level in the hierarchy, the classification system would need many more layers than practical. In addition, substantial ongoing maintenance would be needed to create the correct record subgroup for each accession and to ensure that its position in the archival classification system matched its institutional reporting lines. For example, if the Admissions and Records Office were classified as a record subgroup because its director reported to the Vice-Chancellor, what would the archivist do with the records of the Classroom Space Allocation Office, which reports to the Associate Director for Registration, who in turn reports to the Director of Admissions and Records?

These examples only scratch the surface of the practical difficulties that can occur if the archivist attempts to employ a classification scheme designed not only to reflect the provenance and hierarchy of records but also to describe the organizational structure and hierarchy of the parent institution. Each problem might be solvable consistent with archival theory and institutional needs, but the solutions would be very cumbersome and would likely mire the archivist into a complex "case law" approach that would provide few program benefits. The answer is not to abandon archival classification systems as either antiquated or inadequate, but to regard them as providing a loose structure for workable decisions relating records to institutional structure and organizational relationships. Some general operating principles, however, can help archivists make better decisions in applying archival arrangement principles to local needs.

Understanding the organizational context of these classification problems is particularly important. It is impossible for a static classification system to reflect the complexities and changes that occur in any vibrant organization. The problems may be less severe in governmental settings, where so much of the organizational structure or bureaucracy is a direct result of legislative, judicial, or regulatory mandates which also serve as a source for archival classification systems. Maintaining accurate classification systems will be more of a challenge in higher education because of the highly diffuse foci of colleges and universities. They are considerably less rigid in their design, and offices are often created, eliminated, merged, or divided to accomplish each generation's view of how best to accomplish the institution's program goals and priorities.

Given the widespread attitude in higher education that organizational structure should be subordinate to the institution's educational, research, and service missions, campuses tend to devote far less attention to structure than to program development. At the same time, given the centrality of the academic tradition of personal and professional autonomy for the teaching and research functions of colleges and universities, it should not be surprising that their organizational structure cannot be neatly described in an archival classification guide. Moreover, reporting lines will become less clear and location of related functions will become less consistent as the institution experiments with new programs, revitalizes important central activities, or responds to personnel management problems by moving offices and functions rather than people. Finally, the very cyclical nature of the academic year, with its long summer breaks, and the constantly changing student population, suggest that institutional continuity may be hindered by the fundamental nature of the institutions.[1]

It is important for archivists to be aware of the organizational characteristics of their own institutions so they may identify the local factors that commonly cause changes in the structure and function of offices. Organizational problems may be common in some areas of all schools, but absent in others. Newer or smaller institutions with less clearly defined or evolving missions may be far more prone to the phenomenon of frequent changes. At public institutions, which are subject to detailed statutory rules on structure and process, change in the organizational structure may be more measured. By contrast, there may be more problems in arranging the records of institutions where middle and senior staff are so well established that organizational structure is modified to meet the talents, failings, and influence of particular individuals. For example, a new social science center may be established to accommodate an influential sociologist who has alienated so many of his own department members that they demand action from the dean.

Because the causes of change, even within one institution, are so diverse, it is inadvisable to formulate specific rules that attempt to reconcile the classification system with institutional change. Nevertheless, a general approach would reduce all such classification problems to three basic choices. When a given activity (e.g., Student Employment Services) is moved from one administrative reporting line to another, the alternatives are:

- Keep all records relating to that function in their original place in the classification system, regardless of the function's or office's new place.
- Create a new section in the classification system to reflect the new reporting line and move (at least on paper) all the records to that place.
- Divide and classify the records separately according to whether they were created under the new or the old structure.

While there is a myriad of organizational changes the archivist may face, archival action in each case can follow one of these options.

In deciding which choice is most appropriate, the archivist should focus on the functional characteristics of the office and the records. That is, what institutional objectives does the office accomplish, and how do the records help in this work? As changes in structure occur, one must also determine whether the records continue to relate to the office's mission in the same way. If neither the office's job nor the purpose of the records has been altered significantly by the organizational change, then the records should be kept in their traditional home. When the functional characteristics of the records begin to change at the same time as the purpose and operations of the creating office changes, then a redesign of the classification system, or at least one portion of it, should be considered.

In most cases, resolving these problems should not require extensive research, complex processes, or difficult "either/or" choices. Rather, the archivist should be guided by several general principles. First, despite occasional problems, a classification system reflecting the institution's organization will provide great assistance in arranging the bulk of the institution's records. Second, the application of the system to the records should be flexible, not rigid. Third and most importantly, the archivist must remember that the classification system is not a hierarchical organizational chart.

There is good reason to insist that major organizational units, such as the College of Art and Architecture, are classified as record groups and that departments within these major units, such as the Department of Theatre, are classified as subgroups subordinate to the record group. There is little need, however, to create tertiary, or even smaller, arrangement levels (sub-subgroups) for offices reporting to the department. For example, the records of the Stage Design Office, a subunit of the Theatre Department, may comprise four distinct record series, but there is no reason to create a sub-subgroup for Stage Design. Instead, all the stage design records can be maintained as series on the same organizational level as the Theatre Department's Subject Files or Personnel Files. Thus,

Record Group 11 College of Fine Arts
  Subgroup 11/5 Theatre Department
   Record Series
        11/5/1 Subject File
        11/5/5 Personnel File
        11/5/8 Budget File
        11/5/15 Publicity Scrapbooks
        11/5/16-11/5/19 [Vacant]
        11/5/20 Stage Design—Office Correspondence

11/5/21 Stage Design—Plans
11/5/25 Stage Design—Financial Records

Attempts to make the archival classification system directly parallel to the institutional reporting lines will be very time-consuming, frustrating, and of limited research value. The classification system should reflect only the general provenance of the records, since the subtleties and complexities of a living organization can rarely be illustrated solely by a classification number. These subtleties are best handled through administrative histories, brief provenance notes, and primary and secondary finding aids. A major help in solving many such classification problems will be function and subject indexes to the archives' classification guide and administrative histories. Beyond these general principles, the archivist will find that the most basic and effective tool for reconciling archival classification with institutional structure and change is the set of administrative histories in the institutional classification guide.[2]

Administrative histories are particularly useful for illustrating hierarchy by recording the establishment of smaller offices, centers, and programs created under the authority of the offices represented by record groups and subgroups. For example, if the College of Liberal Arts establishes a "School for Study of Urban Problems," composed of a secretary, a part-time assistant dean, and shared faculty from existing departments, the school's records could be classified under the college's Dean's Office, and the mission and establishment of the school might be described in the administrative history for the college's record group. A similar approach could be followed for many of the smaller offices constantly being created, such as the History Department's new Law History Program or the Undergraduate Housing Office's new Handicapped Students Access Bureau. In other words, as new departments and offices are created, the archivist should attempt to place them within the existing classification system wherever possible and use the narrative of the existing administrative histories to record their presence.

Major institutional changes and the establishment of major new units (e.g., colleges and institutes) that are the result of careful long-range planning should, however, be handled through a broader revision of the classification system and administrative histories. Similarly, when a new center, office, or program has weathered a decade or more of institutional life and appears to be a part of the university's ongoing operations (e.g., an African Studies Office established in 1971), the archivist should revise the classification guide and administrative histories to assign that office a subgroup (or record group) of its own.

Some archives have approached the problem of describing organizational change by placing administrative histories or provenance notes with each accession's finding aid. These are useful for understanding the administrative context of the documents in each record series. However, they can be compiled and updated more efficiently, and examined more conveniently, when they are part of a single repository-wide classification guide/administrative history. Such a centralized tool will accommodate description of units that have not yet transferred records and will reduce the duplication that would occur if separate administrative histories were created for each of the several record series from an individual department. Regardless of the system or tools used, however, the archivist must recognize that despite the imperfection of classification systems, they are extraordinarily useful for controlling institutional records, if applied flexibly.

Because living institutions are constantly experiencing many changes as they adjust their missions and as they accommodate the personalities of their constituencies, it is legitimate to wonder how often the archivist should revise the classification guide and administrative histories. The best approach is to review the guide annually to determine if it still reflects the institution's basic structure. Minor revisions, such as adding or subtracting a simple function or office in the administrative history for a subgroup, may be deferred to when records from those units are accessioned and processed. If even this review schedule is overly ambitious, the archivist should at least maintain a list of revisions that need to be researched and documented as time permits.

Doubtless, creation and maintenance of a repository-wide classification guide with administrative histories is a formidable task. It will be particularly crucial when the archives begins operations or when a program needs over-hauling, such as before renovating the descriptive system. In addition, the task can be a discouraging aspect of ongoing administration because no amount of work will ensure that it is fully current and descriptive of the institution's present and past structure. Nevertheless, the archivist should not abandon the task as impossible or inherently flawed. Instead, the classification system should be seen as providing a broad level of control over the structure of the organization and the major changes it has experienced. Details and precision can be relegated to the descriptive components of the system.

MANAGING THE DOCUMENTS OF STUDENT AND FACULTY ORGANIZATIONS

Adequate historical coverage of a college or university requires attention to the publications and office records of student and faculty organizations. These documents provide evidence of the personal interests of students and faculty, the expression of these interests through affinity groups, and the relation of these groups to the institution. Some of these organizations are focused on, or emerge from, educational and employment functions of the institution. Others contain the germ of movements that change institutional policy and practice and sometimes society as a whole. Still others are centered on student hobbies and recreational concerns, which often stray far from the curriculum. Such organizations reflect the broader influences of the institutional environment on students and faculty

and form key parts of their lives. The records of organizations are important because they illustrate the structural
links between the student's or faculty member's interests,
the organization's activities, and the institution's foci.
They also are critical because they reflect aspects of student, faculty, and institutional life that are often missing
from official institutional records and publications and
even from personal papers of faculty and students.

Despite the importance of such organizational records
to the mission of academic archives, they present many
persistent difficulties for archival management. These
stem from several conditions common to their existence.
Student and faculty organizations, by their very nature,
operate largely outside the administrative framework of
the institution. With the notable exception of unions, they
are almost always voluntary groups with no paid staff to
manage files and publications and no established office
space to house their records. This often means that the
groups are not reliable custodians of their own current
records, let alone their historically valuable documents.
Moreover, the mechanisms an archivist might normally
use to solicit institutional records and arrange for regular
transfers will be only marginally effective for these groups.
Another characteristic of these organizations that has
important archival implications is that their membership,
leadership, program scope, and even their very existence
are constantly changing. The fact that many of these
organizations may become defunct before the archivist
first learns of their existence makes difficult not only the
acquisition of their records, but also their proper description. For example, establishing the proper form of the
name of the organization and its subject focus may be
extremely difficult if all that remains is a file of newsletters and broadsides bearing the organization's acronym
and three variants of what the acronym meant.

In the face of these problems, the usefulness of standard archival techniques will be limited largely to organizations of long standing and with carefully structured
operations. They will be far less effective for the large
number of organizations for which constitutions and min-

ute books are unlikely to exist. Therefore, the archivist must realize that covering only those organizations with well-structured files will leave other important groups undocumented. At the same time, one must recognize that the failure of archival practices to function in these areas is inherent in the nature of student and faculty organizations and thus should not become a cause for undue consternation.

Collection Scope and Acquisition

Virtually all kinds of student and faculty organizations should be included in the archives' collection scope. This would include the records of transitory groups (e.g., Students for Goldwater), long-established bodies (e.g., American Association of University Professors), and organizations with paid staff, such as unions.[3] Given the importance of student and faculty organizations in the institution's life, and the difficulty of documenting them, it will be essential to have efficient means of achieving as much coverage as possible if the archives' collection goals are to be met. A particularly useful approach is to focus most archival efforts on the organizations' publications. Virtually every document prepared by a local organization (or local chapter of a national organization) for internal or external dissemination should be acquired as a publication. These commonly include broadsides, newsletters, programs, and announcements of forthcoming events. While these do not guarantee a great deal of depth about the operation of the organization, they at least provide a good characterization of program activities. Given that a key goal of many organizations is the dissemination and promotion of their interests and views, publications can be a rich source for research. Because they are produced in multiple copies, publications can also be a fertile ground for collecting.

For many organizations, publications may be the only documents the archives holds. However, whenever possible, the archives should also solicit and acquire office records from the organizations, especially constitutions and bylaws, agendas and minutes of meetings, correspondence (except that related to routine membership and business transactions), and other documents illustrating the group's focus and activities. Membership lists, although sometimes useful, are often no more than poorly maintained card files, mailing labels, or computer diskettes that will provide only a weak base for research while presenting preservation, bulk, and accessibility problems. When they are well organized and efficiently designed, they might be retained in their entirety; otherwise, selection of the best parts would be in order. Overall, collection criteria for student and faculty organizations will need to be flexible to deal with the broad variations in how these organizations operate.

The actual processes for soliciting and acquiring both institutional publications and office records have been discussed in the chapter on acquisition practices.[4] Such techniques as sending solicitation letters regularly and placing the archives on mailing lists will be useful with student and faculty organizations, although the effectiveness of these techniques will be limited, and they will require more follow-up because of the rapid turnover in most organizations' staff. Unquestionably, it is a difficult, time-consuming, and frustrating process. It is ironic that as records are passed from officer to officer, each time undergoing weeding and loss, and there is a tendency to keep membership and routine financial records while discarding correspondence, superseded constitutions, and policy documents. To ensure a more orderly receipt of organization records, the archivist might use the "Transfer Guidelines for Records of Student, Faculty, and Staff Organizations" shown in Figure 7.

Archivists often find that the best student and faculty organizational records may be acquired with the personal papers of alumni and faculty. In fact, obtaining student organization papers can be a major goal and justification for soliciting alumni papers. If the files obtained are sizable and cover the organization broadly, and if the alumni or faculty member held the records in an official capacity for the organization, it would be appropriate to separate the records from the personal papers and retain them in a series specifically for the organization's archives. If the files are few and more reflective of personal membership than official service in the organization, they may be retained in the person's papers, with appropriate notes in the repository-wide subject index, if one exists.

Many strategies are potentially useful in obtaining a rich supply of organization publications. The archives can publish a solicitation announcement each semester in student newspapers, negotiate with the office responsible for distributing funds from student activity fees to require archival deposit of publications, "clean" bulletin boards regularly, and "raid" organizations' tables at campus open houses and fairs. Few archives will be able to pursue all of these avenues consistently, but even occasional efforts can yield substantial benefits.

Arrangement and Description

Once organization records and publications are received, establishing archival control presents difficulties similar to those encountered in acquisition. Because of the large number of organizations, the usually small number of documents available from each, and the minimal and unsystematic care given by their creators, a great deal of flexibility is needed in applying archival procedures and techniques. The two largest problem areas, arrangement and description, are best considered as part of a sequence of closely related activities.

The first step in arranging the records of organizations will be to identify the proper record groups and subgroups for them in the archives' classification system. A useful approach is to establish a separate record group for each major type of organization. For instance, Record Group 24 might be Student Organizations, Record Group 25 might be Faculty Organizations, Record Group 26 might be Alumni Organizations, Record Group 27 might be Non-university-Related Organizations. When an organization

Transfer Guidelines for Records of Student, Faculty, and Staff Organizations

The University Archives is the repository for the non-current records of the university as well as for related organizations in the campus and community. The Archives functions as a research center on the history of the institution and the activities of its students, faculty, staff, and alumni. The records of student, faculty and staff organizations form an important part of the campus's historical legacy. The following guidelines will assist members of organizations in identifying those portions of their files that are appropriate for preservation in the University Archives.

Items to be transferred include:

1) Official records: constitutions and by-laws, minutes and proceedings, transcripts, lists of officers and members;

2) Office files: correspondence and memoranda (incoming and outgoing) and subject files concerning projects, activities, and functions;

3) Historical files documenting policies, decisions, committee and task force reports, survey data;

4) Publications: one record copy of all programs, journals, monographs, newsletters, brochures, posters, and announcements issued by the organization or its subdivisions; the Archives should be placed on the mailing list to receive all future publications;

5) Audio-visuals: photographs, sound and video recordings, and films;

6) Personal papers of members which relate directly to the organization's work;

7) Charts and maps.

(continued on next page)

Figure 7. Transfer Guidelines for Records of Student, Faculty, and Staff Organizations (1 of 2)

Transfer Guidelines for Records of Student, Faculty, and Staff Organizations

Records which should not be transferred to the Archives include:

1) Records of specific financial and membership transactions;

2) Letters of transmittal where the date and routing information is on the document transmitted;

3) Requests for publications or information after the requests have been filled;

4) All blank forms and unused printed or duplicated materials;

5) All duplicate material: keep only the original copy and annotated copies;

6) Papers, reports, work papers and drafts, which have been published;

7) Replies to questionnaires if the results are recorded and preserved either in the archives or in a published report; and

8) Artifacts and memorabilia.

Materials should be transferred in the order in which the records' creator maintained them. A letter briefly identifying the materials and describing the activity to which they relate should accompany the transfer.

This list is intended as a general guide. If there are questions about records not listed here or questions about the retention or disposal of specific record series, please telephone the Archivist at _____.

WHEN IN DOUBT, DO NOT THROW IT OUT!

Figure 7. Transfer Guidelines for Records of Students, Faculty, and Staff Organizations (2 of 2)

includes both students and faculty, it should be placed in the record group that reflects its broadest base and focus, or the archives might establish a separate record group for such joint ventures. Overall, the archivist should avoid trying to maintain highly precise systems because the nature of these records will defy such fine distinctions.

Within each record group, subgroups can be developed for the major categories of organizations. For example,

24   Student Organizations
        24/1 Collections (i.e., artificial series containing small files
              of scattered holdings for several organizations.
              These could also be assigned to the record group
              and subgroup used for the administrative offices
              responsible for supervising student organizations.)
        24/10 Academic and Educational Organizations
        24/15 Governance
        24/20 Honorary and Recognition
        24/25 Language, Foreign, and International
        24/30 Music
        24/35 Political and Social Action
        24/40 Professional and Occupational
        24/45 Recreational and Special Interest
        24/50 Religious
        24/55 Residence Halls
        24/56 Residence Fraternities
        24/60 Residence Sororities
        24/65 Service
        24/70 Theatre and Debate
        [etc.]

25/   Faculty Organizations
        25/1 Collections
        25/10 Collective Bargaining and Professional Advocacy
        25/20 Professional and Occupational
        25/30 Music
        25/40 Political and Social Action
        25/50 Recreational and Special Interest
        25/60 Service

       25/70 Social
       [etc.]
26/ Alumni Organizations
     26/1 Collections
     26/10-199 [Geographic Classification]
     26/11 Alabama
     26/20 Boston
     26/45 Chicago
     26/115 New York
     26/116 New York City
     26/150-99 Foreign Alumni Clubs
     26/200-99 [Classes, chronologically]
     26/215 1919
     26/246 1946
     26/700-99 [By College or School—this might also be placed
            in the record group/subgroup for the specific college.]
     26/701 Architecture
     26/795 Zoology

Beyond these two levels of arrangement, the archivist should not attempt to assign record series numbers according to any preestablished scheme. Rather, each organization's records should be assigned a record-series number sequentially based on when the material is first received. For most student and faculty organizations, two record series should suffice for all of its documents—one for published material and one for nonpublished items such as minutes, constitutions, agendas, and correspondence. Larger organizations with long histories, such as the campus YMCA/YWCA and the local chapter of the AAUP, may require subseries, but this should not present special problems because these records will conform more to standard archival practice for modern office records. An example of a list of series of student organizations follows:

24/30 Student Organizations—Music
     24/30/1 Campus Folksong Club Records
     24/30/2 University Choral and Orchestral Society
            Publications

24/30/3 Symphony Orchestra Tour Scrapbook
[etc.]

24/35 Student Organizations—Political and Social Action
    24/35/1 Young Democrats Club Records
    24/35/2 Women's Student Union Historical File
    24/35/3 Black Student Association Publications
    24/35/4 *Up the Wall* [Publication of Students for a Change]

    [etc.]

24/40 Student Organizations—Professional and Occupational
    24/40/1 Agriculture Club Records
    24/40/2 Electrical Engineering Society Publications
    24/40/3 Electrical Engineering Society Minutes and
        Records
    24/40/4 Dairy Technology Society Secretary's Books
    24/40/5 Mathematics Club Meeting Minutes and Protocol
        Books
    24/40/6 Beta Alpha Psi Archives

    [etc.]

24/50 Student Organizations—Religious
    24/50/1 Episcopal Church Foundation Records
    24/50/2 Hillel Foundation Publications
    24/50/3 *Hillel Post*
    24/50/4 Hillel Foundation Records
    24/50/5 YMCA-YWCA Publications
    24/50/6 YMCA-YWCA *Student Handbooks*
    24/50/7 *YMCA-YWCA Weekly News*
    24/50/10 YWCA Subject File
    24/50/12 YWCA Photographs
    24/50/15 YMCA Minute Books
    24/50/16 YMCA Correspondence
    [etc.]

The classification system must recognize the ephemeral nature and fragmentary holdings of records from student and faculty organizations. A simple and efficient technique for the many holdings that are too small and scattered to merit their own record series is to create a single artificial and collective general record series titled "Student and Faculty Organizations File," arranged alphabetically by name of organization. As items are received piecemeal, they can be filed in this general series until their volume and time span justifies separating an organization's documents into a record series specifically for that organization. Maintaining a folder-title-list finding aid for this general file of organization material can be simplified with commercial word processing or database software, which will facilitate frequent updates. The software can also improve access by permitting computer-based searches of key words in an organization's name so that access is not limited to an alphabetical listing of titles. Given the frequent use of a school's name, its permutations, and such generic terms as university and campus in the names of many organizations, computer-based access can be particularly valuable. For example, it might direct the researcher to separate organizations with similar concerns but which are alphabetically far apart in the folder list, such as the Campus Peace Alliance and University Peace Initiative.

Once the questions of classification and arrangement have been solved, the next issue is likely to be the physical and descriptive control of the publications. This can be particularly difficult if one is unwilling to modify standard library and archival rules. An archives that attempts issue-by-issue checking-in and claiming, or establishing a distinct record series for each title, will quickly find that many of the organization publications do not lend themselves to such control. The results will be an extensive investment of staff time, uneven control, and a fragmented system in which access is seriously hampered. It is far more effective to gather all of an organization's publications into one record series for each organization and utilize generic subheadings such as newsletters, programs, handbooks, and broadsides. These groupings will support access to the kinds of information a researcher is most likely to need and will avoid the difficulties that come from attempts to track title changes and maintaining issue-level holdings control. To simplify additions of missing issues in serial runs of newsletters, flags can be placed in the file to indicate gaps. Admittedly, this approach requires examining the actual documents to answer holdings questions rather than using a check-in file, but the volume of such material is generally small enough that this should not be difficult. In addition, the archives has a responsibility to be the fail-safe source of institutional publications, and notations in check-in files are not adequate substitutes for actual physical verification that an issue is held before all other copies are discarded as duplicates. This methodology is not just a short-cut to respond to limited resources, but it also reflects a basic archival emphasis on the body of publications as a cumulative research resource, rather than as discrete items and isolated sources of information.

Descriptive control of the records of organizations needs special attention. Simple access based on provenance, as reflected in the archives' overall classification system, is of little help because each organization's records, however small, can be seen as an archives in itself and thus requires its own classification system. A better way to control these records is through the descriptive system, especially if it includes a repository-wide name and subject index. With such an index, little more will be needed than one index entry for the organization's name to refer researchers to the appropriate series for its records. Organizations represented only by a single folder in an artificial or collective file are best left out of the repository subject index and controlled instead through series-level container lists and finding aids.

Once this basic arrangement strategy has been employed, descriptive control of organizations' records can follow general archival practice. The most fundamental principle will be to use flexible, aggregate series-level descriptions in the primary finding aid so that simple catalog entries can be prepared and updated to ensure the expeditious handling of organizational records. The minimum will be to note the focus of the organization and the types of documents and topics they contain. Subtleties concerning provenance, name changes, dates of tenure of records creators, and subjects of particular documents are best handled through the box and folder listings of the series, where available and as time permits.

The processing of individual accessions of organizational records will generally follow the same patterns as other archival accessions. The major difference is that organizational records may be more comparable to manuscript collections than to well-managed office records. Thus, the archivist may need to impose an artificial arrangement of documents within series rather than allow arrangement to emanate organically from the accession itself. The detailed finding aid may resemble a manuscript register, with provenance and arrangement notes and subseries structure, rather than the simpler box and folder title lists that generally suffice for modern administrative records. More detailed processing instructions should be based on the nature of each accession.

Balancing Collection Needs With Program Resources

Given the number of student and faculty organizations and the generally unsystematic maintenance of their publications and records, it may be both very time-consuming and ineffectual to attempt the same kind of control as in other areas of the archives. The most important consideration is a willingness to bend archival rules without forgetting that the purpose of such variations is to move away from detailed control of each organization's files and toward treatment of organizations' records as a general resource on campus life. If compromises to deal with this material within existing resources are not adopted consciously, an unsystematic and more troublesome approach will be the actual result.

Ideally, the records of each organization should be seen as a discrete archives to document each group fully, but except for the larger bodies of records, these documents will be better understood as small collections under the broader but more amorphous heading of "campus life." Because of the tremendous resources required to deal with the documents of student and faculty organizations, archivists will need to make difficult choices about how much attention to devote to them. If resources are strictly limited, the archives may need to define a narrower focus for the documentation of student and faculty organizations and restrict itself to certain types of organizations. For example, it might collect intensively from recreational and political groups but deemphasize professional and residential organizations. Perhaps a more appropriate exclusion for organizations with extensive files would be to collect their publications but exclude other records beyond constitutions, minute books, and other summary official documents. The volume of material, the institution's character, and the available resources may dictate and shape such policies, but such restricted collecting should be avoided if at all possible.

Despite the challenges posed by faculty and student organization documents, the archivist should never lose sight of their importance. Obviously, they are critical for understanding the history of each organization, but this may be the least significant of their values. Beyond the topical focus of each organization and its connection to the college or university, the records reflect an important cultural characteristic—the tendency for people to come together and then organize around shared interests and avocations. Certainly this phenomenon is not restricted to colleges or universities, but academic archivists are in a particularly strong position to document it because they deal with a universe large enough to generate diverse groups but small enough to limit the number of organizations and records available. As the school brings together large numbers of people with diverse interests, it also provides them with the opportunity to reflect these interests in organizations which in turn are mechanisms that create and preserve records of these interests. Thus, the fact that a group of students is interested enough in reen-

acting medieval tournaments to form a campus organization to create such spectacles tells one something about
the students and the institution, as well as about the
broader society that led them to conceptualize and then
actualize their interests within the institution's setting. In
this sense, the often neglected area of organizational records may represent one of the largest "windows on the
world" that an academic archivist can provide.[5]

STUDENTS AS STAFF

A distinctive characteristic of college and university archives is the use of student employees for many archival
functions. The availability of students provides an opportunity to hire low-cost employees and diversify the archives' labor force with little long-term risk if their work
is unsatisfactory. In many institutions, this may be the
only way to add personnel with the few dollars available.
In addition, work in the archives broadens the students'
education by exposing them to archival practice, historical
documentation, and research methodology. While this educational role may be beyond the core mission of an archives, it is an important contribution to the institution
and may lead to life-long interests or careers in archives.
Finally, employment of students exposes the archives'
regular staff to a breadth of perspectives and talents that
can add significantly to staff's vitality and ability to explore new program areas.

The extent to which students can be used depends on
institutional practice and the flexibility of the archives'
budget. For example, some institutions will provide high-
quality College Work Study (CWS) students, enabling the
archives to hire students at a lower cost than other student
employees. At other schools, CWS employees may be un-
suitable, thus requiring the archives to hire students only
at the full hourly rate. Some archives may be able to shift
funds from one budget line to another so that students
might temporarily fill vacant professional or support-staff
positions. The archives' use of students, therefore, must

begin with an understanding of the budgetary and personnel policies and practices of the parent institution. The
archivist may need to work with campus administration
to see if procedures can be modified to improve the quality
of the student staff available for the archives. Although
specific policies and procedures can be formulated only in
reference to each institution, this section will suggest
areas of archival work that benefit most from student
employees and note management practices that increase
their efficiency.

Types of Student Staff

It is useful to consider the full range of student staff
that may be available before developing a student employment program. Most institutions have students on work-
study scholarships who may be assigned to or selected by
units along with funds to cover all or part of the student's
wages. Often, such staff are available only in limited
quantities. A second major category is student hourly
workers—either graduate or undergraduate—paid in full
from the archives' wage budget. A third category available
at some universities is graduate-student assistants who
are hired to work a preestablished time (e.g., quarter-time)
for a stated contractual period (e.g., nine months). Graduate assistants generally cost more than the hourly students; they may be paid from the archives' budget or
assigned by an academic department at no cost to the
archives. In either case, the archives will have to compete
with other units for the wage budget or the allocation of
graduate assistantships.

A useful strategy in managing student staff is to hire
students from different levels and categories for different
types of work. Undergraduate work-study or regular hourly students may be most effectively used for typing, clerical, and simple processing tasks. Hourly graduate
students, often at slightly higher pay, may be particularly
useful for processing personal papers, answering complex
reference questions, supervising the reference room, and
participating in exhibit preparation. Graduate students

on assistantships, because of the greater continuity that should come with their commitment to the position, are particularly good for larger processing projects, regular reference-desk responsibilities, and other activities requiring sustained effort. This latter category of student employees is particularly valuable since the term of the assistantship enables the archivist and the student to plan longer-range activities. If this type of staff is available, it is well worth the extra cost.[6]

The archives should also look for sources of free student labor for carefully selected tasks. As opportunities arise, students in history, archives, or library classes might be tapped for processing smaller bodies of records preliminarily arranged by the archivist. Or the archivist may work with a faculty member in graphic design or television production to have students develop publicity materials for the archives as a course project. Cooperative projects may be developed with faculty members to utilize their graduate assistants to research and prepare a major exhibit. Most colleges and universities will present many similar opportunities, all of which should be explored. However, volunteer efforts should serve only to supplement paid students because volunteers can create major difficulties for supervision and regulation that do not occur with paid staff. Should volunteers come forward, they are best utilized for special projects that would not otherwise be done, rather than for basic work of the archival program.

Selection of Appropriate Areas of Work

Effective use of students to stretch the personnel budget should begin with an assessment of what archival activities and what tasks within those activities are most amenable to the kinds of student employees available. Common activities and tasks include clerical work (typing, keyboarding data, filing finding aids, photocopying, etc.); "go-fer-ing" (retrieving and reshelving records; boxing records in offices and moving them to the archives; running errands for photocopying, photographic reproduction, and audiovisual duplication orders; archival processing; re-searching for reference inquiries); and specialized projects using the specific skills of a particular student (e.g., foreign languages, computer programming, photography, or graphic design). Not all tasks in these broad areas are equally appropriate for all types of student employees, and the archives should not plan on students being the sole staff handling any one activity. Thus, typing or data entry for some complex finding aids or reports may need to be reserved for experienced regular staff. Similarly, students should be used carefully for researching reference inquiries or assisting with exhibits. Rarely will it be possible or desirable to assign students entire projects requiring them to initiate, plan, execute, and follow up on tasks in multiple areas of archival work. To make most effective use of students, manageable tasks should be defined, segmented, and assigned to those students with appropriate talents.

The processing of archives and manuscripts—perhaps the most common area for student work in archives—is a particularly appropriate one, once tasks are defined. When processing is divided into its components of arrangement, description, and preservation, one can see how crucial the differentiation of tasks is to managing student employees. Arrangement is likely to require more experience and understanding of archival operations than one can reasonably expect from students. This is particularly true for decisions on the appropriate record group and subgroup for accessions, but it also applies to the internal arrangement of each accession. Where students will be quite useful is in examining the accession and advising the archivist about the content and condition of files so that the professional can make sound arrangement decisions. If the order of a body of records has been badly disrupted, students can be employed productively in reorganizing the material, once the archivist has developed a workplan. However, given the tendency of inexperienced staff to have rather cavalier attitudes toward the integrity of the original order, archivists should be hesitant to give student staff unsupervised responsibility for arrangement.[7]

Students are an invaluable resource for many phases of description, especially those focused on preparing container lists or inventories of records and manuscripts. The bulk of their processing work will be examining documents in each folder, revising the folder titles as necessary, and preparing container lists to serve as the core part of the finding aid. More experienced students can expand their work to include drafting of the analytical collection-level and series descriptions that form the primary finding aids. Review by professional staff and careful monitoring will be necessary, however, to make sure that student interest in a particular subject does not lead to overly detailed biographical sketches and notes on scope and content. In most cases, students will not be qualified to prepare MARC-AMC format catalog entries.

The physical protection and preservation components of processing are another very good use of student staff. In addition to weeding duplicates and non-archival materials (preferably according to written guidelines), students are ideal staff for the detailed work of removing staples, paper clips, rubber bands and other harmful materials, photocopying onto acid-free paper, replacing folders, and reboxing documents. This close examination of the collection also can lead them to discover more complex preservation problems. If an archives utilizes more extensive preservation activities, such as encapsulation, on a large scale, students can be quite useful for some assembly-line work, such as cutting Mylar or preparing sleeves.

A set of flexible guidelines for student processing, whether written or unwritten, will enable adjustments to the needs of each repository and accession, as well as to the talents of each student. Archivists will find that students may be the best staff to use in processing if supervisors can preview their work, develop a processing plan, and divide the work into separate and superviseable phases. Using students for substantial portions of the processing work may be preferable to hiring permanent staff solely devoted to processing. Because of the detail of much processing work, it can be quite tedious if performed on a full-time basis, and the part-time schedules of student processors can reduce the mind-numbing impact of processing minutiae on staff morale.

Limitations and Controls

The academic archivist should not embark on the use of student employees without acknowledging their limits. This knowledge will place one in the strongest position to hire, train, supervise, and assign appropriate tasks to them.[8] Perhaps the most important limitation is the extensive training and supervision students require, since they frequently come with no background in archives, library science, or historical research. A brief orientation period should suffice to get students started on basics. This might include reading the archives' annual report or descriptive and promotional material, or viewing audiovisual items concerning the archives. Written instructions, processing manuals, rules, and checklists can be particularly useful in giving students a consistent level of guidance in some work areas, such as typing finding aids and processing records. Inexperienced staff are prone to take liberties with archival principles of appraisal and arrangement, but damage can be limited by providing student processors with a brief list of "do's" and "don't's." In order to compensate for the students' lack of training, regular staff will need to conduct routine supervision and examination of their work so that quality control will be maintained. In the first few months of each student's tenure, the archivist should regard time spent on supervision as an investment in their education. Once this period passes, the archives should reap many benefits from the students—provided they have the basic competencies the archivist saw when making the original hiring decision.

Lack of training and experience is connected closely to a second major limitation of student staff—the rate of turnover. In the best of circumstances, a student may be able to work for the archives for two to four years. More often, a heavy course load or another job possibility, with better pay or more relevant to their career interests, may draw them away after a semester or two. These problems are largely beyond the archivist's control, but they might be minimized through careful screening of applicants and more variety in work assignments to keep students' interests high. At the same time, a clear advantage of the transiency of student employees is that the poor performers also leave, or can be encouraged to leave, with much less trauma than marginal permanent staff. Ultimately, however, the archives must accept the risk of losing good student staff as a condition of employing them. If the problem becomes endemic to certain classes of student employees or certain job activities, hiring and work practices should be modified accordingly.[9]

A related problem is that student work schedules are often irregular. The students' main activity, at least in principle, is their education, and their class and study schedules should take priority over work schedules. In most cases, a more fundamental problem is that students have little experience with workday routines and can be rather lax about appearing on time and on a daily basis. The damage can be contained if the students are asked to submit a schedule of work hours each semester and the schedule is monitored to make sure they adhere to it closely. This tactic, however, cannot solve other workflow problems caused by the seasonal nature of students' schedules. In addition to the vacations and holidays built into the academic calendar, other fluctuations will occur during midterm and final examination time, when the more serious students, who often are the better student employees, devote greater time to their courses. These problems come with the territory and, while frustrating, should not be so great as to preclude using students as staff. The archivist's responsibility will be to judge, on a case-by-case basis, whether the student's deviations from the schedule are for educational reasons and career interests, rather than for expansion of social and recreational activities.

A reservation occasionally voiced about using student employees, especially for processing, is that their presence could threaten the confidentiality of some records held by the archives. Indeed, there are risks that students, in performing their archival work, may see confidential records that, if revealed, could compromise an individual or the institution. An occasional student might even take advantage of work time in the archives to search out such information for personal interest. Certainly, a similar potential exists for other categories of staff, but the risk there may not be so high as with students, who may have less developed professional ethics and less stake in a career at the institution. Nevertheless, these risks are easily exaggerated, since the number of restricted records in an archives should be relatively small and their access should be easy to regulate. Moreover, the adoption of a few general practices should provide safeguards against serious problems. First, an informal assessment of each student's attitude and approach should be part of the employment screening process to reduce the likelihood of hiring irresponsible students. Secondly, new student employees should be reminded orally and in writing that they are expected to approach their work with a maturity and professionalism that would preclude them from taking advantage of their position as employees. Finally, assignments should be developed so that the students' work does not bring them into contact with the few records requiring sensitive handling. For example, the processing of recent (less than 10 years old) central administrative and departmental records, student academic and counseling records, and faculty and personnel files should always be reserved for the permanent staff. Thus, while the issue of access to confidential records may limit the use of student employees, a few simple administrative practices will contain the risks and free the archives to use students in many less sensitive tasks.

To use student employees effectively, the archivist must recognize the many areas of archival work where students will be of limited or no value. It would be unwise to rely on students for appraisal, records management, overall classification and arrangement, general reference room service, or many technical areas of conservation. Students simply lack the breadth, knowledge, and experience to perform efficiently and proficiently in these areas.

The capable archival administrator will, however, find tasks in support of these areas that will be assignable to students. For example, students might examine an office's case files in detail to determine whether certain categories of information were recorded consistently so that an appraisal decision on sampling or disposal can be reached.

Management Basics

Experience with the student employees on one's own campus will suggest a number of procedures to enable the archives to derive the most benefit from this labor force. There are, however, a number of common management techniques that can be quite useful in most academic archives. First, to facilitate recruitment, selection, and supervision of student employees, the archivist should prepare job descriptions for typical student positions. These should identify the basic tasks, the skills, knowledge, and abilities needed for the job, and the supervisory relationships. The job description can be used to advertise positions and develop selection procedures. Second, if no application form is available from the institution, the archivist should develop a simple one. Third, a carefully defined selection process should be followed to make sure applicants are treated fairly and that the archives' needs are considered fully. Fourth, newly hired students should be given a brief orientation to the archival program and specific work areas. Many archives find it useful to have a simple student-employee manual to regularize the delivery of this information. Finally, the archivist or other permanent staff will need to monitor student productivity and provide corrective advice or discipline throughout the student's employment. While such formal procedures might be criticized as overly elaborate for students, they will assure far greater quality. Equally important, they will provide the archivist with valuable experience in standard personnel practices that are critical in dealing with other archival employees.

Despite this recommendation to use student employees as broadly as possible, the strategic value of such programs should be reconsidered periodically. That is, one needs to examine each use of student staff to determine when a point of diminishing returns is reached—when so much preparation, supervision, and revision is necessary that the work could be handled more productively by regular staff. It is also useful to consider what is the largest number of students that the permanent staff can supervise effectively. For example, if there are sufficient funds to hire 10 students working a total 2.25 FTE, one must consider whether there is enough permanent staff to supervise them. In a repository with only one professional and one clerical staff member, supervision of 10 students would be unwieldy and the repository may be better advised to hire one additional full-time permanent clerical staff member. The net result would be fewer employee hours but greater continuity and less time in supervision. Such decisions are, however, strategic and need to be considered in light of all the available resources.

These decisions can be made only in response to specific circumstances, but the use of student employees should be given serious consideration as a general aspect of college and university archives administration. If local circumstances appear to mitigate against broad use of students, the archivist should work with administrators either to permit the variations needed for the archives or to secure sufficient alternative staffing.

STUDENTS AS USERS

The location of college and university archives within educational institutions leads to a user community not commonly encountered in other kinds of repositories—students. Undergraduates, in particular, form a large part of the in-person use of many academic archives.[10] The distinguishing features of most undergraduate use relate to their larger numbers, short inquiries, and repetitious cursory examination of a relatively narrow range of topics. In several respects, their service needs are similar to those of other user communities, but there are enough differences to merit attention as a special challenge in the management of academic archives.

Importance and Characteristics

Student users present a unique opportunity to enrich the academic archives' program and mission, but they also bring many problems. The archives provide an ideal opportunity to introduce students, normally young adults, not just to historical research but to the raw material of history itself. Given the nature of precollege historical instruction, the archives has the opportunity to bring college students into contact with history in a radically different way. For most, their previous courses focused on secondary accounts and predigested samples of primary sources in books of readings, but archives introduce students to the importance of documents as evidence, that is, as mechanisms to span time. Therefore, regardless of the subject of a student reference inquiry, the archivist should use the opportunity to demonstrate that individual documents, and the archives as a whole, are a means to retrieve and partially reconstruct the past. Learning how documents can mediate between the past and the present will be one of the most important lessons students, especially those not specializing in history, can learn in their college years.

Demonstrating the immediate relevance of the past to the present need not be a conscious goal of answering student inquiries. Rather, the archivist should be satisfied if the contact merely shows that the past contains both great continuities with the present and equally important discontinuities. In the most successful uses of archives, the student should go away with the realization that documents not only bring out the similarities and differences, but also hold the clues to understanding the processes that generated this continuity and change.

Other types of archives and museums provide similar opportunities. What is different about college and university repositories is that their setting gives them a clear advantage in access to a large and constantly renewing

source of users. Secondly, most students conceive of themselves in relation to the institution even if they disagree
with its policies and question its character. Thus, the
archives' institutionally related holdings are very strong
bait to lure a student audience. The academic archivist
should exploit students' interest in the parent institution
by linking elements of the students' current lives to documentary evidence of analogous experiences of previous
generations. When students become interested in the past
in this way, they will discover how continuities and
changes are clearly relevant to their own lives, and they
will obtain a personal understanding of history, documents, and archives. To appreciate the importance of this
process, one need only recall the many cases of students
who come to the archives with a simple trivia question that
is readily answerable from old yearbooks, but who end up
spending an hour or two examining photographs, student
handbooks, and scrapbooks from the turn of the century.
While it is hard to gauge the long-range impact of such
use, the frequency with which this happens, and even
leads to return visits, suggests that it is an important
phenomenon meriting the archivist's attention. Obviously,
these benefits do not occur with all or even most student
users, but they occur frequently enough that this form of
proselytization should be a key goal in providing service
to students.

The long-term value of archival research to students'
lives is another important justification for programs to
facilitate their visits to the archives. Nevertheless, a substantial volume of student use will occur without such
philosophical arguments, and more practical and mundane issues will loom large in the archivist's view of
student use. In fact, the typical reaction to student users
may focus on difficulties they raise for archival operations.
The volume of students alone is likely to create management problems at many repositories, and the nature of
their inquiries can compound these difficulties. The kinds
of research that undergraduates conduct and the range of
their topics is quite diverse, but their projects tend to be
less comprehensive and far less exhaustive than the re-

search in which archivists are often trained. Archivists who are accustomed to serving graduate students and scholars conducting research for publication, or administrators seeking historical roots for the campus's future, will need to adjust their expectations to avoid frustration with student users. In this light, one can draw the analogy that student users are to academic archives what genealogists are to governmental archives—high-volume users who place heavy service demands on the program, but whose use generally touches only the surface of the archives and who utilize only the simplest techniques of historical research. From such an understanding of student use, the archivist should plan programs and services that will permit rapid delivery of relevant, but simple, information, just as many governmental archives have developed special services for genealogists.

Academic archivists have also found student users frustrating because of the repetitiveness of the subjects studied and the inexperience of the student researchers. Is there really a value in yet another student paper on the history of Old Main or why puce and lavender were chosen as the school's colors? This concern about repetitiveness is often coupled with the realization that the level of analysis and understanding in student research is frequently quite simplistic—a result of students' inexperience as researchers. They therefore require considerable orientation in the basics of historical documentation and even rudimentary facts about the past. Another important problem is that student use can strain the physical condition and integrity of documents because of the volume of student use and the limited time they have for research, and they are generally unaware of basic preservation needs. These factors may combine to lead to carelessness with fragile archival holdings. Experience may suggest other liabilities of students as archival users, but these problems should not detract from the importance of serving students. Just as with genealogists in governmental archives, students have a right to expect high-quality, attentive reference service from their institution's archives.

Strategies for Serving Students

The first element in programs and procedures to assist undergraduate researchers should be the delineation of the archives' goals in serving this important user group. The most basic goals are:

1. Delivering information to answer the question and fulfill the need (e.g., completion of a course paper) that motivates the student to come to the archives.
2. Educating students by causing them to alter or refine the basic question they pose when entering the archives.
3. Demonstrating the difficulty of arriving at historical certainty, even when documentation is available.
4. Convincing the student of the importance of the past for the present.
5. Illustrating the need for archival programs to support personal and academic research and to help sustain society.

Ideally, all these goals would be accomplished with every student reference inquiry, but in actuality, the archivist will be fortunate to achieve even one with most uses. Even so, they should be the bedrock for the archives' attitude toward, and management of, reference service to students.

To give the archivist a chance to meet these goals, a number of techniques can minimize the problems inherent in managing student use. First, the archivist should conceptualize use and service broadly so that some student research needs can be met without requiring the time of reference staff. Outreach vehicles, especially exhibits, slide shows, and curriculum packets, can help meet this need. They will be quite valuable in supporting student contact with the archives while reducing wear and tear on documents and staff. For example, students coming to the archives for an overview of the campus's history might be directed to an area where they can view an audiovisual production about the school. Permanent and rotating exhibits can be quite effective for introducing students to the history of the institution or local community as well as for illustrating how documents and archives are links to the past.

When one accepts this broader approach to use, it becomes clear that the line between tactics for serving students and outreach methods are often blurred. In fact, the best promotional activities will be those that not only advertise archives and history, but also provide historical information and serve as research sources in themselves. If one kind of student use tends to create more demand than the archives can handle, it should consider how standard outreach vehicles (e.g., curriculum packets or tour books) can answer common questions. If the archives finds that it does not have enough undergraduate student use, it should contact instructors, especially for introductory English composition, speech, and history classes, to suggest a class assignment to write a short paper or speech on an aspect of college history. The success of such an appeal will be higher if the archivist can provide a list of topics that will appeal to students and faculty and engender manageable research projects. Encouraging advanced undergraduate and graduate research projects will require more diligence and consultation with the faculty to choose topics that are both appropriate to the course and supported by the archives' holdings.

In an active archival program, the most prominent feature of student use may be large numbers of first-time researchers looking for quick answers to questions on popular topics. Much of this use can be met through the archives' ready-reference or vertical files and its reference collection of secondary sources on campus history. These sources should serve as the archives' first line of response to student inquiries, thereby simplifying student access to archival material and reducing wear and tear on the archives' holdings for popular subjects of study. Another valuable tactic is for the archivist to make presentations to those classes requiring archival research for course assignments. These orientation sessions, comparable to bibliographic instruction programs in libraries, should explain the nature of archival materials, outline sources relevant to the course's topic, describe archival finding aids, and explain user policies and procedures.

Successful handling of student users may require special talents on the part of the reference staff. Students often ask particularly complex questions but expect simple answers. For example, they may request documents illustrating racial-discrimination practices of the institution before World War II without realizing that many such practices were never recorded in documents or policy, but were more insidious and pervasive in daily operations. In addition, because of the broad scope of the question, the archivist will need to work through an interview process to direct the student to a manageable topic, such as minority student housing policies and practices. The reference interview's follow-up questions will be even more important with undergraduates than other users, and these questions are likely to play a critical role in shaping the very essence of the student's research. Thus, the ideal reference archivist for the scholar doing an exhaustive study of instruction in theoretical mechanics may not be the best reference archivist for the undergraduate writing a class paper on the design and construction of the Engineering Laboratory. While few archives can afford separate staff for each type of user, some specialization is possible even in a two-person operation, and the concept of specialization for users can provide the basis for staff to change gears.

In handling student users, the challenge is to direct them to useful information quickly while avoiding subtleties and complexities that are beyond the scope of their projects. All this needs to be done in a way that neither causes the student to become exasperated with archival research nor fails to give due respect to the seriousness of their interest in, and need for, archival material. Archival managers may want to establish rules of thumb for serving students, such as providing only one box of material at a time, allocating no more than ten or fifteen minutes of staff time to an inquiry, or restricting students to the reference file and published sources. These rules can be useful, but in practice they will need to be abridged so often that they are best maintained as informal, unwritten guidelines.

Some archivists express concern about student examination of nonpublished source material in office records and personal papers because the use might compromise the sensitive or confidential information in the files. This concern is not inappropriate since students often are inexperienced as users, may lack sensitivity in dealing with certain issues, and are occasionally anxious to mount a crusade. Nevertheless, it would be irresponsible to allow these potential problems to lead to rules that would exclude students from using major categories of material or place more restrictions on students than on other kinds of users. Fortunately, a large volume of student inquiries can be answered without their having to examine possibly sensitive records and papers.

When it is necessary for students to examine unpublished material, the archivist should make it available, but may wish to take additional precautions. First, the reference process should include an assessment or evaluation of student users in the same way as for scholars and administrators. This assessment should start with a consideration of what and how much information the researcher appears to need and what relevant sources are available. Then the archivist should determine if less "sensitive" documents can be provided first while the archivist assesses whether the user's information needs also require access to more sensitive and possibly even restricted documents. Inescapably, these decisions are matters of the archivist's judgment and thus inherently subjective. This is not, however, a reason to replace them with hard-and-fast rules denying students access to records that are normally available to other researchers, nor should subjectivity become an excuse not to follow ethical principles in providing reference assistance. Instead, the resolution of the problem will come when the archivist is prepared to critique the decision-making process used in helping each student user, and to regulate personal prejudices about the subject matter or student researchers. Ultimately, the archivist's professional ethics should dictate that students be treated as other users and be provided with information and service commensurate with their needs and the archives' resources. Restrictions should stem only from the nature of records, not from the characteristics of potential users.

It would be imprudent not to recognize that student users present many difficulties for academic archives. The additional service load alone can be quite demanding on program resources. Nevertheless, service to students should be a fundamental part of archival operations since it is central to their mission—presentation of the past to enhance the knowledge of present and future generations. To ignore student users is to ignore one of the best hopes that future generations of the university community will understand, support, and use the archival programs.

Service to students also can aid the archives in demonstrating its value to the university. By its preservation and promotion of the institution's past, the archives can be an invaluable tool for the university to capture the student's long-term interest in the school at an early date. Ultimately, more important than these pragmatic and even exploitative considerations is the archivist's fundamental responsibility to enrich the lives of a major component of the higher education community through exposure to the wealth of history preserved in the archives.

ARTIFACTS AND MEMORABILIA

Documents are and should continue to be the proper center of attention for archives. Their formats may vary, but they all use textual, iconographic, or aural means to convey information and meaning. Archival holdings normally do not include physical objects acquired and preserved primarily for their value as objects. Such nondocumentary materials from the past are commonly called artifacts and memorabilia, although sometimes they have been less logically and less gracefully called "realia" or "three-dimensional objects." In the strictest sense, artifacts are solid objects that are the result of human action, but they also can include remnants of naturally occurring items that have acquired an important historical association with human events (e.g., a fragment of an oak tree that marked the site of the founding of the campus). Because of the nondocumentary character of artifacts, their frequently awkward shapes and sizes, and the complexity of their preservation needs, they have not been welcomed in archives. In fact, archival literature provides little advice on how to handle them beyond the simple but often impractical suggestion of "transfer them to a museum." This is not an unjustifiable course—academic archivists should avoid accepting responsibility for artifacts and memorabilia whenever possible since they are not central to the archives' mission, and they are not well-handled by archival techniques. Moreover, artifacts may be better understood through the concepts of material culture that are fundamental to the museum world than through the concepts of documentary culture that are basic to archives.

Nevertheless, it would be irresponsible for academic archivists to refuse categorically to deal with artifacts and memorabilia. In many cases, they are asked to accept objects directly related to the archives' documentary holdings on the history of the institution, and few campuses have a historical museum to offer proper care for the objects. It will not be long before a new archivist must confront this question as the archives is offered such "treasures" as homecoming buttons, fraternity paddles, sorority pins, banners, flags, uniforms or other academic clothing, fragments of buildings, furniture, scientific equipment, trophies, shovels, and plaques. In some cases, these materials may be among personal papers or even official records accessioned by the archives, but in other cases, they may be isolated donations sent to the archives because it is known as the custodian of campus history. While archivists often can discourage such donations by saying they do not "do" artifacts, sometimes it is necessary to accept them to avoid offending a donor or leaving the impression that archivists are Philistines who really do not care about the past. In other cases, the archivist can

accession the artifact gladly if it is of a manageable physical format and size and has clear value for supplementing
archival documentation, especially as a visual attraction
for future exhibits. In a few cases, such as scientific collections of specimens, the archivist has an obligation to
ensure their preservation for future research, although
the archives may not be the ideal site.

As archivists consider how to deal with artifacts, they
well might begin by recognizing that not all objects described under this heading are of the same type. Archival
decisions can be simplified by dividing the objects into the
following three categories:

1. Information carriers—objects designed to carry textual or
readily apparent symbolic information, including awards, certificates, buttons, badges, banners, flags, and commercial pack-
aging and products (e.g., special soda and beer cans) designed
to "co-market" the product and the institution.

2. Physical remnants of events, places, and persons—objects
once used to accomplish some function related to the institution,
including student uniforms, military corps swords, hats, bean-
ies, footballs, bats, bricks from old buildings, furniture, and, in
at least one case, the physical remains of a person associated
with the institutions' founding.[11]

3. Ceremonial objects—objects deliberately created to formally communicate data about an event or deed to the future,
including trophies, groundbreaking shovels, plaques, gifts from
or to visiting dignitaries.

A single object may fall in more than one category, e.g.,
an engraved gavel used for 50 years to call the Faculty
Players Club to order is both a ceremonial object and a
physical remnant of an event. However, if the archivist
uses the above categories to group artifacts and memorabilia, many decisions can be made easier. For example,
comprehensiveness may be desirable and feasible for in-
formation-carrying artifacts because many are compact
items like archival documents; photographs of the others
often can suffice for archival documentation. Similarly,
since ceremonial items often tell researchers little about

events not already apparent from textual records, generally they may merit less attention, even if their material
or sentimental value is high.

Given the shortage of resources for most of archival
work, it would be improper for the academic archivist to
devote much time to artifacts and memorabilia, but some
basic areas merit brief notice. In appraisal, selectivity
rather than comprehensiveness should be paramount. For
example, rather than attempting to collect all examples of
the college uniform, the archives might select one uniform
and rely on photographs for the balance. In other cases,
such as sorority pins or homecoming badges, comprehensiveness may be a reasonable goal because the objects are
small, relatively durable, and drawn from a narrowly
defined universe. Nevertheless, the archivist's collecting
role should be passive, responding to, rather than soliciting, such gifts.

In deciding on the arrangement of artifacts, the archivist generally should separate these objects from documentary collections after making separation records to
place in the documentary files and provenance records to
keep with the artifacts. Then the artifacts can be housed
centrally, organized by type, and placed in environments
that are most compatible to their preservation. Exceptions
to separating artifacts would be appropriate for items
found in scrapbooks, such as pins and badges, since they
are often a predominant part of the design and composition of these books.

Descriptions of artifacts should be brief, and, as with
the rest of archival holdings, the type of descriptive tool
should vary with the level at which the material is described. A summary series-type description can be used for
the archives' central collection of artifacts and memorabilia, but almost invariably, item-level description will also
be necessary. Detailed finding aids, most easily prepared
by using word processing or database software, will be
essential to maintain inventory control and facilitate user
access. A brief entry for each item should record its type
and name (e.g., Alpha Lambda Delta pin), date, source
(including record series number when it has been sepa-

rated from personal papers or official records), storage location, and date of acquisition. Those items that form long and relatively uniform series (e.g., homecoming buttons and badges) and for which the provenance may be unknown or of little importance should be described in a summary fashion (e.g., "25 Homecoming Badges, 1935-41").

In considering physical care and preservation of artifacts and memorabilia, the academic archivist should start with the recognition that he or she probably cannot satisfy high museum standards. Nevertheless, a reasonable goal will be to provide the same level of care for artifacts as for textual documents. Often, this level of protection can be accomplished by storage of smaller items in archival or museum envelopes and in boxes or in steel cabinets away from light, heat, and humidity. Museum-quality care for larger items, fabrics, woods, metals, and other materials will probably be impossible for most archives. However, the archivist should utilize museum textbooks and catalogs as sources of advice, supplies, and equipment whenever budgets allow attention to artifact preservation.[12]

Artifacts and memorabilia are likely to be used primarily as attention-getting additions to documentary displays and for outreach lectures. Such use provides the major justification for the time and resources that artifacts require, but the archivist should not overlook the fact that artifacts themselves can be the focus of research. For example, artifacts that portray campus symbols over time can be critical for understanding the evolution of symbols and institutional images, such as mascots. Research on such topics can be enhanced greatly when related documentary evidence about design and use of the artifacts also has been preserved.[13]

Academic archivists have good reason to relegate artifacts and memorabilia to a secondary status in their programs, but it will be neither possible nor desirable to avoid them entirely. Political considerations, donor relations, and institutional mandate often will combine to require archivists to assume responsibility for these objects. At the same time, by adapting basic archival practices and imposing limits on time devoted to artifacts, the academic archivist can do justice to this notable category of evidence of the past. Academic archivists should neither shun this responsibility nor become concerned if they fall short of high museum standards, since the artifacts should be seen only as a supplement to their primary focus on documents.

"THE EYES OF HISTORY ARE UPON US"

Historical Consciousness in Higher Education

College and university archivists frequently encounter a curious feature of the higher education community that is both an opportunity and a source of much frustration. Members of the academic community are particularly conscious of, and interested in, exploiting their institution's history. Fortunately, this interest often manifests itself in research in original documents, leading to analytical studies and interpretations of important events and trends. Unfortunately, the more frequent manifestations of this historical consciousness are searches for historical documentation to provide window dressing for public relations efforts or to satisfy personal and institutional nostalgia. The problem for the archives is that it is expected to respond promptly and accurately with information that meets the researcher's preconceptions, whether superficial or profound. The archivist may be left in the position of seeing the repository used, even promoted, but knowing that the institution's past is being misrepresented, or at least that important issues are being ignored while more trivial ones are examined closely and disseminated widely. Managing the archives' resources in response to these pressures is a particularly difficult task. It requires that archivists combine their own understanding of the institution's past with their knowledge of available documentation and then relate this information to their assessment of the merit of the researcher's inquiry.

Success in this area requires not only strong archival and research skills, but also good judgment and interpersonal skills.

By no means is the problem of balancing nostalgic, public relations, and scholarly research interests unique to academic archives. One need only consider such historical celebrations as the American Revolution Bicentennial, the Statue of Liberty rededication, and the Constitution Bicentennial to find clear examples of extensive but predominantly shallow interest in history, which largely miss the true meaning and significance of the original event. Nevertheless, the problem seems to occur so regularly in colleges and universities that it merits special attention from the academic archivist. Given higher education's focus on teaching and research and its emphasis on free inquiry and scholarship in pursuit of truth, it is particularly important that archivists, as members of that community, combat inaccurate and shallow representations of their institution's past.

Indeed, it is because of the importance of the archives' educational role and its responsibility as the primary resource for accurate representations of the past that the archivist must pay particular attention to this problem. If the archives does not adopt strategies to respond authoritatively to both the trivial and the profound research projects that develop from this historical consciousness, it risks great inefficiencies in the use of its resources. Worse yet, it can easily fall prey to the perception that the archives is primarily a resource for whatever historical sideshow the institution is promoting at the moment.

Roots and Manifestations

Despite the unfortunate side effects of this historical consciousness, it places the academic archivist in an excellent position to exploit the academic community's historical interests for the benefit of basic archival goals. To develop appropriate mechanisms that respond to the problems created by this historical consciousness, the archivist must first understand why this is such a dominant trait in academic institutions.

Perhaps one of the most fundamental reasons for the high level of historical consciousness at colleges and universities is that their claims to credibility are based on their ability to refer to long and distinguished pasts. Unlike so many quarters of the business, manufacturing, and service industries, where innovation and change are seen as providing the decisive or competitive edge, credibility and support for colleges and universities are sought through evocations of the past accomplishments of its faculty, alumni, and athletes. When innovation is cited as an asset, it is normally coupled to references to long traditions of innovation or to explanations of how the institution's past success has led to its present ability to innovate. This should not be surprising or inherently objectionable in a realm where the progressive enlightenment of humankind is the daily stock in trade. Every institution should remember its past glories, and it is the archivist's duty to make sure they are documented and available for study and dissemination.

At the same time that recollection of past accomplishments serves an important legitimizing function for the institution, it also contributes to a second major cause of the historical evocations so common at colleges and universities—the need to present a positive public image. Through the selective presentation of past glories, the institution can provide a more positive public image than it could if it had to focus only on present deeds, whose warts are often as readily visible as their virtues. Classic examples of this occur in athletics, where the great star of the 1920s or 1950s is regularly promoted along with recollections of that great game in which he scored so many points. This pattern is not isolated to athletes—there also is the tendency to concentrate on the handful of faculty who may have won international honors, sometimes decades ago. What is inappropriate about such emphasis on past accomplishments is that the accounts of these great moments seldom go beyond a superficial retelling of a well-known story and usually fail to relate the past to the institution's present record in the same area.

Underlying these motivations is a basic human trait to admire great accomplishments and revere the past. Given the fact that colleges and universities project themselves as representatives of the accumulated knowledge of the human race, it is hardly surprising that the images of "storehouse of past knowledge" and "bastion of tradition" quickly become blurred. In addition, one might argue that colleges and universities offer models of continuity in the midst of a changing and strongly iconoclastic society— they provide the appearance of following time-honored traditions (through their annual cycles of classes, exams and graduations, athletic and cultural events, and their strong and often very traditional architectural presence) when the rest of the world appears to be in constant flux. For anyone who has attended a college or university, the mental image of the institution is likely to be one of a place and a time to which one assumes one can always return. Thus, colleges and universities are the focus of great historical attention both because they are vehicles for conveying the wisdom of the past to the present and future and because they occupy a critical place in the life experiences of a large portion of American adults. Many institutions, especially private colleges and universities, recognize the importance of this experience and strive to translate this interest into financial support through their alumni and development offices.

It is important for the archivist to recognize the extent to which trips to the archives can be motivated by inward searches for tradition and stability or by nostalgia for one's own college days or the glory days of an institution one has adopted. By being able to perceive these motivations for research and reference inquiries, the archivist will be able to respond most effectively so that both the immediate question can be answered and the curiosity about the past may be directed toward more productive lines of historical inquiry. On a practical level, understanding these psychological dimensions of researchers' motivations will assist the archivist in classifying types of inquiries for speedier

response and in developing outreach tools that may anticipate and answer many nostalgia-based inquiries.

Problems for Archival Operations

Few archivists would criticize the basic result of the
historical consciousness found in colleges and universities—an increased interest in, and use of, the archives for
historical research. It can, however, present a series of
problems not readily solvable through the written or informal procedures archivists use to regulate their work.
The most common problem is heavy reference demands
that preclude allocation of staff energies to the many other
archival functions that archival textbooks would have one
perform. This will be most obvious at times of key anniversaries or special historical celebrations by major campus units (e.g., the centenary of a college, the renovation
and rededication of a landmark building). While archivists
should devote their energies to meeting researcher inquiries, many manifestations of campus historicism or nostalgia lead to frustrating and time-consuming searches for
trivia or for evidence to fit preconceived notions of the past.

A second critical problem is that dissemination of the
results of research driven by the motives of public relations or nostalgia, especially when done by less sophisticated researchers, can perpetuate misperceptions or, at
least, superficial explanations of the past. This problem is
particularly troublesome with public relations offices and
media personnel, who have the greatest ability to dissem-
inate information but often lack the time, space, training,
or inclination to present the complex picture of the past
that is necessary in any competent historical account. The
opposite problem can develop with sophisticated researchers, whose efforts at producing balanced, comprehensive
histories can lead them to monopolize archival reference
services in their quest for definitive documentation. This
commonly occurs when a local faculty member is commis-
sioned to write the definitive history of the institution.
There is also the possibility of an ironic and unfortunate
consequence that can follow the completion of major schol-

arly histories and anniversary publications, whether sophisticated or superficial. The completed products can
create the impression that the institution knows its history and need not do further research. If a "definitive"
narrative history was written at the last major anniversary, or if the public information office regularly dissemi-
nates historical information, the institution may ask itself: Why do we need more research, and why do we need
an active archival program? To both the experienced researcher and the archivist, the answer is as obvious as the
question is absurd. However, this view is not beyond the
shortsightedness of some campus officers, thus illustrating the need for the archivist to use every public display
of history to inform the campus of how many more issues
remain to be explained and how much more documentation remains to be mined for future studies and public
events.

A final archival problem posed by the historical consciousness prevalent on campuses is that the institution
may become so focused on its own past that it loses sight
of its place in the larger world. The history of every
institution contains at least a few chapters deserving
broad interest from the public and scholars alike—for
example, key scientific experiments that contributed to
the development of the theory of relativity, student demonstrations that triggered national events, or the tenure
of a literary or political notable on the faculty. It is, however, an unfortunate tendency of all institutions to refer
to these readily recognizable events with such frequency
that they begin to assume a disproportionate role in the
life of the college or university. Even when public accounts
of these events are well-researched and balanced, the
attention they receive can easily lead to an institutional
myopia, whereby the event is seen in isolation from other
university history and from the rest of higher education
and American society.

Remedies

While archivists cannot prevent the detrimental effects of historical consciousness, they can take countermeasures that may prevent certain people or events from looming larger than life. First, they must not allow themselves to lose their own perspective on the significance of the person or event, no matter how many times they must answer questions on the subject. Otherwise, there may be detrimental effects on appraisal and description, such as overdocumentation and indexing of the person or event. Many archives show at least a few signs of being the center for the study of a given experiment, social movement, or person rather than a balanced center for documentation of the institution. Secondly, the archivist, perhaps more than any other institutional representative, must maintain a critical perspective on the institution, its past, and its place in the community and in higher education. Sometimes this will result in the archivist's being seen as a critic, gadfly, or curmudgeon, but this is necessary for archivists to fulfill their role as educators. Exhibits and public presentations by the archives will aid in this process, but perhaps the most common manifestation will be the questioning and redirecting of reference inquiries to move researchers away from the simple answers they had hoped to find and towards a more textured view of the past based on a broad range of documentary evidence.

Beyond these general considerations, there are a number of actions the academic archivist can take in response to the more problematic manifestations of historical consciousness in his or her parent institution. First, even when a particular use or dissemination of historical information is not sophisticated or completely accurate, the archivist should recognize that it still represents an interest in the past that should not be discouraged. When inaccuracies or distortions occur, the archivist should respond with polite references to documentation that provides a more accurate picture of the event in question. This can be accomplished through letters to the editor and phone calls to the author of the offending piece. When inaccuracies and distortions become frequent, the archivist will have to decide which are most critically in need of correction and which can be allowed to stand.

A better approach may be to assume an active role in promoting the institution and its past through exhibits, slide shows, and lectures. Such outreach devices may preempt inferior work by satisfying the community's interest in the past while also exploiting this interest to draw attention to the archives as the primary source for historical inquiry. To address the fact that many of the worst offenses against historical accuracy come from alumni and public relations offices, the archivist should cultivate contacts in these offices and pursue cooperative ventures whereby their staff conduct the research and writing but do so in close consultation with the archives.

The problem of superficiality in relation to an institution's past will not disappear, no matter how well-run the archival program. It will require constant diligence. As managers of important but small programs, archivists must work to make sure that their institutional resource allocators are aware of the following four aspects of the phenomenon of historical studies of its past.

1. The dissemination and preservation of selected evidence of the past, whether "definitive" histories or historical photo albums and calendars, are not substitutes for proper archival documentation of the past.

2. References to the past in university publications and events, however valuable for color and image building, must be accurate and balanced, and they are not substitutes for research and careful analysis.

3. Archives can play a major role in the institution as the source of documentary evidence for both nostalgia and history.

4. The archives must document not just the institution's great moments in the past, but also its failures, unheralded successes, and its mundane activities that do not fall into any of these categories. This comprehensiveness of coverage is fundamental to both the archives' mission and the college's role as an educational institution.

The focus of this discussion of the effect of historical consciousness on academic archives has been on problems raised by the quality of the work performed by some archival users. Clearly, this places archivists in a difficult position. On the one hand, they should be simple intermediaries who supply documents to address the questions posed by users and who do not interfere with the subject or interpretation. On the other hand, archivists must serve as the historical conscience of their institutions, ensuring that the past is documented, researched, and described accurately. One must balance these responsibilities in the course of each reference inquiry. At the base of all reference actions will be the twin responsibilities of vigorously supporting the pursuit of truth and educating society about its past.

In a college or university setting, archivists have great opportunities to pursue these objectives. Indeed with the transitory nature of the academic community, there is a continual need to educate the members of the campus about its past. The most transient element of the community, students, are, moreover, at that critical age when life-long interests are developed and consolidated. With minimal efforts, these interests can be expanded to include historical inquiry. The college or university archives offers the best opportunity for placing individuals into contact with the heritage of an institution and a community to which they have just been initiated. To a great extent, the archives also can foster and direct interests in history among the less transitory elements of faculty, staff, and administrators. When the process works properly, students and faculty members will be able to use history as a tool in defining their own identities, either by separating themselves from their institution's past or by embracing elements of it. By responding to historical interests on the campus in ways to meet these needs, the archives will move beyond being a service agency and become an educational program as important as any other component of the campus.

Notes

1. Refer to Laurence R. Veysey, *The Emergence of the American University* (Chicago: University of Chicago Press, 1965), 264-341; and Daniel Alpert, "Performance and Paralysis: The Organizational Context of the American Research University," *Journal of Higher Education* 56 (1985): 241-81.

2. See the discussion of "Administrative Histories."

3. This section's discussion of methodological issues in handling student and faculty organizations is focused on the many smaller, *ad hoc* groups rather than the more institutionalized bodies such as unions. Bodies such as unions will be more amenable to the standard archival practices used for campus offices and large manuscript collections and thus do not require specialized attention in this discussion. The records of all groups, however, are appropriate for academic archives.

4. Refer also to Kenneth W. Duckett, *Modern Manuscripts: A Practical Manual for Their Management, Care and Use* (Nashville, Tenn.: American Association for State and Local History, 1975), 62-67.

5. David B. Potts, "College Archives as Windows on American Society," *American Archivist* 40 (1977): 43-49.

6. A good introduction to the administration of students is Beatrice Sichel, "Utilizing Student Assistants in Small Libraries," *Journal of Library Administration* 3 (1982): 35-45; also useful is Andrew Melnyk, "Student Aids in Our Library," *Illinois Libraries* 58 (1976): 141-44.

7. For a brief report on cooperative processing by students, refer to Richard M. Kesner and others, "Collection Processing as a Team Effort," *American Archivist* 44 (1981): 356-58.

8. Michael D. Kathman and Jane M. Kathman, "Management Problems of Student Workers in Academic Libraries," *College and Research Libraries* 39 (1978): 118-22.

9. Lawrence L. Steinmetz, *Managing the Marginal and Unsatisfactory Performer,* 2d ed. (Reading, Mass.: Addison-Wesley, 1985). This work can be discouraging because of its focus on

workplace problems, but it provides excellent management advice for dealing with all categories of employees.

10. For the purpose of this section, the terms "students" or "student users" will be used primarily in reference to undergraduates. While many graduate students might have as little experience in archives, the focus of their use, unless for personal interest or minor supplement to coursework, will be quite similar to that of faculty and independent scholars.

11. Jeremy Bentham's clothed skeleton and mummified head were donated to University College, University of London, following Bentham's death in 1832, although they are not part of the archives *per se*. Refer to Megley Harte, *The University of London 1936-1986* (London: Athlone Press, 1986) and Southwood Smith, *A Lectured Delivered over the Remains of Jeremy Bentham ESQ.* (London: Effingham Wilson, 1832).

12. The academic archivist's bookshelf should include a basic text on the care of objects, such as A. Bruce MacLeish, *The Care of Antiques and Historical Collections,* 2d ed. (Nashville, Tenn.: American Association for State and Local History, 1985).

13. For thought-provoking discussions of the research importance of artifacts, refer to Thomas J. Schlereth, ed., *Material Culture Studies in America* (Nashville, Tenn.: American Association for State and Local History, 1982).

Programmatic Activities

INTRODUCTION

The preceding chapters have focused on the core activities of an academic archives and have reviewed key issues that the archivist in a college or university will confront. All historical records repositories aspiring to be archives should incorporate such techniques and approaches into their basic operations, especially in appraisal, arrangement, description, preservation, and use. For new institutions and repositories, meeting minimum goals in these areas will require full attention and resources for a number of years. However, once these elements are firmly in place, the archives should move beyond the basics to become involved in several related programmatic activities. These activities include records management, manuscripts collecting, exhibits, outreach programs, and oral history. To varying degrees, these activities have become hallmarks of American college and university archives. In most cases, these programs have helped archives accomplish their basic missions and garner important institutional support and recognition.

Each of these special activities involves a distinctive methodology and set of goals, and each can, and sometimes does, exist independent of archives. Because of the specialized methodologies of these fields, some have evolved into distinct professions (e.g., oral history and records management). For example, a college or university might have a free-standing records management program in a reporting line totally separate from the archives. In the best of conditions, however, the key elements of these programmatic activities will be incorporated into the archival program if not subordinated to it.

These programmatic activities can provide long-term focus and individual character in a mature academic archives, but the extent of the archives' involvement will depend on the balancing of two countervailing forces. On one hand, these activities should be part of the archives' long-term goals because of their relation to the core mission of preserving historical documentation and making it accessible. On the other hand, the development of programs such as records management, exhibits, and oral history must vary with the institution's needs, the archivist's interests and talents, local constituencies, and resources. Despite their importance, these programs are often best postponed until the archives has made substantial progress in its basic mission of documenting the parent institution.

Since each of these activities has its own detailed methodology, the focus will be on identifying their basic elements, delineating their archival implications, and specifying what elements of each activity are so fundamental that they should be incorporated into every academic archives.

RECORDS MANAGEMENT

Of all the programmatic activities that go beyond the core of archival work, records management is the most fundamental to archival goals because it relates to the selection and regular transfer of material to the archives. Some have claimed that archival work is merely a subset of the broader discipline of records and information management, but others note that records management emerged historically from archival work in the U.S. federal government in the mid-twentieth century. Despite these differing perspectives and the fact that relations between these two fields have not been well coordinated in recent years, it is pointless to allow controversies regarding origin to interfere with the academic archivist's involvement in records management. Rather, the academic archivist should accept the existence of records management as a separate but allied discipline and should recognize that close cooperation in a number of areas is necessary for both fields to succeed. Records management is fundamentally important to archival programs because it influences the creation, content, and preservation of the documents that will be available for archival accessioning. Therefore, the archivist should pursue an active role in his/her institution's records management program, and if necessary, institute a program if none exists.

This book cannot provide a comprehensive guide to academic records management. Rather, it will identify basic concepts and techniques and leave details to the literature.[1] Records management can be defined as the processes that assure the creation, organization, maintenance, retrieval, and use of the fewest and best records at the lowest possible cost in salaries, space, and equipment. Its primary goal is efficiency in handling information resources so that needless records will not be created or retained and valuable records will be preserved and made available for use by the creating organization and sometimes by outside researchers.[2]

Records management has expanded considerably in the past four decades to cover earlier stages in the life of a record. From an archival standpoint, records management can be seen as a series of techniques in four major areas:

1. Records creation, including subordinate "managements" for correspondence, forms, reports, and directives.

2. Information access and retrieval systems to ensure that information necessary for administrative operations is readily available for use. It includes work in files management, mail management, and indexing systems.

3. Records protection, focused on identifying and protecting (by microfilm and off-site storage of duplicates) those records that are vital to the ongoing operations and continued existence of the parent institution.[3]

4. Records disposition, involving the ultimate fate of records, normally including such options as office retention, transfer to records centers, preservation in an alternate format such as microfilm, and archival transfer and preservation.

Importance of Records Management to Archival Programs

Archivists have a stake in all these areas. For example, a well-established program for filing systems will ensure that records received in the archives will be more accessible, and a good forms-control program will result in more compact and informative documentation. However, the most common focus of records management in academic institutions has been on the key area of records-disposition programs—the preparation or review of schedules to authorize the destruction or transfer of records. Scheduling programs are important to archives because they focus on orderly handling of records, but archivists should remember that disposition is only one component of records management.

There are many reasons why academic archivists should be interested in developing records management programs. First, there are strong theoretical and practical links between archives and records management. Archivists and records managers utilize some of the same inventory, appraisal, and descriptive techniques. Both disciplines deal with the documentary accretions of institutions, even though each may focus on different points in the life of a document. This theoretical link is often articulated in terms of the life-cycle concept; that is, each record passes through several stages from its creation and active use in an administrative function to its final disposition in archival boxes awaiting researchers or in trash cans awaiting recyclers.[4]

Second, the accomplishment of the key archival functions of appraisal, arrangement, and description can be affected greatly by the quality of current records handling practices. Records management is of great assistance because it aims at controlling records before they reach the archives, and it can reveal the current administrative context of the documentation held by the archives. Through involvement in records scheduling, archivists can extend their control over documentation much further than if they remain in a passive and curatorial role. Records management provides appropriate safeguards to ensure that historically valuable materials are not lost, disordered, or destroyed without prior knowledge of the archivist.

Third, there are a number of practical reasons for archivists to become involved in records management. Not only will a records management program facilitate many archival tasks, but it will also provide important public relations advantages. Because the theory and goals of records management are tied to the scientific management school's emphasis on operational efficiency, involvement in records management will enable the archivist to claim the archives is making a substantial contribution to the institution's efficiency. While arguments of efficiency may be of greater value in business than in academia, college and university archivists have little to lose by being identified with improved management of resources for current operations. This identification can serve as an antidote to unfavorable stereotypes of archivists and demonstrate that the archivist is vital to the present and future of an institution. There is also considerable public relations value in pointing out how records management work enables archivists to discard far more records than they keep. Some archivists have found that their credibility increases with each office clean-out and each trip to the dumpster made possible by the completion of records schedules.

Fourth, insofar as archives are frequently the only records program at a college or university, the archivist may need to assume some responsibility for vital records protection. The first step is to identify the small body of the archives' holdings that are vital for the institution's and archives' continued operations. Then these records should be protected, often through remote storage of duplicate or microfilm copies, so that operations could resume in the event of a disaster.

Nature and Extent of an Academic Records Management Program

A complete records management program would include provisions for records creation, disposition, protection, and retrieval. These are admirable goals but probably beyond the basic interests and resources of academic archival programs. Considering the archival emphasis on preserving only documentation with long-term research value, most academic archivists should focus their records management efforts on records-disposition activities.

The two best approaches are a records-disposition and scheduling program assigned to the university archives, or a comprehensive records management program independent of, but closely coordinated with, the university archives. The exact nature of the records management program and the scope of the archivist's role in it will depend however on local conditions beyond the archivist's control, especially:

1. Legislation and regulation passed by an external body. For instance, public colleges and universities are often subject to state records, privacy, and freedom-of-information acts.

2. Historical precedent within the institution. If a college accounting office already has a plan for the disposal of financial records, the archivist may have difficulty in persuading the institution to vest broad records-disposal powers in the archives. If campus practices have solved some of the bulkier and more visible records problems, it can be difficult for the archives to make the case to initiate a comprehensive records-disposal plan.

3. The "gestalt" or cultural attitude of the organization may be such that there is little inclination toward archival retention of records or little interest in the efficiencies resulting from a systematic records program. A few academics may shun records management as symbolic of the encroachment of the business world or as excessive for the seemingly modest records needs of smaller institutions.

The archivist, therefore, must be flexible in undertaking records management tasks since he or she may have little control over outside bodies that have already been assigned responsibility or attitudes that can determine institutional responses to the archives' proposal.

Regardless of institutional setting, it is essential that the archives have a well-defined association with records management activities. For example, if the institution is a public college or university, state records laws may place the disposition of the campus's records under the authority of a state-wide board, and designate staff and procedures for inventorying, scheduling, and disposing or retaining of documents. Unless the archives has been able to influence the drafting of these procedures, the campus archivist may not have been given a significant role in the review process. Similar circumstances may occur in institutions that have developed a records management program as part of administrative operations independent of the archives. In either case, the archivist's goal should be to ensure that institutional or governmental policies require consultation with the campus archivist as a part of the appraisal and scheduling of records. Admittedly, if a state or local program has already been developed, the archivist may find considerable resistance to altering existing policy to secure a central role in campus records retention decisions. Nevertheless, such authority is so fundamental to the health of the archives that the archivist should be willing to wage this battle until a satisfactory policy is developed. When an external records management program is already firmly established, even if it is not operating well, there are more severe limits on what the archives can do. More often, however, there may be no formal program. Then the archives should initiate its own proposal for a full records management program.

Establishment of a Program

If a records management program does not exist and there are no state, local, or institutional procedures for deciding on the records-retention periods, the archivist

should secure the interest and support of campus administrators by emphasizing the basic goals of records management. The first step is to prepare a proposal that
outlines the need for and content of a records management
program. In brief, the proposal should contain:

- A history of the organization's handling of
  records, including: an account of problems caused
  by the lack of a systematic approach to records
  management, the potential cost savings, and
  historical evidence of how records management
  could have increased the organization's efficiency
  and ability to accomplish its goals.
- An outline of the kind of program needed to
  address these problems, including a list of the
  elements of records management, such as records
  inventories, disposition schedules, vital records,
  forms, and reports management.
- Specifications of what resources will be needed,
  including administrative authorization and
  policy support; personnel; space, equipment,
  services, and supplies; a storage facility; and
  micrographics.
- A timetable for phasing in the records
  management program, i.e., what should be done
  first, second, and third, and what can wait.

After obtaining general support for the proposal, the
archivist should prepare and secure approval of a formal
charter for the program. How one secures approval will
vary from institution to institution, but both patience and
lengthy negotiations may be necessary. At a minimum, the
document should be reviewed and approved by the chief
financial, legal, and academic officers.

Records-Disposition Programs

In academic archives with limited staff and many
existing demands, it would be imprudent to try to establish a full-scale records management program. Rather,

attention should focus on the area most critical both to custodians of current records and to archival researchers—a records-disposition or scheduling program. This is a minimalist approach to ensure that the archivist has a role in decisions regarding the ongoing disposal or transfer of campus records without overburdening the archives with additional tasks.

Establishing a records-disposition program requires the same basic steps as outlined for a complete records management program. While the program will require both personnel resources and policy support, the latter should be the first priority. The archivist should work to secure approval of a records policy from the highest level of the institution, presumably the board of trustees. The policy should define institutional records; assert institutional ownership of all records so defined; state that no record may be destroyed without prior written approval; and delineate the archival, legal, fiscal, and administrative approvals necessary for records schedules. The policy must be tailored to institutional circumstances, but a model statement would include language such as that in Figure 8.

Because of the large number of administrators and faculty with interest in records issues, obtaining approval of such a policy can require months, if not years, of negotiation and delicate planning to ensure that the archives is not seen as usurping the authority of other offices. In these negotiations, the archivist will need to accommodate administrators' interests, but must also be persistent in defining records clearly and ensuring that the archivist is provided with veto power over decisions to dispose of documents regardless of how the institution decides to proceed.

Once such a records policy is approved, the archives and appropriate university offices should develop a more detailed statement assigning responsibilities for each step scheduling records—inventory, appraisal, and drafting, reviewing, and approval of disposition recommendations. Once this document has been approved, both statements should be incorporated into institutional policy and proce-

Model University Records Policy

1. For the purposes of this policy, records shall be defined as all documents, regardless of form, produced or received by any agency, officer, or employee of the university in the conduct of its business. Documents include all forms of recorded information, such as: correspondence, computer data, files, financial statements, manuscripts, moving images, publications, photographs, sound recordings, drawings, or other material bearing upon the activities and functions of the university, its officers, and employees. Not included in the definition of records as used in this policy are: faculty research notes, library, museum, and specimen material made or acquired for reference, research, or exhibition purposes, and extra copies of publications and other documents.

2. Records produced or received by any agency or employee of the university in the transaction of university business become university property and subject to university policy for retention/disposal, access, and publication. Records produced or received by faculty in administrative and university committee service capacities are university records and subject to this policy.

3. No university records shall be discarded, destroyed or transferred from the custody of the university except upon the prior written approval of the University Archivist, pursuant to a finding and recommendation by the administrative unit involved that such records have no further administrative value. The archivist shall withhold the approval of any such action until satisfied that the records involved have no value for other administrative offices and that they need not be retained for legal or accounting reasons, as determined by appropriate officers. Where appropriate, the archivist may arrange for the transfer of records to the University Archives as an alternative to destruction.

4. The University Archives, under the direction of an archivist, is the depository for records having research or historical value and includes records transferred to its custody. The University Archives also includes professional and personal manuscripts of members of the academic and administrative staffs and records of faculty and student organizations that may be given to the university for preservation and use.

Figure 8. Model University Records Policy

dure manuals and publicized periodically in campus newsletters.

Records Scheduling Procedures

To handle records disposition work, the archives will
need to develop forms and procedures. The most helpful
forms will be those for the summary listing of records and
the series-level description of records in offices. The "Summary Records List" (Figure 9) can be a simple table. It
should include columns for physical location, type of storage equipment, inventory number of equipment (where
available), volume, inclusive dates, and brief title. Each
row on the table will be used to describe a single drawer,
box, or shelf.

When used for physical drawer-by-drawer and room-
by-room surveys and combined with rough maps of offices,
these forms can be very useful in gaining control over large
bodies of records.[5] The information from these Summary
Records Lists can be combined with data gleaned from the
files and office personnel to complete more detailed Records Inventory Work Sheets (Figure 10), which provide a
series-level description for each record series or filing unit.
Figure 11 contains instructions for completing the Records
Inventory Work Sheet.

Information on the Records Inventory Work Sheet can
double as the basis of the series-level summary descriptions used for the archives' primary finding aid. When
used for records management, the description should be
kept simple and contain only the information needed for
records identification and appraisal. Thus, records management inventories may be sparser and limited to the
name of the file, its function, dates of coverage, volume,
arrangement, and types of documents. An essential part
of the information collected on the Records Inventory
Work Sheet will be a description of the functions that led
to the creation of the records and the purpose of the file.
Overall, the description should be generic rather than
specific so that individual subjects, persons, and activities

SUMMARY RECORDS LIST

Department/Office: Govt. Architecture Planning   Person Completing Inventory: J. Grimm Date: 8/7/90 Page 1 of 3

Bldg.	Room	Area	Storage Equipment	Volume	Years	Brief Title
ARCH	309	NoW3	2ltr	2.5	1986-90	Subject Files, A-Z
ARCH	309	NoW3	2ltr	3.0	1977-86	Subject Files, C-K, T-Z
ARCH	309	NoW4	1ltr	1.5	1975-85	Subject Files, A-C, L-S
ARCH	309	NoW4	2lgl	4.0	1970-84	Contracts + Projects Files 70-5 to 84-15
ARCH	309	NoW5	3lgl	6.0	1972-85	Contracts + Projects Files 70-1 to 85-5
ARCH	309	Desk	1ltr	1.0	1988-90	Vouchers + Monthly Statements
ARCH	308	SoW9	1ltr	1.0	1986-90	Project Personnel Files, A-Z
ARCH	308	Closet	2 boxes	2.3	1980-87	Vouchers + Monthly Statements
ARCH	308	Closet	1 box	1.5	1979-85	Personnel Files, A-J (1974-78), B-W (1979-85)
ARCH	307	West	3crdfl	1.0	1948-90	Project File Microfiche w8-90-15
ENGR	19	SoE1	3 boxes	3.0	1970-80	Vouchers + Monthly Statements
ENGR	19	SoE2	4 boxes	5.0	1970-79	Personnel Files, L-V (1974-79), A-Z (1970-75)
ENGR	21	No1	5ltr	6.0	1948-76	Subject + Administrative Files, A-W
ENGR	21	W1	4lgl	8.0	1948-80	Contracts + Projects Files 48-1 to 78-19
ENGR	21	E5	2 boxes	6.0	1970s	Rolled Architectural Plans

Total Volume: 51.8   Total Separate Record Series: 6

Figure 9. Summary Records List

UNIVERSITY ARCHIVES
RECORDS INVENTORY WORK SHEET

CONTROL INFORMATION

Record Group (college or major administrative unit)
Public Affairs

Record Sub-Group (department, office or unit)
Office of Publications

Record Series Title (name of file)
Project Files

Contact Person and Phone
Carol Menaker
3-0289

Location
24 E. Green, Suite 17

Dates of File
1976-78, 1980-

PHYSICAL DESCRIPTION
Number & size of files, drawers, or documents
40 ltr file drawers, 10 Bernoulli cartridges, oversize art file bins

Volume (in cubic feet)
136.8

Annual Growth
12.5 cu. ft.

Physical Condition Good. Mixed formats and oversize artwork

CONTENT DESCRIPTION (Indicate: formats and types of material, dates of responsibility of creating office, functions, subjects, duplication, missing or purged material.)

Project files for publication design and production jobs prepared for campus units by the Office of Publications contain project cost information, printed samples, bid specifications, correspondence, vendor delivery receipts, prepress art boards and proofs, plate-ready negatives, and electronic microcomputer files of camera-ready copy for publications.

Arrangement By type of document and by project number thereunder

Index, file guides, or relationship to other files Billing info in Fin Records

USE:
Number of times retrieved: 25+ weekly ____ monthly ____ annually. (current projects)
Oldest documents used on monthly basis: 3-4 years

Legal, accounting or regulatory use, or audits of file? Yes/No Yes Explain: Audits within 18 months for some jobs.

RETENTION RECOMMENDATION Retain 5 years and destroy, provided that:
a) one copy of all publications is sent to Archives
b) summary project costs and policy correspondence are placed in Subject File

Figure 10. Records Inventory Work Sheet

RECORDS INVENTORY WORKSHEET: INSTRUCTIONS

DEFINITIONS:

Record Group: A large body of organizationally related records established on the basis of provenance to reflect major administrative units and core functions of the institution.

Record Sub-Groups: Smaller bodies of organizationally related records placed within a record group to reflect subordinate administrative units that collectively form the record group. Sub-groups can be delimited by lines of authority as well as by function, geography, or chronology.

Record Series: A systematic gathering of documents that have a common arrangement and common relationship to the functions of the office that created them. Record series are the filing units held by offices at all levels in an institutional hierarchy.

RECORD SERIES TITLE   A short, familiar title, descriptive of the informational content of the file. In assigning a title, be specific. Do not lump several together as "Miscellaneous Financial Records," "Routine Correspondence Files," or "Ledgers." Do not list forms as records series unless the form listed is the only document in the file.

DATES OF FILE   Inclusive dates of documents. If an active record, omit the final date, e.g., 1955- .

VOLUME   Total cubic feet (e.g., 1.5 for letter-size drawer, 2.0 for legal-size drawer, 2.0 for lateral letter-size drawer, 1.0 for photocopy paper box, .25 for a 12" 5 x 8 card file, or .1 for a 12" 3 x 5 card file).

ANNUAL GROWTH   Annual accumulation for most recent year in cubic feet.

CONTENT DESCRIPTION   The description should explain:

A) why the record is found at its present location, (e.g. "office copies of documents submitted to and received from" or "original copies sent to another office");

B) its procedural or functional significance;

C) substantive content of the file to explain its value and potential use.

Select from the following terms, using those that are characteristic of the bulk of the file:

(continued on next page)

Figure 11. Records Inventory Work Sheet Instructions (1 of 2)

applications	ledgers	releases
announcements	letterbooks	requests
bills	maps	schedules
bonds	motion pictures	scrapbooks
books	newsletters	slides
bulletins	notes	sound recordings
cases	notices	statements
circulars	orders	studies
claims	payrolls	summaries
computer data tapes,	photographs	surveys
disks or other media	plans	videotapes
correspondence	proceedings	vouchers
inventories	programs	warrants
journals	receipts	worksheets

Use these terms in a semi-narrative fashion to describe the records. Combine the names of record forms with modifying information (e.g., "office copies of outgoing correspondence" or "record copies of minutes of board meetings"). Then note: the titles of the officers/employees who created the records; the principal functions that the records were created to accomplish; and the specific subjects and persons documented in the series.

ARRANGEMENT Chronological, alphabetical, numerical, or by status (active or inactive). Also list secondary and tertiary arrangements thereunder.

LEGAL AND AUDIT USES If known, explain the nature of the legal, accounting, or regulatory use by citing local, state or federal statutes or regulations that require the retention or an audit of the information in this record series. Indicate how long the record must be kept to meet such uses. Note instances in which the record series has been used for proving claims in a court of law or administrative proceedings.

RECOMMENDATION Give the number of years the record series must be retained in active office space for administrative, fiscal, or legal reference, and suggest the most appropriate actions for its subsequent disposition (e.g., transfer to archives, destroy, or reformat).

Figure 11. Records Inventory Work Sheet Instructions   (2 of 2)

are not identified unless they are a primary focus of the file.

Preliminary inventorying should be delegated, whenever possible, to the clerical staff currently holding the records. This delegation will be especially important in institutions with insufficient staff to handle records management, and the process can be facilitated if the archives provides samples of records descriptions and schedules prepared for other offices. The assistance of the files' current custodians throughout the inventorying and scheduling process is crucial because they are most familiar with the function and content of each file, the level of use, and the files handling practices that might hinder proper records preservation. Furthermore, if the files' custodians are required to conduct the preliminary survey, they will be compelled to locate, identify, and evaluate all of their office files, even those that may be neglected because they are no longer needed in daily operations. Office staff, however, should not be expected to understand the theoretical basis of archival work, especially the concept of the record-series and the method of deciding on the historical and archival value of the records.

The clerical staff's inventory will provide a solid basis for the archivist's follow-up inventory. The archivist's inventory should include a drawer-by-drawer, box-by-box examination of the files to verify the information on the Records Inventory Work Sheets and to determine which file descriptions should be combined or divided to reflect distinct record series or accommodate special scheduling considerations. Beyond the examination of the files, the most valuable aspect of the office visit is the opportunity to question the staff closely and obtain appraisal information on the function and use of each record series. It also gives the archivist an opportunity to provide advice on files management that can lead to better quality documentation and more orderly records transfers.

After the preliminary survey and the follow-up inventory, the archivist can begin assembling the inventory sheets to further combine or divide record series for the preparation of a Records Disposition Schedule (Figure 12).

College or Administrative Unit Liberal Arts and Sciences	APPROVALS: (*sign and date*)
Department Anthropology	Archivist
Office	*William J. Moher* 7/2/90

I find and recommend that the records described in this request have no further administrative value and request that authority for their disposal be granted pursuant to the University Records Policy as approved by the Board of Regents.	Campus *John G. Finder* 7/10/90
Rochelle B. Richman 6/28/90 (*head of college, department or office*) (*date*)	*R. T. Chapel* 7/28/90

Record Series Number	Description of record series, inclusive dates, annual accumulation, arrangement, and disposition recommendation
1	Subject File, 1959–
	Subject File includes correspondence, reports, memoranda and publications relating to departmental administration, curriculum, academic policy, departmental and campus committees, affirmative action, space, equipment, graduate and undergraduate programs, professional organizations, honors, lectures, grant proposals, relations with academic and administrative units, faculty sabbaticals, departmental governance, and salaries.
	Annual Accumulation: .5 cubic feet Arrangement: Alphabetical by subject Recommendation: Retain 20 years and transfer to Archives, provided that routine documents may be destroyed after 3 years.
2	Budget File, 1970–
	Budget File contains correspondence, memoranda, Business Affairs internal budget statements and budget working papers showing objects & amounts of proposed expenditures for salaries, equipment, supplies, and other purposes.
	Annual Accumulation: .2 cubic feet Arrangement: Chronological Recommendation: Retain 8 years and destroy.

Figure 12. Records Disposition Schedule

This work will be a logical extension of standard archival description and appraisal practices. If appraisal establishes that the records have archival value, little additional work will be necessary beyond drafting the final records-disposition recommendation. If the records do not have archival value, the archivist will need to go through several additional steps to determine the length of time they will need to be retained for administrative, fiscal, and legal reasons. Answers in each of these areas will come from experience with similar records, knowledge of legal and regulatory requirements for records retention, and consultation with the institution's auditors and legal counsel.

The archivist must be able to recognize legal and fiscal values in records but should not be expected to make final decisions on these values without the advice of specialists who are charged with protecting the institution's interests in these areas. Thus, a basic element of the records management program should be a means for the archives to obtain legal and business office opinion on the retention recommendations it drafts. This review can be accomplished through a formal records management committee or through informal agreement of these officers to use correspondence to comment on draft retention recommendations.

After obtaining archival, legal, and fiscal agreement on draft schedules, the archivist should obtain the signed approval of the director of the office that created and maintained the files. Sometimes this is a delicate matter since it may call for longer retention or earlier archival transfer than the office desires. The best response to such objections is to remind the administrator of the purpose and the statutory basis of the archives' records management program and the rationale that the university legal and fiscal officers used in the review process. Following departmental approval, the archivist will need to indicate final approval by signing the schedule. Depending on the administrative structure of the archival program, the archivist also may need to secure signatures from the offices of president, chancellor, or regents, as well as state and local records board. Even if a long series of reviews and signatures is necessary, the program should be structured so that the bulk of inventorying, appraisal, and setting of retention periods is conducted by the archives.

Evaluation and Reporting

Once schedules have been approved, both the archives and the office will be freed from further complex appraisal decisions about the files. However, neither unit should neglect completed schedules or the issues of evaluation and reporting. Ideally, the archivist should review all disposition schedules regularly with campus offices to determine whether the retention periods are still adequate for the changing archival, legal, and administrative needs and whether new series need to be added or old ones deleted. In practice, however, few archives can be this ambitious—one review every ten years may be all that is feasible.

To monitor the continuing relevance of the records schedules, the archives might require offices to submit a certificate each time a group of scheduled files is ready for disposal. In institutions where records scheduling is performed by staff from outside the archives (e.g., by state records management personnel) or where general schedules are used, these certificates can provide the only opportunity to review records before they are disposed. For example, a preexisting schedule may call for the destruction of personnel records after eight years, but a certificate requesting permission to discard the English Department's 1976-84 personnel records would enable the archivist to postpone the disposal long enough to ensure that the files for a particularly notable scholar are preserved.

The archives' records management program should also include a series of internal evaluation and reporting mechanisms. The records management field is fond of generating a broad variety of statistical measurements, many of which are unnecessary. An archivally based records management program might limit its statistics to the number of offices and series scheduled, the annual volume scheduled for archival transfer or destruction, and the number of surveys conducted each year. While translation of these measurements into cost savings will carry less weight in a university than a business setting, a few such statistics may help to make points about the value of the records management program. The most useful figures will be the dollar value of office space released by regular destruction of files. The buildings or architect's office should be able to provide the current construction cost of a square foot of office space and its expected life so that the archivist can determine an average cost of space. Since office space generally can accommodate no more than one cubic foot of records in a single square foot of floor space, the cost of a square foot of floor space could be multiplied by the overall volume of records scheduled for annual disposal to obtain a cost savings. For example, if the current cost of office space is $15.00 per square foot and the archives has scheduled 1,000 cubic feet for annual destruction, one could claim credit for an annual savings of $15,000 to the institution.

Structural and Pragmatic Considerations

Most of the records-scheduling activity should be based on series-by-series inventorying, description, and appraisal. General schedules, which establish a retention period for a category of records wherever they are found throughout the institution, should be avoided except for record series consisting of a single type of form. General schedules should not be used for seemingly common series merely because the same kind of file (e.g., departmental majors files or promotion and tenure records) appear throughout the institution. Often there are wide variations in the content, structure, and value of these files from one office to the next. Thus, careful appraisal will necessitate scheduling series by series even though the blanket or general schedule is appealing because it involves less work.

An archives-based records management program is unlikely to have the resources to develop records disposition recommendations for all files of all offices on a campus. When comprehensiveness is impossible, the archivist should take a strategic approach. That is, review the institutional structure to identify administrative units with large or important bodies of records and then prepare a calendar to schedule the files in these offices gradually. The particularly important units include president or chancellor, business affairs, registrar, personnel, grants and contracts, student affairs, and college deans. Other prime targets should include offices that create bulky but generally insignificant records. This two-pronged approach will give the archivist assurance that the most important records are preserved while providing the opportunity for favorable press as a result of clearing out large hoards of files. Given the vagaries of institutional behavior, it is important to build credibility with both the research and the administrative service offices simultaneously.

An important aspect of establishing a records management program is to use an advisory committee to review records-retention schedules, microfilm applications, and other policy issues. The committee need not meet formally but can conduct its business by mail. It should include representatives of the legal department, financial or auditing department, data processing, central administration, and archives. This kind of committee can be especially important in establishing the archives' credibility and securing the political support needed for a new program.

In developing and maintaining a records management program in a college or university, the archivist must recognize that records management impinges upon several constituencies and interest groups. Especially important are financial officers, personnel administrators, academic records personnel, and student affairs staff.[6] Each of these groups has its own professional organization that often has developed recommendations on records disposition and access. The challenge for the archivist will be threefold: to obtain these other professionals' recognition of the archivist's authority in records issues; to obtain their expertise on records-scheduling questions; and to be free from their issuing any directives that hamper archival access to, and control of, campus records. Often these professionals are represented by large staffs with prominent institutional positions. In these circumstances, the archivist must be quite sensitive to how he or she establishes his or her authority and expertise, and it is best to proceed in a consultative rather than regulatory mode.

A range of educational activities will be useful because successful implementation of records management requires the informed cooperation of administrators and clerical personnel. These activities can take the form of handbooks and workshops that present the goals and techniques of records management in a straightforward manner. Because of the high turnover among personnel who handle files, the instruction should be scheduled frequently and kept simple.[7] It is equally important to prepare workshops and presentations for higher-level administrators even though these must be kept brief and to the point.

Records management activities, whether running a program under the archives' auspices or coordinating with larger institutional or governmental programs, can require a sizable investment of the archivist's time. The work, however, is so fundamental to the archives' mission of documenting the parent institution that it should not be ignored. Not only will it put the archivist in a stronger position to preserve important documentation, but it will also provide a broader base for appraising records throughout the institution. There can be considerable public relations value in records management involvement—it enables the archives to demonstrate a role in current documentary operations and in reduction of the institution's records-handling costs. It puts the archives in a stronger position to defend itself against critics who claim that it is indiscriminate in its acquisitions and retains too many records. Most importantly, the archives should have a central role in records management because the control of current records is an integral part of the archivist's responsibility for the documentary heritage of the college or university. Finding resources even for a scaled-down records-scheduling program may be difficult, but the responsibility should not be ignored.

MANUSCRIPTS PROGRAMS

One of the most distinctive characteristics of American college and university archives is their extensive involvement in the acquisition, preservation, and use of large bodies of documents beyond the institution's official records. Commonly called manuscript collections, these holdings of non-record material account for a significant part of the historical documentation held by academic archives. The importance of manuscript collections to academic archives emerges from the nature of the governance and administration of higher education, the academic focus on research, and the historical development of academic archives programs.

In fact, few academic archives are pure archives in the way that many governmental and business archives are. These latter focus overwhelmingly on the records created by elected officials and employees of the parent organization. Therefore, a book on college and university archives must address the administration of non-record materials that may find a home in the repository. Manuscripts are an appropriate and even necessary part of academic archives, but their management will be understood best if the archivist approaches them as a distinct program area with its own goals and objectives, even though they share methodology and attention with institutional records. For the purposes of this book, the term *manuscripts programs* will describe the series of policies and procedures used to define collecting areas and then to appraise, acquire, arrange, describe, preserve, and provide for user access to the broad range of non-record documentation found in many academic archives.

Even though definitions often become blurred in practice, it is important to start with an understanding of terminology. In theory, there is a sharp distinction between official record items (archives) and other documents in the repository that were not created as records of the parent institution (manuscripts). Archives consist of documents created to assist in the conduct of the organization's official business and which contain information needed for operations and accomplishment of the organization's mission. Manuscripts are documents created outside the routines of daily business, or created for private purposes, or subsequently collected to document consciously an event or action.[8] The distinction is theoretically important and practically useful as a way of categorizing the kinds of materials on which archivists focus. As archivists consider how to handle individual accessions, the distinction can be helpful in choosing the appraisal, description, and access approaches that best suit the character of the material and its likely research use.

Attempts to draw neat lines, however, can be frustrating and counterproductive. Experience with faculty papers or campus organizational records, where the lines between official duties and personal pursuits are often very hard to find, will convince the academic archivist that the distinction should not be carried too far. For example, many collections of faculty papers contain not only personal papers related to research and personal interests but also official records of the professor's department, perhaps from service as department chair. The records of student and faculty organizations, strictly speaking, are not the university's records and might, in a purist's perception, seem inappropriate to an academic archives, but they are essential because of their inextricable ties to the institution's governance and programs. Thus, regardless of the precise categorization of a given body of documents, the collections commonly called manuscripts should be given an important place in how college or university archives conceptualize and publicize themselves. The adept academic archives administrator should welcome both archives and manuscripts as central to a program's operations.

Types of Manuscript Collections

In an academic archives, manuscript collections can be classified in four categories, based on the relationship of their creator to the institution:

- University-related collections of personal papers of faculty, staff, students, and alumni; and records of campus organizations.
- Personal papers or collections that are unrelated to the institution but which emanate from individuals who have an association with the institution (e.g., alumni papers).
- Non-institutionally related subject collections and personal papers.
- Records of outside organizations, especially academic or professional associations with members on the university's faculty, and records of businesses and organizations without any formal connection to the institution.

These four categories reflect the broad types of manuscript collections by creator; a more precise classification is highly problematic because lines of provenance often overlap. Adding to the difficulty is the great diversity in their condition and in the subjects, documentary forms, and kinds of evidence and information they contain. Nevertheless, the difference between these collections and university office files is often dramatically apparent as soon as the archivist opens the first box.

Several examples can provide an overview of the range of manuscript collections appropriate in academic archives. They can include the personal papers of a senior faculty member who had the clerical staff or personal inclination to maintain systematic files covering university service, professional association activity, interaction with scholarly colleagues, research, and instruction. The papers of an equally important professor, however, may contain little more than the fragmentary remains of haphazard filing systems containing only a few documents that the creator thought were historically important. The small bodies of official records from student and faculty recreational and special-interest organizations exhibit similarly broad variations. Commonly, they are unsystematically filed groups of publicity announcements, minutes, membership and financial records, meeting announcements, correspondence, and stacks of publications.[9] Student and alumni papers frequently contain a few scrapbooks and important letters, but occasionally can consist of large and well-organized collections documenting long careers in business and public service.

Beyond student and faculty papers, manuscript collections in colleges and universities most often are focused on local and regional history, professional organizations, labor organizations, politicians, businesses, and ethnic groups. The documentary forms and condition of these nonuniversity collections can vary as much as, if not more than, those of faculty, staff, and students. Local history collections may include family papers, genealogies, photographs, maps, and architectural records. The records of labor unions, businesses, and large professional, scholarly, and voluntary organizations are likely to be better organized and reflective of the breadth of activities of their creators, but there can be great variations depending on the size, age, and financial status of the organization. For these reasons, the most useful categorizations of manuscript collections will be those prepared by each repository based on its experience and collecting scope. The process of delineating such categories is crucial to maintaining control over the archives' involvement with manuscripts.

Determining the Role of Manuscripts in Academic Archives

Manuscripts programs have played an important role in the historical development of college and university archives. Many have evolved from preexisting manuscript collections, while many newer archives were coestablished with manuscript collections so that the twin programs often bear such names as "Special Collections and Archives" or "University Archives and Research Collections." These circumstances have often meant that archives are subordinated to manuscripts programs. Although unfortunate, the relative place of the two programs must recognize the age, character, and location of both the institution and the archives. For example, in a century-old university with a medium- to large-size student body, the archival holdings are likely to be larger than the manuscripts. In a twenty- or thirty-year-old college, where the volume of institutional records is low, it would not be inappropriate to focus more on non-institutionally related manuscripts of local, regional, or national interest.

Ideally, the college or university archivist should be given a central role in deciding on the creation, expansion, maintenance, and priorities of the manuscripts program. The scope and history of repositories, however, can mean that some specialized collecting areas (e.g., labor history, popular culture, or ethnic history) have already been incorporated in programs entirely separate from the archives. It would be inadvisable for the archivist to claim control of these programs, but their existence should not preclude the development of an archivally based manuscripts program.

The crucial first step in establishing the program's goals and objectives and determining its relation to the archives will be the definition of its collecting scope. Most archivists will have to work with preexisting collections, but the keystone of all ongoing management should be development, review, and revision of a documentation policy. A useful approach is to divide plans for manuscript collections into successive phases. The archives should focus first on collections directly related to the college or university. Later, it may be possible to expand to cover externally created collections with no subject or organizational link to the college or university. If powerful constituencies (e.g., the university library or history department) already have committed the archives to broad collecting, dividing possible manuscripts programs into these two groups may be a useful way to redefine priorities.

Phase One: Campus-Related Personal Papers and Organizational Records

The most fundamental phase of manuscript collecting should be the personal papers of faculty, staff, students, and alumni relating directly to their participation in university events. A program with this limited collecting focus should be an integral part of all college and university archives. Of all areas of manuscript collecting, these personal papers are the most vital, and the one area to which the archives can most readily lay claim.

The archivist should be aggressive in collecting faculty, student, and alumni papers, not allowing other campus or library units to assume control of them, regardless of the subject-collecting interests of these other units. For example, the music faculty papers should be part of the college archives, not part of the music library's collection of modern composers' manuscripts. If the archives neglects responsibility for such papers, it invites disrespect and misperceptions, and weakens its ability to meet its institutional mandate.[10]

Academic archivists will not, however, encounter much competition for most student, staff, faculty, and alumni papers; the more common problem will be that even such a limited collecting scope can quickly expand to include all the professional, personal, and avocational interests of these members of the academic community. Given the nature of American colleges and universities, where a central governing role is given to faculty and professional staff who also are encouraged to pursue individual research and professional service activities, documentation of higher education requires the collection and preservation of evidence of external activities. Often, practical concerns lead the archives to accept the expansion in scope involved in faculty papers—it is far simpler to acquire a person's papers as a single unit. In other instances, an archivist interested in only a small set of papers may have to accept a large and diverse collection or risk alienating the donor. Maintaining the collection as a whole also will ensure adherence to the archival principle of *respect des fonds*. Meanwhile, the archivist may find that the extra-institutional documents are the most interesting items in the collection.

Once the archives has expanded its scope to include these personal papers, the next step will be to collect the records of student and faculty organizations. These should be acquired and preserved as soon as resources are available because they are essential for understanding aspects of the institution's life not covered in office files. Their integration into the academic archives represents a natural and healthy maturing of the archival program.

Phase Two: External Manuscripts and Archives

A second phase of manuscript collecting—papers of individuals, subject collections, records of organizations with no direct relationship to the institution—is appropriate for academic archives that have mastered the official records, personal papers, and organization files necessary to document their parent institution. As a repository of primary source material and a center for research, the academic archives is a logical home for historical documentation about the world beyond the campus walls, especially if no other institutional units are filling this role.[11] The entree into this broader collecting area may come after other manuscripts are offered to the archives, because it now has demonstrated its methodological expertise and practical ability to preserve and make accessible the college's documentary heritage. Collecting areas include local history, politics and government, labor, business, or professional and social organizations. Many times, the focus of the collecting program, as well as the requisite donor contacts, will emerge from the research interests and personal acquaintances of faculty, alumni, and campus administrators. The initiative for a particular acquisition may come from the archivist's knowledge of the subject area, or it may come from faculty or administrative staff, whose interest in a topic, person, or organization is so great that they wish to ensure that its documentation is preserved.

Clearly, this sort of manuscript collecting takes the archives beyond its core mission of caring for college or university records, but it is a legitimate goal. When there are no other repositories for the particular subject, the archives has a basic responsibility to preserve what it can within available resources. In addition, these kinds of manuscript collections can bring several advantages: they connect institutional archival activity with broader interests in historical documentation; they can elicit additional resources and create visibility that institutional records alone will not provide; and they give the archivist an expanded role in the institution and community.

The appropriateness and extent of collecting noncampus materials will depend on the presence of other manuscript programs. Thus, a university in a city with a strong historical society would be ill-advised to establish an urban history manuscripts program. However, a college in a small town whose historical society is focused on artifacts and genealogical research could perform a valuable service by beginning a program for the papers of local individuals, businesses, and organizations.

Very often, a key factor determining how broadly the archives should collect will be whether the campus library has already collected manuscripts. If there is a program following modern archival and manuscript practice, the archives may want to limit the scope of its manuscript collecting to avoid duplication and competition. If the other campus units do a poor job with manuscripts, as often is the case, the archivist may want to move gradually to assume responsibility for all manuscript collecting.

There are strong reasons for established archives to build a program for campus and noncampus manuscripts, but the archivist must be aware of several inherent liabilities. The most important and far-reaching is that a manuscripts program inevitably will dilute the resources and attention available for institutional documentation. Collecting manuscripts will give the repository a second mission and thus contribute to the institution's and the public's fuzzy perception of the archives' basic purpose. This issue will become particularly important as the archivist has to decide whether to invest hard-won new resources in the archival or the manuscript program. Even more troubling is that the campus records program often suffers inattention from resource allocators, archives staff, outreach campaigns, and users when it is juxtaposed to manuscript collections. Institutional records often are inherently less glamorous than manuscript collections, with their special subject foci. If the archivist cannot balance and protect the archival part of the program, it would be better to abandon, or at least deemphasize, manuscripts activities.

Administering the Archives' Manuscripts Program

With proper management, these liabilities can be reduced and manuscripts programs can be made to benefit the archivist's overall goals. The key will be the archivist's ability to balance the manuscripts with the records program and with available resources. The most fundamental step will be to develop and enforce a documentation policy that defines the manuscripts program's subject scope and intensity of coverage. The collection scope should be realistic, based on the present and likely future resources of the archives. A grand plan for collecting local political papers would be unwise if the archives had a large backlog of unprocessed university records.

Ideally, the subject focus of the manuscripts program should emerge from institutional and local strengths. Thus, the archives at a scientific and technologically oriented university may develop a manuscripts program focused on the history of technology or theoretical physics. Often such subject or theme collections are natural extensions of strengths in official record holdings from the relevant academic departments. The environment and constituencies of an institution often suggest a collection scope. For example, an urban university archives may become the nucleus for ethnic or regional history collections. A rurally situated, land-grant institution may develop a collection of farm mechanization records. The

archives of women's liberal arts colleges may become the
focus of manuscript collections on suffrage or social work
movements. Archives at religiously affiliated schools may
become centers for the documentation of religious, mis-
sionary, or evangelical movements. Archivists looking for
suggestions on how to develop a collection scope need only
examine directories of archival repositories to see many
examples of how theme collections have evolved from the
institutions' surroundings or mission. At the same time,
many existing collections reflect something far less than
a rational collecting policy and instead illustrate how
personalities and opportunities play a major role in shaping repositories.[12]

Aside from the development of a documentation policy,
the most important factor in managing manuscripts will
be to recognize the usefulness and limits of standard
archival procedures for arrangement, description, and
use. Beyond acquisitions, where more specialized work is
needed for solicitation and for gift agreements, there is
often little difference in archival and manuscript techniques. For example, both require a similar respect for
maintaining the arrangement developed by the documents' creators. Although description is often cited as an
area of legitimate difference, this ignores one important
underlying similarity of archives and manuscripts—they
are both bodies of raw, undigested information as yet
unfiltered for presentation in a focused manner, as would
be the case for books and journals. Because archives and
manuscripts are generally not self-conscious mechanisms
for presenting concepts and information, both require
flexible and summary descriptive procedures to extract
the most likely research topics embedded in the documents.

Control of most twentieth-century manuscript collections can be simplified by using the practices that have
emerged from the public archives rather than from the
historical manuscripts tradition.[13] These techniques are
more efficient, and they are more compatible with the
nature of documentation in many modern collections.
Still, there are important differences in handling of manu-

script collections. Arrangement schemes for manuscript collections, especially personal papers, may need to be more complex than for archival record series and may require the establishment of several, often artificial, subseries, to reflect the diversity of activities of the documents' creator.

Manuscripts frequently require more elaborate descriptive work than archival records. Not only do they contain more diverse subject matter, but provenance may not be so useful an access tool. The placement of manuscript collections within a repository's overall classification system, therefore, is unlikely to assist in retrieval of information about their subject content, function, and organizational purpose. In addition, the simple box and folder inventory lists that are quite adequate for archival records may need to be expanded into more complex registers with annotations, narrative introductions, and subject indices when dealing with personal papers. Manuscript collections also lend themselves more than archives to control by conventional library cataloging and description through standardized subject terms, such as the *Library of Congress Subject Headings.*

Finally, for both practical and theoretical reasons, manuscripts can engender an array of user access problems that are less common with archives. Restrictions on access are often a condition of the acquisition. Moreover, since manuscripts frequently reflect more of the individual's personal role in events than do official archival records, the creator may have more right to maintain privacy than if the actions were part of official responsibilities in a large organization.[14] As noted previously, however, the archivist should work to minimize access restrictions, whether for records or manuscripts.

In practice, there will be so few examples of pure archives or pure manuscripts that many other variations in archival versus manuscripts techniques will be necessary, and hard and fast rules will be difficult to formulate. The most successful repositories will mix archival and manuscript methodologies, depending on the nature of the material in each accession or portion of an accession.

Rather than rejecting the distinction between archives and manuscripts as only of theoretical value, however, the archivist should use the distinction as a tool to determine the proper methodological approach case-by-case.

Keeping Manuscripts in Their Place

As a text on the management of college and university archives, this book has emphasized the importance of official institutional records and closely related personal papers in setting the tone for the repository. From this perspective, it is appropriate to criticize the rather large role that manuscripts programs have played at some institutions. Too often, manuscripts have created problems for the academic archivist because they have diverted attention and resources from institutional records, which should be the first focus of the academic archives. Despite these drawbacks, the development of a manuscripts program is not only unavoidable at most institutions, but also it can be a logical extension of the archives' basic mission. Through a carefully balanced program for manuscripts, especially faculty papers, the archivist can serve scholarly disciplines by preserving the record of their development. A manuscripts program enables the archives to enhance its role as a laboratory for instruction in historical research and as a center for advanced scholarly studies. Finally, the archives can obtain valuable institutional credibility by demonstrating that the college or university contributes to the life of the community through the preservation of its documentary heritage. If the archivist has established solid control over the college or university's records and papers, the development of a more extensive manuscripts program is an appropriate area for entrepreneurial endeavors. The modern academic archivist has a good product to offer—preservation of and accessibility to the past—as well as the means to fulfill a basic need of society in a most efficient and effective manner.

OUTREACH

Basic texts on archives often leave the impression that there is little more to archival work than executing a series of techniques in reaction to problems posed by documents, their creators, and users. Such a view ignores the fact that archivists must take considerable initiative if they truly are to fulfill their role as custodians of a documentary heritage. Recently, archivists have recognized the need to be active, or even proactive, in many areas of archival work, such as in identifying and selecting records.[15] This is particularly important for the key archival domain of use, because use is the ultimate goal of all archival activities and therefore at the core of the academic archives' mission. In fact, the responsibility to see that material in one's archives is used is so fundamental that considerations of use should influence the conduct of the full range of archival activities.[16]

A modest level of use will develop on its own, but use is unlikely to reach its full potential unless the archivist takes special action. Beyond the essential step of adopting a positive attitude toward use, academic archivists also need to initiate contacts with, or reach out to, the many publics in the world outside the archives. The educational and promotional activities pursued to fulfill this key responsibility have been commonly grouped under the heading of outreach. Although subordinate to the domain of use, outreach deserves special attention as a program area because it emphasizes the actions needed to promote the primary archival goal of use. Considering outreach separately also allows one to study how best to administer the breadth and variety of activities that promote the archives' documents and services. If the term outreach carries too much of a religious overtone, these activities might instead be described as public programs or public relations. The terms *marketing* and *advertising* are less appropriate, because the purpose of outreach is to educate as much as to promote.

The primary goals of outreach are to:

- Encourage direct and indirect use of the archives.
- Educate persons outside the archives about phenomena documented in the archive.
- Demonstrate the usefulness of archival information for understanding the past and present.
- Communicate information and insights from specific archival holdings.

Common outreach activities include exhibits, publications, open houses, lectures, audiovisual presentations, and instructional programs. Some projects have the primary goal of persuading the public as to the value of history and historical study. Others are aimed simply at reminding the community of the existence of the archives.

Outreach programs have a fundamental role in the mission of archives as information resources. Indeed, archivists' obligation to promote the use and dissemination of historical documents is rooted in their acceptance of the charge to preserve documents. Archivists have a basic responsibility not just to collect and care for documents, but also to ensure that the value of these information resources is brought to the attention of the broadest possible public. Outreach is a critical step by which the archivist ensures that evidence of the past is used by present generations to shape the future.

There are also important long-range political reasons for outreach, arising from the tremendous need to gain understanding and acceptance of the archival program from institutional and external constituencies. Given the limited awareness of what archives are and why they should exist, an outreach campaign can be an important weapon in the struggle to secure greater resources. At some institutions, outreach's greatest value may not become apparent until those occasional critical moments when administrative changes call into question the archives' professional status or even its very existence. At other institutions, outreach efforts may be critical to building clientele and support for underutilized archives.

As members of educational institutions, academic archivists have a particularly strong obligation to initiate outreach programs. Fortunately, they should find a fairly receptive audience in institutions whose primary goals are learning and discovery of knowledge. In addition, archival outreach at colleges and universities is facilitated by the fact that these institutions are generally of a manageable size with a well-defined and constantly renewing audience for the archives' public programs. Academic archivists have yet another advantage—campuses often provide access to inexpensive or free facilities and services needed for technical aspects of outreach programs, especially those requiring audiovisual, printing, and artistic assistance.

Planning Outreach Programs

Successful outreach will require more than the mere recognition of the archivist's core responsibility to support use of records and manuscripts and more than disconnected efforts to accomplish specific outreach projects. It merits special attention as a distinct activity so that overall program planning can balance outreach with other archival responsibilities.

Outreach should begin with defining goals. For example, are the activities intended to increase the number of users, deliver archival information to persons who never come to the archives, increase public understanding of archives and history, or some combination of these or other goals?[17] The setting of goals should be coordinated with the important task of identifying the audiences that the archives needs to address. Virtually any group outside the repository staff is a potential audience, but to fulfill the goal of encouraging greater use of holdings, the primary audiences for academic archival outreach might include campus faculty and students, alumni, scholars at other institutions, local high schools, and the public at large.

When planning outreach, key audiences that often are overlooked are the internal ones—the administrators of the parent institution and even the parent department.

Considering how frequently policy and financial support
are impeded by communication problems between archivists and librarians, outreach can provide significant benefits when it is aimed internally. Thus, an important
collateral goal for outreach projects should be to demonstrate the importance of the archives' unique mission,
services, and holdings and to emphasize that archival
materials are crucial to the library's own mission. The
health of the archives may also depend on outreach activities directed at campus administrators to convince them
of the importance of archives for preserving the institution's history and increasing the efficiency of its information-handling practices.

Once the goals and audiences of the outreach programs
have been defined, the archivist will need to determine
what resources are available for specific projects. Beyond
the obvious need to secure funds for products such as
exhibit materials, publications, and audiovisual presentations, the archivist will need to decide how much time the
staff can afford to devote to outreach. As with all other
archival functions, the time allocated to outreach must be
balanced against other pressing needs, such as reducing
a backlog of unprocessed records, microfilming a core
collection, or finishing a campus records inventory and
schedule. Furthermore, it may be unwise to embark on
outreach aimed at increasing use until the archives is well
in control of its holdings and has sufficient staff for the
greater reference workload.

Only after these issues have been addressed should the
archivist proceed to determine which projects are most
suited to the repository's overall outreach needs and resources. For example, a relatively new college archives
with little student use should concentrate on lectures to
classes and arrangements with faculty for course assignments from archival holdings. An established university
archives with few scholarly users but many undergraduate users should bypass course-centered activities and
concentrate on presentations to graduate seminars and
publication of specialized lists of sources for advanced
research.

Types of Outreach Activities

One of the most exciting aspects of outreach in academic archives is that so many options are readily available. The types and extent of involvement will depend on goals, program resources, available talent, and communities to be served, as well as the archivist's personal interests. The most successful programs will be those that vary the activity according to each audience's needs, the occasion, and the subject material.[18] In addition to exhibits, which are examined in the next section, common outreach activities include publications, open houses, lectures, audiovisual presentations, instructional programs, and curricular materials.

Publications and printed publicity materials are particularly effective in reaching large audiences, especially those off-site. These diverse outreach mechanisms include introductory brochures, news releases, photo histories, chronologies of the institution, calendars, note cards, bookmarks, and similar items. Often they will draw heavily from archival photographs and drawings to capture the reader's attention. There is a considerable market for publications with such trappings of history, even if they do not inspire any deep understanding of the past. At the same time, items such as press releases and brochures can give the archivist the opportunity to communicate directly with the public and present the case for archives without the filtering and stereotypes that often occur in pieces prepared by journalists and news bureau staff.[19]

Open houses can be held at the archives, possibly in connection with another event. These can be quite useful in attracting members of the campus and community to the archives for a general orientation and an invitation to future research visits even if they do not now have a specific research project. Open houses provide an additional incentive to develop outreach tools, because they can incorporate several outreach techniques into one event, such as the opening of an exhibit, presentation of a lecture, issuance of a new brochure, and the viewing of a slide show. The success of such events depends on advance publicity through contacts with faculty, news releases, newspaper articles, and community calendars. They are likely to elicit the greatest response if advance publicity can note that the archives will be offering something free to those who attend—for example, advice on the preservation of family documents or orientation on local history or genealogical research.

Lectures can be used to describe archival holdings or institutional history. Their greatest public appeal may be when they provide detailed analytical information about events documented in the archives. Lectures also can include talks to classes and seminars to encourage research; presentations to student, faculty, staff, and public audiences on aspects of institutional history; and speeches by researchers on results of their work in the archives. Historical lectures work particularly well as contributions to lunch-time speaker series, "friends of the archives" meetings, and orientation sessions for new students, staff, and faculty.

Audiovisual presentations, including slide shows and videotaped productions, educate as well as exploit the appeal of visual materials. These productions are particularly useful for student orientation and meetings of alumni, trustees, and library and archives donors. Because they do not always require the in-person participation of the archivist, they are effective for traveling displays and permanent installations, such as in visitor centers and student unions. The production and technical problems inherent in audiovisual projects may necessitate use of external talent, but the first step will always be for the archivist to outline the subjects to be featured and select the topics and documents with the greatest public appeal.

Instructional programs are most useful for reaching undergraduate and secondary school students. In these activities, the archivist provides instruction or support for instruction through regular college classes or noncredit workshops. Sometimes the archivist will work alone, but often these programs require contacts with faculty, especially those in humanities fields, to encourage the instructor to assign archivally related topics to students looking for projects. Survey courses in history, English, and architecture can often find a place for the assignment of a brief paper on a popular campus building, event, or tradition. To assist the process, the archivist may develop a set of problem statements that describe a research question and list possible sources to examine. Related instructional activities include lecturing to advanced and graduate students about archival resources and presenting minicourses on campus history through continuing-education programs offered by the university and outside bodies (e.g., YMCA). These contacts may lead to increased use, so the archives needs to be prepared to provide efficient reference service.

Curricular materials are invaluable for delivering archival documents directly to large numbers of college or high school students who need archival material for class assignments. Curriculum packets normally contain interpretive text on a historical topic (e.g., the role of women and minorities in the institution), facsimile copies and transcriptions of documents, and research or discussion questions. A major advantage of curriculum packets is that they permit the archives to reach large bodies of novice users systematically without placing a strain on the archives' documents or reference staff. Before embarking on such a project, however, the archivist should first approach the instructors of the students most likely to benefit from the curricular package; otherwise, considerable effort may be wasted in preparing a product that meets no one's needs. In addition, the archivist needs to realize that preparation of the material requires extensive work. If the packets are not just to display documents but also to provide a basis for analysis, the archivist will need considerable time to research the topic, assess the audience, select documents, and write the study guide. Experience and talent in dealing with students and teachers will be particularly important in these endeavors.

The above projects only touch on the major categories of public programs. Since the essence of outreach is creativity in bringing historical documents to the attention of audiences outside the archival program, good projects will not be limited to these activities. Rather, outreach will be most successful when it emerges from creative responses to local needs and opportunities.

Completing Outreach Projects

Step-by-step instructions for producing particular outreach tools are beyond the scope of this book, especially since each requires technical skills in areas outside the core of archival work. As a general rule, however, archivists should resist the temptation to try to do it all by themselves. Because outreach programs are intended to impress the public and attract them to the archives, two areas of public relations work are critical. First, the archivist should study the target audiences to understand their needs and learn what approaches will be most successful. Second, more often than not, a polished product will be as critical as its documentary content. Thus, while informally prepared brochures may be adequate as handouts for people who already know about the archives, a far more polished product is needed whenever the archives wishes to capture the attention of outsiders who do not yet know of the archives' existence, holdings, or uses.

Archivists must therefore recognize that outreach programs require many extra-archival talents and that their own expertise in records and history will not ensure attractive or successful public programs. Instead, one of the most important steps in outreach is for the archivist to acknowledge the need for assistance of experts in other fields, especially in writing and editing, photography, graphics, layout and design, audiovisual production, and broadcast media. For example, the advice of communications specialists should be sought to understand the interests of potential audiences and to obtain technical advice on issues such as the optimal length for press releases and exhibit catalogs or for the choice of type styles and the use of white space in publications. The archivist's role will be to define outreach goals, conduct background research, develop themes for presentations, and select documents.

Within the limits of available resources, a few strategic
outreach products will merit considerable investment of
time and money, even though the benefits of simply produced materials should not be overlooked.

Fortunately, academic archives are in a good position
to secure professional or near-professional technical assistance at relatively modest costs. Most institutions have
public information offices, which can provide some publicity services for free (e.g, writing and dissemination of news
releases) and others at modest cost (e.g., brochure design
and production). If the archivist is willing to compromise
on some production standards and schedules, good products can even be developed as part of individual or group
class projects. For example, the archivist might enlist the
support of a faculty member to locate a journalism or
graphics student to prepare an archives brochure or design a newsletter as a course project. This approach may
be even more effective in dealing with highly technical
areas, such as multi-projector slide shows or videotape
productions, where archivists often lack skill and or the
cost of commercial production is prohibitive. Such cost-
cutting may require more of the archivist's time for planning, research, and review than if professional services
were hired, but the monetary savings can permit activities
that otherwise might be impossible. Also, because students often have little experience with archives, and thus
few preconceived notions, their insights may be fresher
and thus lead to far more attractive and effective outreach
tools.

The outreach activities chosen by each archives should
reflect highly personal and local choices as to what public
relations needs are greatest and what can best be accomplished with available resources; it will not be possible to
pursue outreach programs in all areas on a regular basis.
Thus, the best practice is to focus available talent and
resources on a few areas and develop others as time and
resources permit and as program needs require.

EXHIBITS

The emphasis in outreach on diversity of offerings and its frequent dependence on extra-archival skills can have the unfortunate effect of making some archivists despair of ever being able to create the tools needed to reach new audiences. That is why academic archivists should consider exhibits, the most traditional outreach activity, as their first public program. Even if the technical challenges of other projects can be overcome, exhibits are readily accessible and can fulfill an important educational role. They are also excellent ways to increase the public visibility of archives while simultaneously describing important issues in the history of the parent institution. In addition, exhibits bring many internal benefits in the areas of staff development, research, and understanding of the holdings.

Most college and university archivists acknowledge the importance of exhibits, but their involvement has varied greatly. Some mount exhibits only for major campus anniversaries. At other institutions, exhibits are a central program focus, accounting for vast quantities of staff time, even dwarfing acquisitions and processing. While neither extreme is desirable, the best academic archives should balance exhibits with their other programs.

Two obstacles often discourage academic archivists from preparing exhibits. First, many lack adequate and accessible cases in which archival materials can be displayed. Certainly, the facilities and resources for exhibits will vary from institution to institution and occasion to occasion, but even the smallest archives should be able to mount occasional exhibits in borrowed cases or contribute archival materials to exhibits sponsored by other units. Even institutions lacking an equipment budget should be able to secure the few hundred dollars needed for a modest, glass-enclosed bulletin-board wall case for display of archival documents in a public corridor. Some initiative and creativity will be needed, but the archivist should not miss the opportunity to demonstrate the archives' contributions to documenting history and aiding research.

A second and often related obstacle is that archival exhibits have difficulty competing with the increasingly dynamic exhibits found in science museums, historic restorations and museums, and living-history installations. The documentary material that must be the center of an archival display is inherently static and less able to seize the attention of viewers. This problem can be compounded by the fact that academic archives often lack the funding for the technical and graphic features that make many museum exhibits so inviting. However, academic archives should be able to overcome this barrier, given their location within academic communities, which are supposed to be literate and interested in the written word. Visual interest can be heightened by interspersing textual material with iconographic, graphic, and artifactual items. Overall, archival material can have substantially greater visual impact than the books and dust jackets in the typical library displays which are often found in the same building as archives.

Exhibits bring several important benefits. They publicize holdings and stimulate research. They provide the non-archival world, both inside and outside the institution, with a means of grasping what the archives does and why it exists. They serve as an important public relations tool by stimulating interest in campus history and educating the campus and outsiders about the institution's accomplishments and failures. Equally important, exhibits educate the archives staff and thereby enhance its ability to appraise, describe, and interpret holdings to assist researchers.

Types of Exhibit Work

Involvement in exhibits can take several forms, each requiring a different level of commitment and producing a different impact. Academic archivists have a number of attractive options:

1. Interpretive exhibits on a single theme may be displayed in the vicinity of the reference or search room. These may be informal and need not require extensive preparatory research, artistic and graphic materials, and catalogs or captions. They might cover the history of a department, a campus tradition such as homecoming, or a newly processed collection of alumni papers.

2. Interpretive exhibits also can be mounted in exhibit cases located elsewhere and shared with other units (e.g., in the library's public area, the student union, or a campus visitors' center). These may be identical in scope and content to the first group, but their off-site location adds security challenges and their greater visibility may necessitate more attention to a sophisticated design.

3. Historical sections may be developed for use in broader exhibits sponsored by other units. For example, the archives may select manuscripts and photographs on chemical laboratories to augment a college's display promoting its role in science education.

4. Traveling exhibits can be prepared for one-time display at a conference or for repeated showings in multiple locations. These will require considerable advance planning, attention to security, and flexibility, as display equipmemt and locations can rarely be predicted in advance.

5. Historical material may be contributed to permanent institutional displays in such locations as student unions or alumni and faculty centers.

6. Materials such as photographs, architectural drawings, and scientific field notes may be loaned for off-site exhibits sponsored by other institutions.

7. Elaborate exhibit catalogs may be published to serve as stand-alone research or public relations products.

8. Exhibits illustrating preservation problems and solutions can be very useful in drawing public attention to the challenges of archival work and in providing information that will allow the viewers to improve the care of their own historical documents.

All types of exhibit activity require blending archival knowledge with artistic and public relations skills. The physical and intellectual demands of each activity impose a substantially different workload that should be assessed before the archives undertakes any project.

Over a period of years, most archives will have the opportunity to be involved in many of these types of exhibits, but few will be able to pursue all on a regular basis. Because exhibits require large amounts of time for research, selection, and presentation, the paramount consideration should be a series of guidelines to help balance exhibit activities with other program needs. First, the kinds of exhibit work an archives pursues will be very dependent on available facilities. A critical step is to recognize that all exhibits are not equal, and thus the archives might adopt a multi-tiered strategy, doing some exhibits quite casually and devoting considerable effort to a select few for more formal settings. For example, the archivist should devote less attention to a one-month exhibit on football traditions in the archives' reference room than to a twelve-month display on a college centennial in the student union building.

Another valuable strategy is to choose two types of forums as the foci of an ongoing exhibits program. For instance, the archives could produce occasional major exhibits, perhaps annually, in high-visibility areas covering broad themes (e.g., student life, collection and use of faculty papers, or major campus anniversaries). At the same time, there could be less elaborately researched exhibits on a monthly or quarterly basis in a few cases near the reference room. Using a minimum of exhibit materials, graphics, and interpretive text, these smaller exhibits can treat topics of narrower scope, such as anniversaries of an important scientific experiment, an event, a building, or the centennial of the birth of an important faculty member or athletic coach. If publicized properly, such casual exhibits can be effective tools in attracting users and in demonstrating the purpose and diversity of an archives to the casual visitor. Smaller-scale exhibits also permit experimentation with subjects and techniques while the staff develops expertise that will be invaluable when the archives mounts a major exhibit.

Exhibit Preparation Procedure

Regardless of the display's size and audience, the work of preparing and presenting exhibits is best understood when divided into the following phases:

- Definition of the topic.
- Delineation of staff responsibilities.
- Background research.
- Division of the topic into units that can be covered in separate cases.
- Decisions about "target" types of documents for which to search.
- Location and selection of documents.
- Assessment of visual impact.
- Adjustment of content and visual features, including selection or preparation of backing materials, graphics, artifacts, etc.
- Physical preparation, including security, document protection, copying, and enlargement of copies.
- Description, including preparation of identifying cards, transcription or highlighting of sections of text, and production of a catalog for more elaborate exhibits.
- Publicity, including announcements in media, listings on calendars of events, and formal openings when appropriate.
- Administrative control, including detailed inventories of contents, unless a catalog is prepared.
- Return of items to proper location and informal assessment of quality and success.
- Report and record-keeping so that the exhibit may be reconstructed to display again or answer researcher questions.[20]

A good deal of attention must be given to physical preparation and description. The former requires a sensitivity to preservation concerns and techniques to ensure that documents are not lost or stolen or damaged through exposure to excessive heat, light, or humidity. Preservation issues are very important because the display cases can expose some of the archives' most valuable and interesting documents to far more risk from environmental or security hazards than they would face in their storage boxes. Whenever the risks outweigh the advantages, photographic or electrostatic copies should be substituted.[21] Good exhibits also depend on artistic and graphics talent, which are not necessarily part of an archivist's background and expertise. Consultation with those skilled in artistic fields will be very important for the highly public displays; the more casual search room displays can function quite well with little design assistance.

Descriptive captions are crucial to successful exhibits and can become quite elaborate, with numerous explanatory cards and lengthy catalogs. In these cases, the exhibit becomes not only a public relations or outreach activity, but also a stand-alone research project. For most occasions, however, the archivist should not hesitate to limit the description to simple one- or two-line caption cards identifying each document. Photographs, especially of familiar campus buildings and subjects, often need no caption beyond the date and the name of the building or person. If a few summary cards provide a brief interpretation of the display's subject, short descriptive captions will be adequate for most other items. Whenever possible, exhibits should allow the documents to speak for themselves—after all, it should be the documents, not the archivist's research notes, that are on display.

Managing Exhibits

Successful administration of exhibits starts with a recognition that they require substantial amounts of time, but that the archivist should vary the amount of work in each phase depending on the location, audience, scope, and purpose of the exhibit. Flexibility is also needed so that budgetary and resource constraints do not preclude a modest exhibit program. Even if there are not resources for special mounting materials, published catalogs, and large cases, a number of valuable exhibits can still be mounted. If the archives limits its exhibits to the larger public occasions when sufficient funds are available, it will deprive itself of many opportunities to demonstrate its holdings and program.

Instead, the archivist should be ready to obtain the maximum benefit in the minimum time. One method is to look for occasions to create exhibits on recurring themes (e.g., homecoming or commencement) and use the same format to incorporate different material each year. There also may be opportunities to reuse the components of one exhibit, after a decent interval, for another exhibit or audience. Finally, archivists should be ready to prepare impromptu exhibits in response to major events on campus (e.g., winning of a conference championship, burning or flooding of a campus building, or naming of a faculty member to receive a national or international prize). Given a small amount of space in a public area, the archivist often can quickly select a handful of documents to illustrate historical traditions to which the current major event can be linked.

The subject matter of the archives' holdings is another important influence on the format and location of exhibits. A university archives with institutional records but no manuscript collections may be restricted in the audiences its exhibits can attract. By contrast, a college archives with a local or regional manuscripts collection may have so many opportunities for exhibits of interest to the general public that college topics may be subordinate. In either case, however, the archives should pursue an active exhibit program to bring its holdings to the attention of communities broader than just those doing scholarly research or course papers in the archives.

Since exhibits are public relations devices, it is not surprising that their internal benefits are often overlooked. Even in the unlikely event that no one comes to view an exhibit prepared by the archives, exhibit preparation has great value as a staff development tool. Through researching, selecting, and assembling the materials, staff can obtain a deeper understanding of how well the archives' holdings elucidate, or leave unexplained, the essence of historical events. Working with exhibits also should show the staff the difficulty of communicating the meaning of historical documents to the public. The perspectives so gained will increase the staff's effectiveness in appraisal, description, and user service. In addition, exhibits have a management value as morale boosters that should not be underestimated. When a processor is encouraged to devote time to an exhibit, an important diversity is added to an often tedious job at the same time that the archival program can exploit the processor's special knowledge of a collection. Just as the best exhibits depend on the availability of staff with special subject and technical knowledge, the best archival programs will rely on exhibits to stimulate the staff as well as carry the archives' message to its several publics.

ORAL HISTORY

Like many other basic archival texts, this book presents a very full agenda for the conscientious academic archivist, and it is hard to imagine that one would be expected to consider yet another program area. Oral history, however, is an important activity that deserves attention as part of the college or university archives' mission. Failing to consider oral history puts the program at risk of leaving an incomplete documentary record. While embarking on oral history too early in a program's life can create distorting pressures, it should be considered as the archives matures. At a minimum, archivists should assess how they can incorporate oral history techniques and projects to ensure as complete a record as possible of their colleges and universities.

Nature and Practice of Oral History

The use of oral interviews as the basis of historical writing is at least as old as Thucydides' research on the Peloponnesian Wars, but in its modern form, oral history consists of recording interviews of individuals to capture their accounts and perspectives on events, people, and places of historic interest. It relies on written, sound, or video recordings of an interview that follows a systematic set of questions based on prior research, and it presumes that the resultant records will be preserved for future research use. Oral interviews of historical figures are often conducted by subject-area specialists, journalists, and amateur enthusiasts, but high-quality oral history requires considerable time, expertise, and research.

Just as it would be incorrect to assume that any taped interview is an oral history, it would be presumptuous to suggest that a general text such as this can do justice to the complex methodology of oral history. Instead, this section will identify the contribution oral history can make to an archival program, summarize its technical components, and suggest how the academic archivist can determine the proper scope for oral history.

Before proceeding to administrative and policy issues, it is appropriate to identify the basic steps of oral history programs and projects. The components of creating oral documentation are considerably more demanding than the mere compilation of a set of interviews. The archivist should be aware of the processes involved in each step before embarking on any such project. Fortunately, texts and articles are available to provide details on personnel and equipment needs, as well as thorough outlines of procedures.[22] As a basis for program planning, the following list summarizes the steps in producing oral histories:

- Selecting the themes, the interviewees, and the interviewers.
- Contacting potential interviewees, securing agreements to participate, and securing releases for any resultant tapes and/or transcripts.

- Researching for interview questions.
- Interviewing.
- Indexing, abstracting, and/or transcribing tapes.
- Proofreading and editing transcripts by the oral history program staff and interviewee.
- Ensuring preservation (e.g., copying interview tapes from cassettes to open-reel archival tape and making copies for use).
- Establishing user access regulations.
- Preparing summary descriptions, catalog entries, and indices to groups of related interviews.
- Providing reference service for users.

The technical and intellectual processes for each of these steps can be quite complex, but the basic goal of all oral history is quite simple—to provide systematic evidence to address questions left unanswered by traditional written documentation. The importance of securing oral evidence from participants in an institution's history stems from the nature of human communication. The background and key motivations surrounding decisions often are not fully recorded in office files and other records traditionally acquired by archivists. These gaps in the written record are exacerbated by technological and legal considerations, which can mean that oral communications, important early drafts of key policy documents, or potentially sensitive explanations of personnel decisions are often absent from the records transferred to the archives.[23]

Oral history interviews are an important means to fill the inevitable gaps in the written documentation of an academic institution. By securing interviews of individuals who have participated in the institution's development, archivists can obtain important recollections and reflections of major participants in events. Examples range from a single interview of a retiring president commenting on key events in his or her term to a series of interviews with women faculty hired before 1980. In such cases, there may be substantial paper files generated by these individuals, but files will tell only part of the story. Oral history also is invaluable in gathering information on people and events not commonly represented in the written record. For example, interviews might capture students' accounts of current social and study life, or custodial staff perceptions of changes resulting from anti-discrimination practices or increased use of contractual services.

Although interviews can compensate for gaps in the written record, oral historians have long recognized that an interview is no guarantee of accuracy and that the records of an interview may well be less useful as evidence than records created in the course of the event under study. To make oral histories more reliable as evidence, several steps are necessary, including extensive preparatory research, gathering evidence from several participants or observers, and constructing questions very carefully. Archivists contemplating a few interviews as "fill in" should remember that the value of oral history as evidence rests almost solely on the quality of the efforts that went into the interview.[24]

Programs Versus Projects

All college and university archivists should consider establishing or participating in an institutional oral history program, but few will be able to mount extensive programs, given the many other demands on the limited resources typically available to them. However, once an archival program is successfully undertaking the full range of core archival activities, an oral history program should be considered if sufficient additional resources are available.

A useful tactic is to distinguish between a full-fledged oral history program with special staff and a far more limited effort consisting of discrete projects with occasional interviews conducted by the archives' regular staff. A few institutions, such as Columbia University and the University of California, Berkeley, have developed full oral history programs that often cover subjects well beyond campus history. A full oral history program will require not only substantial personnel and equipment, but also sufficient institutional or foundation support to sustain the program over time. There will be little value in short-term funding for an extensive series of interviews if funds are not also available for transcribing and indexing or if the program will not be vibrant five years hence, when follow-up interviews are needed. For example, interviews of freshmen's expectations of higher education will be far more valuable if they can be followed by exit interviews of the same individuals five years later and if the process can be repeated for later cohorts of students.

Program-based Oral History

If resources are available, the first step in an oral history program will be definition of a collecting scope, possibly with the assistance of an oversight committee. Because so much of the value of oral history is incremental, the program's long-term success will require a carefully crafted and executed policy. In developing a full-scale program, it is appropriate to consider expanding the oral history scope well beyond that of institutional history. In fact, this may be necessary to attract the interest of potential funding sources. The most natural expansions are along lines represented by the repository's faculty papers and other manuscript collections, especially for issues not easily documented through conventional written records.

The staff and budget needed to maintain such a program will depend on its scope, but a minimum of two full-time positions (one professional and one clerical), plus student assistance, would be appropriate for all the activities needed to develop and maintain an oral history program at a medium-to-large institution and to provide modest coverage of themes in manuscript collections.

Project-based Oral History

Many college and university archives, especially new programs and those with full-time staffs of less than four, should be hesitant to start a full oral history program. Too often, these archives can neither spare existing staff nor secure new positions. In such cases, archivists would be ill-advised either to attempt a broad oral history program or to deprecate themselves for not doing oral history. This does not mean, however, that established archives should ignore the value of conducting oral history interviews, as circumstances and resources permit. Occasional oral history interviews should be incorporated into normal program operations to ensure that important issues are covered and to demonstrate that the archives is aware of the need to provide comprehensive documentation.

This kind of oral history activity will be most manageable and useful if it focuses on interviews in connection with major retirements and donations of papers. This may result in a "great man" bias, but it can still be useful to explore issues that tend to be slighted in office correspondence and personal papers. In such small-scale or project-based oral history, the archivist must conduct interviews as time and other responsibilities permit. Because full transcripts probably will be impossible, the archivist may settle for indexing and abstracting major themes on the tape by using timing or footage indications.[25] In addition, a project-based operation will require a narrow subject focus so that the resources spent on oral history serve the archives' central mission.

Relations with Other Interviewing Programs

When only a limited oral history program is possible, the archivist may seek to acquire interviews conducted by non-professionals, especially from campus and local media sources. While regular news reports would not normally qualify per se, broadcast interviews can be useful when one individual or event has been covered in depth. Such interviews may be far from oral history; for example, they may not be based on research in archival documentation, or they may utilize imprecise or ingratiating questions. Even so, these accessions can provide insights not available in the traditional written documentation, and the interviewers might be viewed as a rather loosely controlled field staff. In addition, sometimes even inexperienced interviewers can uncover important caches of manuscripts to add to the archives' holdings.

Whether attempting a full-fledged or a barebones program, academic archivists may face their most troubling oral history problem when responding to the desire of amateurs and enthusiasts to mount projects on their own. Campuses are replete with individuals who have in-depth knowledge of important subject areas and close connections with interest groups and constituencies whom the archivist often cannot reach. When these well-intentioned individuals succumb to the "history bug," they may seek the archives' assistance or endorsement in documenting their field through oral history. The subject knowledge and personal contacts of these individuals can be invaluable to an oral history program, but these people frequently have a very simplistic understanding of oral history and its relation to archival documentation. In these circumstances, the archivist may be faced with a choice of diverting resources to support development of a professional oral history project or disappointing the individuals and creating the impression that the archives is unsympathetic to history and preservation. Neither alternative is particularly attractive, but the archivist must maintain the archives' resources for the program's highest priorities. A willingness to provide general advice and to accept the tapes generated by such projects can soften the blow of the archives' unwillingness to assume responsibility for the project. The resulting interviews may not be of the highest quality, but archivists should limit criticisms of such projects to general comments that resources are inadequate for oral history to be properly managed as part of the archives.

Ultimately, the decision on the extent of the archives' activity in oral history is a management choice. It should be based on balancing three factors: the advantages, costs, and necessity of oral documentation. An important advantage of oral history projects is that they place the archivist in more direct contact with participants in the institution's history. Such contact has a double benefit. It can lead to the transfer and preservation of more records and it can enable the archivist to better assess the quality of documentation coming to the archives.

Considerations of oral history will often focus a great deal of attention on its apparent high costs, but it is not necessarily appropriate to compare oral history costs with traditional processing costs. It has been suggested that if one were to consider the full costs of acquiring, arranging, describing, and storing institutional records and manuscripts, oral history interviewing would seem quite competitive.[26] Despite the ancillary benefits and the inevitable expenses, the overriding concern should be the necessity of oral history for the full and proper documentation of institutions. It cannot substitute for the primary documents that form the bulk of the archives, but it is the best method to address the many questions that traditional archival documents leave unanswered. Once the archival program is on solid footing, the main question for the academic archivist should be how to obtain resources for this critical supplement to archival work.

Notes

1. The two best texts for records management are Ira A. Penn, Anne Morddel, Gail Pennix, and Kelvin Smith, *Records Management Handbook* (Aldershot, England: Gower, 1989); and Wilmer O. Maedke, Mary F. Robek, and Gerald F. Brown, *Information and Records Management,* 2d ed. (Encino, Calif.: Glencoe Publishing, 1981). The first is the more readable, but the second has many useful sample forms. A brief review of records management for the academic archivist can be found in William Saffady, "A University Archives and Records Management Program," *College and Research Libraries* 35 (1974): 204-10. The academic archivist also should regularly review *Records Management Quarterly,* the journal of the Association of Records Managers and Administrators. A comprehensive survey and detailed bibliography on college and university records management can be found in Don C. Skemer and Geoffrey P. Williams, "Managing the Records of Higher Education: The State of Records Management in American Colleges and Universities," *American Archivist* 53 (1990): 532-47.

2. For the purposes of this book, records management will be regarded as synonymous with information management. There are merits to both sides of the arguments on the question of whether records or information are the commodities to be managed. From an archival standpoint, however, this controversy should be seen as merely the most recent in a series of efforts by records managers to expand the scope of their activities, as well as the most recent manifestation of experts in newer technologies and systems to assert control over records management as they reconceptualize the world in their terms.

3. Archivists should recognize the difference between archival and vital records. The former are documents of enduring research value. Vital records are documents necessary for the resumption of an organization's operation following a disaster. Records vital for normal operations (e.g., register of accounts payable and receivable) may have little archival value, and records of critical value to historians may have little value for current operations.

4. The life-cycle concept is often mentioned in discussions of archival appraisal and records management, but only rarely is it explicated in detail. Early evidence of the concept, without necessarily mentioning the name, can be found in G. Philip Bauer, "The Appraisal of Current and Recent Records," *National Archives Staff Information Circulars* 13 (June 1946); and Philip C. Brooks, "Archival Procedures for Planned Records Retirement," *American Archivist* 11 (1948): 308-15.

5. A good example of this form and a detailed explanation of its use can be found in William Benedon, *Records Management* (Englewood Cliffs, N.J.: Prentice-Hall, 1969), 17-25. Also, refer to Penn et al., *Records Management Handbook*, 46-60; and John A. Fleckner, *Archives and Manuscripts: Surveys* (Chicago: Society of American Archivists, 1977), 18.

6. For example, business procedures and accounting procedures are outlined in Lanora F. Welzenbach, *College and University Business Administration,* 4th ed. (Washington, D. C.: National Association of College and University Business Offices, 1982). Student records issues are raised in American Association of Collegiate Registrars and Admissions Offices, *Retention*

of Records: A Guide for Retention and Disposal of Student Records (Washington, D.C., 1987). A review of this work by Sharon Pugsley is in *American Archivist* 50 (1987): 610-11. Also, refer to Donald D. Marks, "AACRAO's Guide for Retention and Disposal of Student Records: A Critical Review," *Midwestern Archivist* 8 (1983): 27-33.

7. For example, the records management offices for the University of California and University of Missouri issue handbooks for records custodians on each campus, and the University of Illinois and Auburn University have conducted workshops for clerical staff on the basics of record handling.

8. The term *manuscripts* is subject to considerable confusion. Despite its etymological roots, it is often applied to both handwritten and typewritten (or word processed) documents. Furthermore, the archival profession has used *manuscript collection* to apply to any form of unpublished recorded information including computer data, audiovisual programs, and photographs. For purposes of convenience, this broader meaning of the word *manuscripts* will be used here. Refer to the definitions of *archives* and *manuscripts* in the "Introduction." Also, refer to Kenneth W. Duckett, *Modern Manuscripts: A Practical Manual for Their Management, Care and Use* (Nashville, Tenn.: American Association for State and Local History, 1975), xi-xii, 337, 342-43. Also, refer to "A Basic Glossary for Archivists, Manuscript Curators, and Records Managers," *American Archivist* 37 (1974): 415-33.

9. See the section on "Documents of Student and Faculty Organizations" for a detailed discussion of these records.

10. The subject of faculty papers has been covered in several journal articles. An excellent review of the basic issues can be found in Mary E. Janzen, "Pruning the Groves of Academe: Appraisal, Arrangement and Description of Faculty Papers," *Georgia Archive* 9:2 (Fall 1981): 31-40. For a discussion of the relation of academic archives to special-subject repositories also interested in faculty papers, refer to Jane Wolff, "Faculty Papers and Special-Subject Repositories," *American Archivist* 44 (1981): 346-51. Also, refer to Frederick L. Honhart, "The Solicitation, Appraisal, and Acquisition of Faculty Papers," *College*

and Research Libraries 44 (1983): 236-41; and Harley Holden, "The Collecting of Faculty Papers," *Harvard Library Bulletin* 19 (1971): 187-93.

11. A passionate statement of the need for college and university archives to collect manuscripts can be found in David F. Noble, "Higher Education as an Industrial Process: What University Archives Reveal about the History of Corporate, Scientific America," *Midwestern Archivist* 2:2 (1977): 35-53.

12. Judith E. Endelman, "Looking Backward to Plan for the Future: Collection Analysis for Manuscript Repositories," *American Archivist* 50 (1987): 340-55. For an introduction to formulating collecting policies, refer to the section on "Acquisitions" and Linda J. Henry, "Collecting Policies of Special-Subject Repositories," *American Archivist* 43 (1980): 57-63.

13. The best discussion of the practical implications of these two traditions is Richard Berner, *Archival Theory and Practice in the United States: A Historical Analysis* (Seattle, Wash.: University of Washington Press, 1983).

14. The classic Weberian idea of a bureaucracy is useful in understanding why records created in an official capacity are less appropriately restricted. These reflect actions completed in fulfillment of the responsibility of an office and should be available so that those actions can be scrutinized. By contrast, documents created in a private or observer capacity will be more reflective of personal views and more appropriately held private. Nevertheless, these neat lines between official capacity and personal action become blurred quite quickly in daily academic life.

15. F. Gerald Ham, "Archival Strategies for the Post-Custodial Era," *American Archivist* 44 (1981): 207-16, is one of the best recent pleas for archivists to take an active stance. This is an important perspective, but Ham's dichotomy of "custodial" and "post-custodial" eras overlooks and unduly diminishes the value of the concept of "custodianship."

16. A clear statement of the centrality of outreach goals to archival programs is Timothy Ericson, " 'Preoccupied with Our

Own Gardens': Outreach and Archivists," *Archivaria* 31 (Winter 1990-91): 114-22.

17. An important point in setting goals is to consider how an outreach project can provide solutions, rather than simply products, for the people the archives is trying to reach. Refer to Elsie T. Freeman, "Buying Quarter-Inch Holes: Public Support through Results," *Midwestern Archivist* 10 (1985): 89-97.

18. For a more detailed description of outreach possibilities and suggestions for how to develop them, refer to Ann E. Pederson and Gail Farr Casterline, *Archives & Manuscripts: Public Programs* (Chicago: Society of American Archivists, 1982). Descriptions and samples of outreach activities focused on colleges and universities can be found in "Academic Outreach: The Use of Archival Material on the College Campus," photocopy. Copies can be obtained from Timothy L. Ericson, University of Wisconsin-Milwaukee Archives.

19. For an overview of the types of publications that may be useful in promoting an information center, refer to Systems Procedures and Exchange Center, *Library Publications Programs,* SPEC Kit 145 (Washington, D. C.: Association of Research Libraries, 1988).

20. Gail Farr Casterline, *Archives & Manuscripts: Exhibits* (Chicago: Society of American Archivists, 1980) provides detailed guidance on each of these steps.

21. With some experience, the archivist can learn how to doctor photocopies (e.g., by copying onto old yellowed paper or staining new copies with coffee or tea) to approximate the aging of originals. On the use of copies, refer to Casterline, *Archives & Manuscripts: Exhibits,* 29-33. On preservation concerns, refer to Casterline, *Archives & Manuscripts: Exhibits,* 19-22, and Mary Lynn Ritzenthaler, *Archives & Manuscripts: Conservation* (Chicago: Society of American Archivists, 1983), 60-62.

22. Especially useful are William Moss, *Oral History Program Manual* (New York: Praeger, 1974); Cullom Davis, Kathryn Back, and Kay MacLean, *Oral History: From Tape to Type* (Chicago: American Library Association, 1977); and Frederick

J. Stielow, *Management of Oral History Sound Archives* (West-port, Conn.: Greenwood Press, 1986).

23. William W. Moss and Peter C. Mazikana, *Archives, Oral History and Oral Tradition: A RAMP Study* (Paris: UNESCO, 1986), 5-12.

24. For an excellent discussion of how oral history compares to other forms of evidence and how particular oral history interviews and projects can be evaluated, refer to William Moss, "Oral History: An Appreciation," *American Archivist* 40 (1977): 429-39. Also, refer to Trevor Lummis, "Structure and Validity in Oral Evidence," *International Journal of Oral History* 2 (1981): 109-20.

25. Dale E. Treleven, "Oral History, Audio Technology, and the TAPE System," *International Journal of Oral History* 2 (1981): 26-45. For a description of the more traditional full-transcript method, refer to Willa K. Baum, *Transcribing and Editing Oral History* (Nashville, Tenn.: American Association for State and Local History, 1977).

26. William Moss has suggested that, for nearly equivalent costs, comparable "evidential yield" may be obtained from 20 hours of oral history interviews as from 60 cubic feet of personal papers. While he spoke somewhat in jest, his point is both that cost factors have been overemphasized and that the nature of the documentary and historical problems should be the driving considerations. William Moss, "Talking Bullish to Bears—Oral History and Archivists (paper presented at the Fifty-second Annual Meeting of the Society of American Archivists, Atlanta, Georgia, October 1, 1988).

Conclusion: Facing the Academic World

The easy part of managing an historical records program in a college or university will be learning the theory and methodological basics of archival work. This book, when combined with other basic texts, should provide an ample basis for understanding the technical aspects of academic archives. Far more difficult and challenging will be translating this knowledge into a viable archival program in the real world, where little follows the script found in texts such as this one. This, in fact, is the most basic problem facing the archivist. No matter how important professional goals and practices may be, an archival program will not prosper in isolation from the many contending influences in living institutions. Therefore, perhaps the most critical part of the academic archivist's job will be to define, develop, and maintain relationships with administrative, faculty, and professional units within the parent college or university.

SIZE AND RESOURCES

Sensitivity to these relationships is critical to the survival of archives in colleges and universities because competition for attention, resources, and position is particularly strong in the highly professionalized environment of higher education. It is especially important to define a clear role for the archives and build relationships with

other bodies because academic archives are, and will continue to be, small programs that are easily overshadowed
by other campus units. Few other campus units are in such
an anomalous position—the archives commonly has dis-
proportionately small resources for the breadth and depth
of its mandate and responsibilities, which extend across
the whole institution for its entire lifetime. To bring this
point home, one need only contrast the size and resources
of a typical archives to those of other campus offices with
similar institution-wide responsibilities, such as public
relations, alumni, or personnel services.

A fundamental responsibility of the archivist must be
to work vigorously for greater resources. At the same time,
the relative smallness of the program and its resources
must be accepted as a fact of life or the archivist's position
as a manager will be seriously weakened. Focusing on
shortages of resources can be far more paralyzing to a
program than the lack of resources itself. Indeed, throughout higher education, the long-term prospects for dramatically increased resources are quite poor. When the situation does improve, the resources are far more likely to
grow in small increments which, with luck, will exceed
inflation and keep pace with the growth in holdings. Major
capital and operating additions to the program's budget
will be rare.

Even if academic archives could double or triple their
staff, equipment, and services budget, most would still be
very small units in relation to other campus programs
with comparable institution-wide authority and responsibility. This should not discourage archivists from striving
for better support. Instead, understanding and accepting
the relative size of archives should be a cornerstone for
building stronger relations with other segments of the
campus. It then becomes clear that achieving archival
goals will require assistance and support from a number
of non-archival campus constituencies at the same time
that the archives establishes its professional autonomy.

INSTITUTIONAL AND PROFESSIONAL COMMUNITIES

The need to develop a strong position for the archives becomes even more apparent when one examines the influences exerted by the many professional groups encountered in academe. There are numerous professional communities encountered by the academic archivist, including the disciplinary communities in each of the academic departments, ranging from architecture to zoology; groupings of professionals in allied service and research-oriented programs, such as museums, libraries, placement, and public relations; and technically oriented offices focused on administrative functions, such as admissions and records, business operations, and medical records. The relative influence of these groups will vary so much from institution to institution and field to field that describing exactly how the archivist should relate to them would be impractical. However, by looking at two of the professions that most regularly impinge upon academic archivists—historians and librarians—one can see why it is so important for the archivist to develop a strong and independent role.

Historians or, for that matter, those from other humanities disciplines oriented toward historical research material have traditionally exerted great influence on the collecting scope of academic archives. This phenomenon has contributed to the establishment of many archives and the building of many important collections. However, these disciplinary groups also frequently make ambitious demands on the archivist's ability to collect and make accessible large bodies of documents to support their particular research areas. It would be a serious mistake to reject steadfastly the interests of scholars in adding to the archives' collections, but the archivist needs to be cautious in embracing faculty-based collecting interests in areas that go beyond the documentation of the parent institution. Without proper control, often in the form of a documentation policy written and enforced by the archivist, the repository can quickly become a loose federation of manuscripts on American cinema, farm mechanization, urban ethnic politicians, environmental action groups, and the like. In the process, both the focus on and the resources for institutional documentation can be lost or relegated to secondary or tertiary status. The answer is not to flee from disciplinary interests in manuscript collecting and devote oneself solely to institutional records; rather, the archivist, not the faculty, should have the authority to select from among the many potential collecting areas in a way that maintains an archival balance in the program. Unfortunately, there are no formulae to simplify this task, and each archivist must choose the best course for his or her own institution.[1]

Libraries exert many pressures on archives, and looking at libraries' focus on reader services provides insight into how archivists should manage their relationships with other professional bodies found on campus. Because of their institutional mandate to serve the information needs of students and faculty, libraries quite properly have a very strong interest in public-service activities, such as reference-desk staffing, weekend hours, circulation, and outreach services. While all academic archives should have a strong public-service orientation, their mandate to meet the administrative documentation needs of the parent institution often can conflict with libraries' emphasis on service. This tension is most likely to occur when an archives is located within the college library. Staff time that had been allocated previously to critical archival activities, such as records scheduling or processing, may be redirected to meet library service goals, such as extended hours or general reference-desk work.

Academic archivists need to cooperate closely with libraries and should be willing to assist in some service functions. However, the success of this relationship depends on an acknowledgment by the campus administration and the library that the archives has institution-wide and long-term administrative responsibilities and that it should not be treated the same as a departmental or branch library. Furthermore, all parties should understand that the redirection of the archivist's time to library activities represents a clear diversion of key resources. Rather, the archives and the library should accept each other as peers operating at the same institution-wide level to meet many allied needs of the campus.[2]

These two examples of archives-campus relationships demonstrate that the archivist needs to establish a position as an independent professional. This argues that the archivist should be oriented primarily to the outside professional body of archivists for guidance on program direction. However, relating to the professional body of archivists is not merely a matter of identifying and then implementing the standard wisdom and practice of the archival profession.

What makes management of an archives particularly difficult is that those external organizations, government agencies, and individuals that have assumed the role of representing the archival profession often place as much pressure on an archival program as the many other professions the archivist encounters. What the archival profession has to say about the management of historical records programs unquestionably should have a pivotal role in guiding the academic archivist. At the same time, however, the composite body called the archival profession needs to be understood as another manifestation of the general phenomenon of professional bodies creating demands on program management—a phenomenon which, if not brought under the control of the individual archivist, can fragment the archives as one tries to satisfy proliferating expectations.[3]

DEFINING A ROLE FOR THE ARCHIVIST

The essence of superior management of an academic archives is not found in compliance with the interests of any one of the groups exerting pressure on the archives. Rather, the key is for the individual archivist to determine how far to go in accepting the opportunities and resisting the pressures that each group offers. This decision will require not so much archival, historical, library, or systems expertise, but the ability to define and maintain relations with other groups. Given the fluidity of the forces influencing archives, specific suggestions on managing relations will be less useful than a general statement of two principles that must underlie how archival programs should relate to these forces and other campus programs.

First the archivist must be recognized and accepted as a professional, and the archives must be seen as a professional enterprise. The nature of a profession is the subject of an enormous body of literature and well beyond the purview of this book.[4] For present purposes, however, a "professional" archival program should be understood as meaning that the archivist serves the institution by developing its historical records program with reference to an external body of knowledge and practice that has greater breadth and depth than the mere techniques and procedures needed to manage a single institution's documentary heritage. The archivist needs to look beyond internal practitioners to communities outside the institution for guidance in making the best decisions for the archives and the institution. In practical terms, recognition of the professional nature of archival work may reside in an institution's personnel system classifying the archivist as a professional, academic, or faculty position and providing the financial support for continuing professional education and development.

Intrinsically related to the recognition of archival work as a professional enterprise is the granting of considerable autonomy to the archivist in defining the archives' mission and goals, as well as the means needed to accomplish them. In other words, the archivist must be granted authority commensurate with the program's institution-wide and time-spanning responsibilities. A practical manifestation of this autonomy will be that the archives, regardless of its size, is considered a peer when it must work with other similar campus programs, such as the library, admissions office, or personnel office, to accomplish its basic responsibilities.

The second key principle in determining the archives' relations with other campus units is that the archivist must take primary responsibility for all decisions affecting the basic direction of the program. Only the archivist can steer a course that maintains a balance among the many forces bearing down on the program. Overcompliance with any particular interest group, whether administrators interested in records management, librarians interested in public service, faculty interested in collecting manuscripts, or the archival associations interested in their educational and regulatory programs, can weaken the core of the archival program. At the heart of the best archival programs, regardless of local resources, will be the archivist's vision and ability to exploit these outside interests to develop a program that maintains that delicate balance among preserving the past, serving current administrative needs, educating future generations, and serving as an information resource center. This sort of balancing clearly involves compromises and local approaches to the methodologies suggested by this and other archival textbooks.

At the same time, to be a vibrant part of an institution's future, an archivist must persistently draw concepts, solutions, and questions from outside one's current spheres of activity. Only by constantly expanding services and sources of ideas for the archives can the archivist create a program that moves beyond mere custodianship of the records of the past to management of a cultural heritage on which the future can be built.

It is precisely this dimension of academic archival work—selecting which practices to follow and which influences to accept—that renders it a professional activity. An academic archives is managerial work that requires decisions and actions based on a thorough knowledge of the technical aspects of archival practice combined with a deep understanding of the realities of one's own institution. Because the circumstances, problems, opportunities, and talents of each academic archivist are so diverse, each program will develop distinctive characteristics. Attention to the practices and guidelines outlined in this book can facilitate academic archival work and help eliminate the insupportable idiosyncracies of local practice. By itself, however, neither this nor any other text can assure the strengthening of academic archival practice. That can occur only through the careful exercise of the archivist's judgment in response to each circumstance that presents itself.

PROFESSION AND MISSION

An academic archival program should be described as professional not because of its adherence to externally developed standards, but because the archives has been developed by balancing resources, opportunities, external standards, and institutional interests. Perhaps the most important recommendation of this book is that its findings should be considered in all archival decisions but its recommendations should never be implemented exactly as presented. Textbook answers are seldom real solutions. Each archivist, of course, bears the responsibility for being informed about the goals, theory, and techniques of archival practice, but the final and perhaps hardest step is to find the best way to meet these goals within one's institution. No literature or professional organization can accomplish this; only a dynamic, knowledgeable individual can. When such a balance occurs, replete with intangibles and variables, and the program grows, it is clear that a professional is at work.

Such a redefined professional approach is imperative because academic archives are, despite their small size, critically important institutions in late-twentieth-century American society. The documentary heritage of a single institution of higher education may seem insignificant compared with the cultural patrimony represented by the National Archives or Library of Congress, but the best building blocks for all citizens' understanding of the relevance of the past are those within each citizen's reach. Academic archivists have the mission to seize upon the heritage of their own institution as a means to educate their communities in how the past explains the present and suggests alternatives for the future. To overlook this opportunity to enrich so many people, especially the many young minds in the process of maturing, will leave the future of higher education far weaker than its past. To make this vision the motivating force of academic archival work will ensure strong programs that contribute much both to the archival profession and to the institutional and local communities.

Notes

1. For an overview of the many dimensions of archives-faculty relations, refer to Maynard Brichford, "University Archives: Relationships with Faculty," *American Archivist* 34 (1971): 173-81, reprinted in *College and University Archives: Selected Readings* (Chicago: Society of American Archivists, 1979): 31-37.

2. William J. Maher, "Improving Archives-Library Relations: User-Centered Solutions to a Sibling Rivalry," *Journal of Academic Librarianship* 15 (1990): 355-63.

3. William J. Maher, "The Current State of Academic Archives: A Procrustean Bed for Archival Principles?" *American Archivist* 52 (1989): 342-49.

4. For an introduction, refer to Thomas J. Haskell, ed., *The Authority of Experts: Studies in History and Theory* (Bloomington, Ind.: Indiana University Press, 1984). For application to archivists, refer to William J. Maher, "Contexts for Understanding Professional Certification: Opening Pandora's Box?" *American Archivist* 51 (1988): 408-27; and Richard Cox, "Professionalism and Archivists in the United States," *American Archivist* 49 (1986): 229-47.

Appendix 1

Management Basics: A Selective Bibliography

Archival work is a specialized activity requiring expertise in both historical and technical fields, but equally important is the archivist's skill as an administrator. The academic archivist must be able to define goals for the program, plan the use of resources, balance program elements to ensure that internal and external constituent needs are met, and communicate with campus administrators to acquire resources and report on accomplishments.

A review of management theory and practice is therefore an appropriate part of a basic text on college and university archives. However, given the broad variations in academic archives' staff size, budget, holdings, and institutional situation, it is not possible to provide a simple set of recommendations for how to function as a manager. Until recently, the archival literature has been of little assistance in applying management techniques to accomplish archival goals, although the 1991 publication of Thomas Wilsted and William Nolte's *Managing Archival and Manuscript Repositories* may well compensate for this long-term neglect.

The reasons for this neglect are complex, but an overriding consideration is that a large number of archivists work in programs that have very small staffs and are often subordinated to a larger organizational unit, frequently a library. It is not surprising that many archivists in these settings have supposed that the management practices of business or government were quite irrelevant to their concerns. This line of reasoning neglects the fact that even the smallest programs require their directors to perform the functions traditionally associated with a manager's responsibilities—to set goals and objectives, plan programs and services, direct people, and evaluate performance of personnel and programs. Thus, while archivists in small repositories may have little need to implement specialized management practices, such as Planning Programming Budgeting Systems (PPBS), it is still very useful for them to understand the rationale and logical processes that link the setting of goals to the planning of programs and the evaluation of services.

As a starting point, management can be defined as administering an organization to guarantee its continued existence and ensure that its goals are met. Management commonly encompasses planning, organizing, coordinating, directing, and controlling. The term is most commonly associated with the for-profit, corporate world, but much of the administrative activity in nonprofit service organizations can be understood and analyzed in terms of corporate practice. Indeed, many have argued that given the importance of management, there are more similarities than differences between business and public service organizations.

Although the terms *management* and *administration* are not uncommon in archival journal articles and conference sessions and even in this book, the actual focus of these references is primarily on technical archival procedures, rather than on the broader issues of program direction.[1] Nevertheless, the shortage of archival literature on management is not so limiting as one might think because many of the problems in academic archives management are similar to those discussed in the literature of general management. Once the findings of management writings are adjusted for differences in size and mission, the archivist will benefit considerably from a modest sampling of management writings. This appendix presents a brief review of some of the literature that academic archivists should examine as they confront the management aspects of their work.

SCOPE AND LIMITS

To introduce academic archivists to management theory and suggest how its principles may be adapted to the academic setting, the following bibliography provides a highly selective sample, with brief commentary, of management and related archival literature. It is intended to equip academic archivists with basic tools to improve their programs so they can make more efficient use of their limited resources and personnel.

This bibliography directs archivists to writers whose comments have relevance to public-service institutions, such as archives. Several items related to the management of libraries have been cited because of their similar nonprofit status, information focus, and service orientation. Because the situation of academic archives is quite similar to that of the small or special library (both being subordinated to considerably larger organizations), items related to the management of such units have been included because of their potential value as daily handbooks.

To ensure accessibility and wide representation, journal articles are emphasized, but also included are a few monographs and readers that should be readily available. The time span has been drawn broadly to accommodate a variety of sources, but most items date from the mid-1970s or later. Virtually all articles on management issues in the *American Archivist* and *Midwestern Archivist* since 1976 have been included. Because of the abundance of library articles on management, only the few of greatest relevance have been included. Those wishing to investigate the library management literature further should start with

Beverly Lynch's *Management Strategies for Libraries: A Basic Reader.* When she omits an important item, the bibliographic citations in the selected articles provide ample direction to the remaining sources. Citations are in chronological order in each category.

BASIC MANAGEMENT WRITINGS

Mintzberg, Henry. *The Nature of Managerial Work.* New York: Harper and Row, 1973.

An essential work, offering a fascinating study of managers and leaders in a variety of settings (from presidents and corporation executives to industrial workers and street gangs). Mintzberg debunks the classical view that management is a series of highly structured activities of organizing, planning, and controlling. Instead, he argues that management is not carefully regulated but highly varied and dynamic. He stresses that the core of management work is the performance of ten roles in three categories: interpersonal, informational, and decisional. In the course of developing his argument, Mintzberg provides an overview of classical management writers such as Henri Fayol, Lyndall Urwick and Luther Gulick, and Herbert Simon.

While much of subsequent management literature has hesitated to accept Mintzberg's view as a model for managers' behavior, his emphasis on how time is spent provides an excellent framework for understanding the role of the archival manager. An excellent summary of this book is found in Henry Mintzberg, "The Manager's Job: Folklore and Fact," *Harvard Business Review* 53 (July-August 1975): 49-61, which contrasts four folklores to the reality of management.

Katz, Robert L. "Skills of an Effective Administrator." *Harvard Business Review* 52 (September-October 1974): 90-102.

This classic essay summarizes three broad skills that effective managers must possess. Archivists will find much relevance in Katz's outline of how critical are the technical, human, and conceptual skills needed for successful program administration. This article provides a basis for archivists to assess themselves as managers and evaluate potential candidates for archival positions.

Drucker, Peter. "Managing the Public Service Institution." *College and Research Libraries* 37 (1976): 4-14.
Drucker outlines key characteristics of management in institutions devoted to public service rather than profit. He notes the importance of identifying the institution's or program's public, setting service objectives, balancing the tension between administrators and professionals, and instilling in the staff a sense of the institution's mission.

Simon, Herbert A. *Administrative Behavior: A Study of Decision-Making Processes in Administrative Organizations*. 3d edition. New York: Free Press, 1976.
This classic work argues that organizations can be understood through their decision making processes. Archivists may also find his discussion of the role of information in decision-making to be useful in appraisal.

Lynch, Beverly, ed. *Management Strategies for Libraries: A Basic Reader.* New York: Neal-Schuman, 1985.
This reader assembles articles and extracts from classic texts by authors such as Max Weber, Frederick Taylor, Herbert Simon, Peter Blau, Henry Mintzberg, and Victor Vroom. These are combined with writings that apply business management theory and practices to librarianship. Many practices described in this book will be beyond the needs of the small archival program, but it will familiarize the archivist with management techniques. In addition, its coverage of larger organizations can improve archivists' understanding of the institutions and processes they are documenting.

LIBRARY ADMINISTRATION AND SMALL LIBRARIES

DeGennaro, Richard. "Library Administration and New Management Systems." *Library Journal* 103 (15 December 1978): 2477-82.

DeGennaro writes from personal experience with the application of "new" management techniques (e.g., management by objective, PERT, PPBS, and participative management) to libraries. He emphasizes the importance of political, rather than quantitative and psychological factors in effective management. His focus on common-sense solutions instead of mechanistic formulae is particularly refreshing.

Riggs, Donald E. *Strategic Planning for Library Managers*. Phoenix, Ariz.: Oryx Press, 1984.

Even in the smallest programs, the archivist should be aware of the importance of planning to the success of management activities. Riggs' book is a readily accessible description of this fundamental management responsibility, and it emphasizes organization for strategic planning, strategy formulation, implementation, contingency plans, and evaluation mechanisms. Also useful are his clear definitions of basic terms, such as mission, goals, objectives, and policies. While the book covers some areas in greater detail than others, its sample forms, checklists, charts, and well-designed typography make it a very practical guide. This book can be used as a companion to Paul McCarthy's *Archives Assessment and Planning Workbook*, cited below.

White, Herbert S. *Managing the Special Library: Strategies for Success within the Larger Organization*. White Plains, N.Y.: Knowledge Industry Publications, 1984.

White's understanding of archives is weak (refer to the review by Karen Benedict in *American Archivist* 49 [1986]: 327-29), but this text can be of considerable value to

academic archivists who, like special librarians, direct
small programs within much larger organizations. Particularly useful are his sections on budgets, staffing levels,
communication, reporting, and the relation of the
program's mission and objectives to those of the larger
parent institution.

Ahrensfeld, Janet L., Elin B. Christianson, and David
E. King. *Special Libraries: A Guide for Management.* 2d
ed. Washington, D.C.: Special Libraries Association, 1986.
This guide is written primarily to explain the rationale
for, and operations of, library units to managers of corpo-
rations, large government offices, and private associations, but its greatest value is as an example of the kind
of handbook archivists should prepare to justify archives
to management. In addition, academic archivists may find
useful guidance in its chapters on "The Library as an
Organizational Unit" and on staffing, space, and equipment.

St. Clair, Guy, and Joan Williamson. *Managing the
One-Person Library.* London: Butterworths, 1986.
Although written for a library audience, much of this
work can be adapted easily to academic archives, especially in relation to the difficulties of managing a small
professional program within a larger organization. The
most useful chapters are those on professional isolation
and independence, self-management, time management,
and communication and public relations.

Stueart, Robert D., and Barbara B. Moran. *Library
Management.* 3d ed. Littleton, Colo.: Libraries Unlimited,
1987.
This basic text on libraries can serve as a valuable
reference book for archivists, especially for its concise
outline of the history of, and major trends in, management
theory.

PERSONNEL ISSUES

A basic text on personnel management will be an important item for the academic archivist's bookshelf, even when there is a personnel office in the parent institution or department. Such a text can be quite important for outlining the theory and legal issues that underlie such areas as employee selection, nondiscrimination, evaluation, discipline, and supervision. Three good texts are listed here, but the reader is advised that personnel practices are constantly evolving, especially in response to changing legal issues, and that other good texts may be available in the local library.

Cascio, Wayne F., and Elias M. Awad. *Human Resource Management: An Information Systems Approach.* Reston, Va.: Reston Publishing, 1981.

Schuler, Randall S. *Personnel and Human Resource Management.* St. Paul, Minn.: West Publishing Co., 1981.

Megginson, Leon C. *Personnel Management: A Human Resources Approach.* 5th ed. Homewood, Ill.: Richard D. Irwin, 1985.

Edwards, Ralph M. "The Management of Libraries and the Professional Functions of Librarians." *Library Quarterly* 45 (1975): 150-60.

Archivists need to be aware of the implications of their aspiration to professional status while working within bureaucratic organizations. Edwards describes the tension between library management and the essence of librarianship as a profession and contrasts bureaucratic and professional methods of library work. This article also provides a good mechanism for understanding how the nature of a professional's work changes on assuming management responsibilities.

Raelin, Joseph A. *The Clash of Cultures: Managers and Professionals*. Boston: Harvard University Business School Press, 1986.

This is a highly readable compendium of Raelin's studies of the tensions between the nature of professional work and employment within large organizations. Because Raelin has so capably captured the causes and effects of the clash between the professional's need for autonomy and the organization's need for control, this work should be primary reading for academic archivists. It sheds important light on the nature of professions and professional institutions, such as universities, without becoming lost in trite discussions of whether particular occupations are professions.

ARCHIVAL WRITINGS ON MANAGEMENT

Wilson, Dwight H. "No Ivory Tower: The Administration of a College or University Archives." *College and Research Libraries* 13 (1952): 215-22; reprinted in *College and University Archives: Selected Readings*. Chicago: Society of American Archivists, 1979.

Wilson's essay typifies the articles on administration or management that focus on technical archival elements, rather than management issues, but his outline of the program elements needed in academic archives is still valid. His suggested plan for the first year, while ambitious, reflects the importance of planning as a basic management activity.

Von Kohl, Marilyn. "Problems of Regional Archival Networks: Some Comments on the Manager's Role." *Midwestern Archivist* 2 (1977): 49-57.

Von Kohl looks at the rather considerable management problems that occur in archival networks where staff are highly decentralized and there are tensions between managerial and professional roles. The article is most interesting because of its convincing argument that the answers to many problems in archival settings can be found not in archival theory, but in management theory and practice.

Maher, William J. "Importance of Financial Considerations in the Administration of Archives." *Midwestern Archivist* 3:2 (1978): 4-21.

Although not written with specific reference to the management literature, this article suggests that cost studies of archival processes may be useful management tools. It provides examples from the University of Illinois Archives and argues that financial or budgetary considerations offer a critical means of increasing the archivist's control over the program.

Worthy, James C. "Management Concepts and Archival Administration." *Midwestern Archivist* 4 (1979):77-88. Reprinted in Maygene F. Daniels and Timothy Walch, eds. *A Modern Archives Reader*. Washington, D.C.: National Archives and Records Service, 1984: 299-308.

Worthy, a consultant and professor of management at Northwestern University, provides a good introduction to this area by focusing on three areas: management by objectives, participatory management, and performance evaluation. While his treatment is not specific to archival settings, he focuses on individuals directing programs with small budgets and staff.

Holbert, Sue E. "Comments on Management Concepts and Archival Administration." *Midwestern Archivist* 4 (1979): 89-94.

This is a short commentary by a government-records archivist on James C. Worthy's management suggestions for archivists. Holbert provides archival examples that both illustrate and rebut Worthy's recommendations.

Gildemeister, Glen A. "Recruiting and Hiring in Archives: Qualifications, Procedures, and Techniques." *Midwestern Archivist* 5 (1981): 113-21.

This article is of interest because it is one of the few archival discussions of personnel issues, and Gildemeister comments on the history of this neglect. The core of his article focuses on the steps to be followed in filling archival vacancies. This information may not be new to readers of basic personnel texts, but its application to archival institutions and the inclusion of a sample job description make it valuable to the academic archivist.

McCrank, Lawrence J., ed. *Archives and Library Administration: Divergent Traditions and Common Concerns.* New York: Haworth Press, 1986. Also published as *Journal of Library Administration* 7:2/3 (Summer/Fall 1986).

Ten essays, most written by archivists, provide insight into the sources of tension between librarians and archivists as well as suggestions for areas of greater cooperation. Academic archivists attempting to manage their programs within a larger library will find useful perspectives in the essays by Paul McCarthy, "Archives under Library Administration," and David Klaassen, "The Provenance of Archives under Library Administration."

"Proceedings of the 10th International Congress on Archives." *Archivum* 32 (1986).

Three papers delivered at the 1984 International Congress on Archives (Bonn, Federal Republic of Germany) are particularly useful because they combine an explanation of the relevance of management principles to archives with practical examples: Michael Swift, "The Use of Management Techniques and Technical Resources in Response to the Challenges Facing Modern Archives" (pp. 119-34); Colin Pitson, "The Application of Business Management Techniques in Archives" (pp. 135-43); and Marijan Rastic, "Management of Smaller (Local) Archival Institutions" (pp. 151-55).

Taylor, Hugh A. "From Dust to Ashes: Burnout in the Archives." *Midwestern Archivist* 12 (1987): 73-82.

This article examines archival management problems caused by stress-related declines in employee productivity and compares the causes of archival stress to those prevalent in the more studied area of librarianship. Not only does Taylor provide useful guidance on an important staff development issue, but in the process he provides one of the very few examples of the practical application of management studies to archival work.

McCarthy, Paul H. "The Management of Archives: A Research Agenda." *American Archivist* 51 (1988): 52-69.

McCarthy provides a overview of basic management concepts, useful references to management literature, and suggestions of areas of archival work that can benefit immediately from use of a management perspective. He also outlines a broad agenda of management-related archival problems that could become the focus of archivists' research. The article is most useful for its thought-provoking questions and rhetorical statements.

Wilsted, Thomas. "Commentary." *American Archivist* 51 (1988): 70-72.

This commentary on Paul McCarthy's outline of a research agenda on archival management is more a restatement than a critique. Wilsted especially notes the need to improve archival data-gathering and reporting and to determine how management needs differ in large and small repositories.

Davis, Susan. "Development of Managerial Training for Archivists." *American Archivist* 51 (1988): 278-85.

After demonstrating that archival work requires a knowledge of management theory and practices, Davis explores the question of where archivists should receive this training. She makes a brief but clear case for the relevance of management issues to archival work and outlines a realistic view of current archival education. The outline of continuing education offerings from professional organizations is detailed, but she overlooks the best and most accessible source for academic archivists—courses at the archivist's parent institution.

Yakel, Elizabeth. "Institutionalizing an Archives: Developing Historical Records Programs in Organizations." *American Archivist* 52 (1989): 202-07.

Because Yakel starts with the recognition that institutional archives are inherently small programs, this article is particularly useful for academic archivists. It emphasizes the importance of setting archival goals and outlines management steps to ensure the program's survival.

Mc Carthy, Paul H., ed. *Archives Assessment and Planning Workbook.* Chicago: Society of American Archivists, 1989.

This is an excellent "do-it-yourself" tool for archivists to evaluate the performance of their programs and make plans based on the results of their own assessment of their progress. Through a series of data sheets, checklists, and planning worksheets, archivists can easily participate in long-range planning activities linked to major functional areas of archival work. The *Workbook* will also be useful when college and university archivists are asked to assess their own programs as part of institution-wide self-evaluations.

"Case Studies in Archives Program Development." *American Archivist* 53 (1990): 548-60.

These case studies of three institutional archives (Yale University, Archdiocese of Boston, and Utah State Archives) are pragmatic accounts of how an archival program actually develops. John Dojka's description of Yale is the one most relevant for academic archivists, but all the essays shed light on practical management issues, including institutional setting, planning, communication, and professional standards.

Floyd, Barbara. "The Archivist as Public Administrator." *Midwestern Archivist* 15 (1990): 17-24.

To assist archivists in applying management practices to the administration of their programs, Floyd describes the development and educational content of the field of public administration. Particularly useful is her perspective that politics often supplants profit as the overriding consideration in public institutions as compared to businesses for which most management literature has been written. Although a public administration approach to specific management tasks (e.g., budgeting and planning) is noted, the emphasis is more on broad observations concerning how public administration helps archivists to understand the institutions and processes they document.

Wilsted, Thomas, and William Nolte. *Managing Archival and Manuscript Repositories.* Chicago: Society of American Archivists, 1991.
As an introduction to the full-range of management tasks, this new work is a basic item for the academic archivist's bookshelf. Wilsted and Nolte provide brief but clear descriptions of management activities and link these to the kinds of problems common in archival repositories. In addition to considering such management basics as organizational structure, planning, and budgeting, Wilsted and Nolte look at specifically archival issues—administering space, managing professionals, and the technology of information systems.

JOURNALS

For periodic updates on management theory and practice, archivists should scan a number of journals in business management. Three that often contain interesting articles are *Harvard Business Review, Human Resource Management,* and the *McKinsey Quarterly.* Equally useful will be occasional reviews in the *Journal of Library Administration,* especially its book reviews and the occasional column, "Management Literature on Selected Current Issues."

Notes

1. A review of two major American archival journals, *American Archivist* and *Midwestern Archivist,* from 1976 (the found-

ing date of *Midwestern Archivist*) through 1990 provides clear evidence of this lack of interest in management questions. With the exception of analyses of processing costs, *American Archivist* contained only four articles dealing primarily with management theory or practice, all in 1988-90, and the *Midwestern Archivist* contained only six such articles.

Appendix 2

Guidelines for College and University Archives*

INTRODUCTION

In recent years, increasing numbers of colleges and universities have established archival agencies for the management of their noncurrent but permanently valuable records and papers. Indeed, the staff of academic archival and manuscript agencies now constitutes the largest membership bloc in the Society of American Archivists. During the period of growth, many archivists have also adopted a wider view of their role in the academic community. College and university archives today are thus the scene of considerable change, growth, and development. The Society of American Archivists Committee on College and University Archives therefore sees the need for a statement outlining goals, guidelines, and standards for such archives, in order to channel these developments along such common lines.

A subcommittee composed of practicing college and university archivists drafted this document, which was approved by the full committee at the annual meeting in Nashville, 3 October 1978.

Guidelines for College and University Archives (Chicago: Society of American Archivists, 1979)

The statement of goals and guidelines is not a step-by-step guide to establishing an archives; nor should it be used as a yardstick by which existing programs might be measured. Nevertheless, it is an outline of complete archival facility, and it is thus hoped that this document will provide some indication of the present orientation of archival management in American colleges and universities. These institutions vary widely in size, resources, and organizational structure. Each archives will therefore vary in degree depending upon the historical evolution of its parent institution and the burdens stemming from that evolution. This statement is intended to serve both college archives and university archives; both pursue the same goals, though universities will require larger staff and will often devote greater resources to their archives.

This report concludes with a discussion of records management. This section is included for the benefit of those archives that become actively involved in this field. All archives should develop a working relationship with the records managers of their institution; many will find it useful to undertake this function themselves.

The subcommittee acknowledges a very heavy debt to *Core Mission and Minimum Standards for University Archives* by the University of Wisconsin System Archives Council. Indeed, many passages in this document were adopted directly from their work. We hope that others will build upon our work as we have built upon the Wisconsin statement.

I. CORE MISSION

College and university archives share the following core mission:

A. To appraise, collect, organize, describe, make available, and preserve records of historical legal, fiscal, and/or administrative value to their institution.

B. To provide adequate facilities for the retention and preservation of such records.

C. To provide information services that will assist the operation of the institution.

D. To serve as a resource and laboratory to stimulate and nourish creative teaching and learning.

E. To serve research and scholarship by making available and encouraging the use of its collections by members of the institution and the community at large.

F. To promote knowledge and understanding of the origins, aims, goals of its institution, and of the development of these aims, goals, and programs.

G. To facilitate efficient records management.

II. ADMINISTRATION

A. Administrative Relationships

In order to fulfill its mission, each college and university archives should have a clearly defined status within the administrative structure of its institution. This status should be defined in a statement of rights and responsibilities approved by the appropriate governing board of the university. Successful archives presently exist that report to a variety of university officers, including the president, the chief academic officer, the chief administrative officer, and the chief librarian. Whatever the place of the archives in the administrative structure, the status of the archives should reflect the following considerations:

1. The administrative structure should provide the archivist with sufficient authority to negotiate for the transfer of records from all university offices. It is especially important that the archivist be explicitly provided sufficient independence and authority to perform the duties outlined in this document, including the authority to accept custody of confidential university records.

2. The administrative structure should provide the archivist with financial and personnel resources that will enable the archives to fulfill its responsibility to the university.

3. The administrative status should facilitate service to the entire university.

4. The administrative status should permit easy access to service and equipment which support the operation of the archives.

5. The administrative status should allow for effective coordination with other university offices that may have related functions.

6. The administrative structure should promote resolution of the administrative difficulties presented by multicampus institutions. Autonomous campuses should maintain a central administrative structure, one archives should be designated as the depository for its records. Colleges and universities with branches in the same town should usually maintain a single archives.

B. Acquisition of Archives

1. Collection

Collection includes the procedures and activities required for acquiring records and papers for the university archives.

a. A written collection policy should be developed by the archivist of every institution, though other operations should not be neglected pending completion of such a document. It should include:

i. An analysis of the current holdings of the archives with identification of particular areas of weakness in the documentation of the university's history, preferably by office or by chronological period. This analysis should include the official records of the university; the records and papers produced by university-related organizations, groups, and individuals while they are actively connected with the university such as the private papers of faculty produced while serving on the university staff; and materials such as still photographs, motion picture film, audio and video tape, oral history interviews, machine-readable records, and manuscript collections relating to the university.

ii. A statement of the limits of the archives' collecting responsibility.

iii. A statement defining acceptable donor restrictions and indicating circumstances under which restrictions may be imposed.

iv. A statement defining policy on copyright and literary rights. If possible, copyright and literary rights should be assigned to the institution or its appropriate governing board.

b. A written plan should also be developed for improving the documentation in the areas of weakness by targeting offices and groups for collection emphasis and establishing priorities in the acquisition of new holdings.

c. The collection policy should be updated as needed.

d. A contact file should be maintained containing information on every office, organization, or individual with which the archivist has discussed records transfer or donation. The information should include dates of contact, agreements on transfers or donations, current status of contact, and supporting correspondence or phone memoranda.

e. An accession register should be maintained, recording the date, title, office, bulk, condition of record, transferring officer or donor and any restrictions on access.

f. It is often useful to prepare a short brochure for university offices outlining archival services and records transfer procedures.

2. Appraisal

Appraisal is that process by which an archivist determines the administrative, legal, fiscal, historical and long-term research value of records and selects these records for retention in the archives. In selecting records, priority should be given to records that meet one of the following considerations:

a. The record should document the development and growth of the university.

b. Priority should usually be given to those records that reflect the development and activities of those university offices and committees that cut across departmental divisions and that formulate or approve university-wide or division-wide policy as well as faculty and administrative involvement in those activities.

c. Archives may accept records in imminent danger of loss or destruction for temporary storage pending a decision on ultimate accession or disposal.

3. The following is a suggested checklist of appropriate records for a college or university archives. The relative importance of these records will vary from institution to institution.

Documentation need not be restricted to these areas, and the archivist should not substitute this list for an analysis of the particular needs of his institution.

a. Minutes, memoranda, correspondence, and reports of the governing board of the university.

b. Records of the office of the chief executive including correspondence, administrative subject files, and reports.

c. Correspondence, subject files, and reports of the office of the chief academic affairs officer.

d. Correspondence, subject files, and reports of the chief administrative officer.

e. Correspondence, subject files, and reports of the chief officer of units of the school operating with a high degree of independence, such as medical and law schools and major research institutes.

f. Minutes, memoranda, and reports of all major academic and administrative committees, including the faculty senate and its committees.

g. Correspondence, subject files, and reports of the office of the chief student affairs officer.

h. Accreditation reports and supporting documentation.

i. Annual budgets and audit reports.

j. Departmental records, including minutes, reports, syllabi, and sample test questions.

k. Personnel records of retired, resigned, or deceased faculty.

l. Records of the registrar including timetables and class schedules, noncurrent student transcripts, enrollment reports, graduation rosters, and other reports issued on a regular basis.

m. Alumni records including minutes of the alumni association.

n. Reports of the admissions office.

o. Reports of the office of institutional research.

p. Reports of the university development office.

q. Records of student organizations.

r. All publications, newsletters, or booklets distributed in the name of the university, including: catalogs, special bulletins, yearbooks, student newspapers, university directories and faculty/staff rosters, faculty and university newsletters, alumni magazines, and ephemeral materials.

s. Audiovisual materials documenting the development of the institution such as still photographs and negatives, motion picture films, oral history interviews, and audio and video tapes.

t. Security copies of microfilm produced by any campus vital records program.

u. Maps and plot plans documenting physical growth and development.

v. Reports of research projects, including grant records.

w. Artifacts relating to the history of the institution if there is no museum affiliated with the school.

C. Processing

Processing encompasses the procedures undertaken for the arrangement, description, and preservation of collections and records series to be maintained in the archives.

1. Arrangement

a. Records should be organized according to the recognized archival principals of provenance and original order. Where no apparent order exists, the order should be determined by the potential uses of the record.

b. All folders and containers of records, papers, and materials should be clearly labeled in some appropriate manner. All materials now boxed or folded should likewise be labeled.

c. Arrangement of collections and series on the shelves in the archives may be arbitrary so long as records may be quickly retrieved and serviced.

2. Finding Aids

Finding aids are guides, catalogs, lists, inventories, registers, and indexes designed to describe the holdings of the archives to potential users; to enable the archivist to retrieve information; and to enable the archivist to build on the work of the present generation.

a. A minimum basic finding aid would consist of the information contained in the accession register arranged by title of collection or record series and placed in a card catalog, loose-leaf notebook, or other device that permits easy access to the relevant information.

b. When possible, a finding aid for each collection or record series should be available to researchers. The detail provided in this finding aid will vary depending on the staff available and the archivist's judgment of the importance of the series and the potential volume of use.

c. When possible, a university archives should make available to researchers an organizational chart or index showing the current administrative structure of the university and preferably detailing the historic changes in that structure.

3. The following minimal procedures should be carried out during processing to preserve records. Standards for the physical environment of the records are contained in Section V.

a. Records should be inspected for the presence of vermin, mold, and mildew and steps taken to eliminate any such organisms.

b. Especially brittle, damaged, or torn documents should be repaired or copied in accordance with approved methods. Polyester encapsulation is recommended for any torn or brittle document whose intrinsic worth merits the cost. By itself, polyester encapsulation protects only from physical wear and tear. Thus documents should also be deacidified whenever possible. Non-rustproof staples or fasteners, rubber bands, and paper clips should be removed and folded documents opened and flattened.

c. Unbound papers such as correspondence should be placed preferably in acid-free folders, and then boxed in document cases or covered boxes lined or constructed with acid-free materials.

D. Access to Archives

1. Access to unrestricted material in university archives should be on equal terms to all researchers who abide by the rules and regulations of the archives.

2. Access to unpublished material in the university archives may be restricted by the office in which the material originated, or by the donor of personal papers.

3. Restrictions on access should be recorded in writing and copies filed in the archives and in the office making the restriction.

4. Restrictions on access should be for a fixed term and be determined at the time of transfer or donation. Archivists should avoid agreements to restrict access to material for the lifetime of any person or persons, as well as other agreements that appear difficult or impossible to administer.

5. Only the originating office or other authority may grant access to restricted material. Such permission should be in writing and should be signed by the officer granting access or the donor and should be retained indefinitely in the archives.

6. The archivist should encourage minimal access restrictions consistent with the legal rights of all concerned.

7. Archivists must be informed of and base policy upon state and federal law affecting privacy and freedom of information.

E. Security and Use Procedures for Archives

Every archivist should consider theft and damage prevention when planning all procedures and facilities for the use and storage of archives. See Section V for facility and equipment recommendations.

1. Archival material should be used in the reading area only.

2. All users should be required to complete a standard registration form recording the user's name, address and a listing of the records series requested and used. This form should be retained indefinitely in the archives for use in the event of theft and for statistical purposes. Procedures for access to this information should follow "Standards for Access to Research Materials in Archives and Manuscript Repositories," *American Archivist* 37 (January 1974): 153-54. Persons should also consult Sue E. Holbert, *Archives and Manuscripts: Reference and Access* (Chicago: Society of American Archivists, 1977), p. 13.

3. The reading area should be supervised at all times when records are in use.

4. Records should be returned to the stacks or to a restricted temporary storage area immediately after use.

5. If possible, the reading room attendant's desk should be located at the exit of the area.

6. Readers should not be permitted to use ink in the archives, including ball point pens.

7. If possible, readers should not be allowed to bring coats and briefcases to their work desks.

8. Eating, drinking, and smoking should not be permitted in the archives.

9. The archives stack area should be restricted to staff only.

10. Each archives should develop photocopying policies that insure the security of their material.

11. Patrons should be informed of the provisions of the copyright law.

F. Conservation and Restoration

Few archives are able to afford the personnel and equipment to undertake more than the most simple restoration of their holdings. Staff should be trained in proper procedures for handling such basic conservation procedures. The emphasis in college and university archives must be to minimize further deterioration; however, all archivists should be cognizant of trends in conservation techniques.

1. Priorities for minimizing deterioration:

a. Minimize fluctuations of temperature and humidity (See Section VA1b for temperature and humidity guidelines).
b. Minimize delay in applying procedures outlined in Section IIC3.
c. Provide polyester and encapsulation for more important and fragile documents as described in Section II C 3b.
d. Only trained personnel should undertake restoration.

2. All archives should develop a plan of action to be followed in the event of fire, flood, or other disaster.

G. Nonprint Material

College and university archives receive a variety of nonprint materials as part of conventional record groups. In order to document fully the history of the school they serve, such materials should be actively sought as widely as possible.

1. Still photographs

a. Photographs received as part of a record series may be left in the series or moved to a central file if a record is made of their original location.
b. Still photographs should be stored in acid-free envelopes or folders, in metal filing cabinets or acid-free boxes, pending further testing and development of new materials.

c. Appropriate agencies should be solicited for donation of photographs such as yearbooks, student newspapers, athletic, alumni, and public relations offices.

d. The archivist should attempt to identify deteriorating photographs and separate them from the main collection pending copying and/or treatment.

e. Unmounted transparencies should be treated in the same manner as still photographic negatives.

f. Mounted transparencies (slides) should be filed vertically in appropriate boxes.

2. Still photographic negatives

a. Nitrate base negatives should be identified, copied, and disposed of.

b. Safety base negatives should be stored in acid-free envelopes of appropriate size pending testing and development of new materials and filed in metal file drawers or acid-free boxes.

c. Negative envelopes made of polyester or other inert plastic are acceptable if the humidity in the storage area is tightly controlled.

d. Glass plate negatives should be placed in acid-free envelopes, emulsion side away from the seam and stored vertically without pressure from other stored plates.

3. Motion picture films

a. Nitrate film stock should be identified and copied and/or disposed of.

b. Safety base film may be stored in metal cans on appropriate shelving.

4. Audio and video tapes

a. College and university archives should seek audio and video tape recordings relating to their institution.

b. Archives holding significant collections of audio and video tape recordings should be provided with easily accessible playback facilities, preferably within the archives.

5. Machine readable records

a. These records should be appraised in cooperation with the university's computer center and should be retained in the most convenient and usable format available.
b. Magnetic tapes should be inspected by the computer center at least once every five years.

6. Oral history interviews

An institutional oral history program may provide a valuable supplement to any college or university archives. Participation in such a project should not be allowed to detract from efforts to collect a complete official record.

a. University archives should cooperate with any institutional oral history program undertaken by their school by accepting deposit of tapes and transcripts and by assisting in the preparation of interviews.
b. College and university archivists may undertake their own interviewing program, if resources permit, and the program does not interfere with the normal operation of the archives.
c. Archivists should avoid agreement to transcribe tapes unless special funds are made available for the purpose.

III. SERVICE

The university archives serves both an administrative function and a research/education function.

A. Administrative Service

The following are the basic service functions to university administrators and to faculty and student governance bodies:

1. Providing an informational service based on the holdings of the archives. From these holdings information may be provided to answer questions about the history of the university, the development of policies and procedures, the history of the programs, organizations, and individuals connected with the university.

2. Providing reference service on all records in the archives' custody in the following ways:

a. Answering a request for a specific piece of information in a record whenever possible.

b. Copying a specific piece of information in a record.

c. Returning a particular segment of a records series to the office of origin when the cost of duplication is prohibitive. The archivist should attempt to avoid this alternative whenever possible.

3. In universities lacking a formal records management program the normal operation of the archives will provide rudimentary service in this area.

4. University archives should prepare and distribute to all university offices a reference policy specifically outlining its reference services and the procedure for making a reference request.

B. Educational/Research Service

1. The archives should serve all interested persons as an information resource on the history, development, and physical growth of the university, and its policies, programs, and organization.

2. The amount of reference service provided to researchers will vary with the type and volume of requests, but should at a minimum provide detailed guidance on the possible sources of the information sought and an explanation of how to use the records involved.

3. The archives should serve as an educational laboratory where students may learn not only about a particular subject, but also about the resources available and the techniques for using them.

a. The archivist should provide, where interest justifies it, information sessions for students on researching archives and manuscripts.

b. The archivist may develop cooperative programs with individual departments or faculty members which will increase the use of archival resources while providing instructional guidance for the users.

C. The archivist should encourage the use of the archives by all interested persons.

In addition to providing the services discussed above, the archivist should publicize services and collections by such means as the following:

1. Developing and distributing an informational handout on the archives, its services, and holdings.
2. Reporting the holdings of the archives to appropriate national and regional guides.
3. Arranging for exhibits or displays at least once a year.
4. Publicizing services and holdings reporting any significant activity, event, or accession to the campus newsletter, student newspaper, and news service.
5. Devising attractive and clear directional signs to guide potential users to the archives.
6. Including the archives in all descriptions of campus resources such as a library handbook or campus catalog.

IV. PERSONNEL

A. Archivist: Director or Curator

Every college and university archives should have a full-time professional archivist as director. This person should have strong professional credentials including archival training and experience and familiarity with research methodology. He or she should be able to deal forcefully but cooperatively with administrators, alumni, faculty, students, and the public.

B. Support Personnel

1. Smaller archives: In addition to the director, smaller archives require at least one assistant. This person need not be a professional archivist, but should be capable and willing to act as secretary, typist, processor, and reference person. The assistant should be able to answer questions and supervise the archives in the absence of the archivist.

2. Larger archives: Once the archives is fully operational, even smaller colleges and universities will need additional staff. These might be:

a. Assistant or Associate Archivist(s). Professional archivist(s) who can accept responsibility and act in most areas for the archivist when he or she is absent. This person may specialize in certain areas and may be required to process collections.

b. Full-time secretary-typist. Types correspondence and finding aids; may maintain the archives' administrative files and payroll records, and may tend the reading room, among other duties.

c. Reading room attendant. If the volume of use requires it, a full-time paraprofessional may be employed for this purpose. This person must be able to respond to the public in a friendly manner and be able with training to answer routine reference questions received by telephone or personal visit.

d. Processors. Persons to prepare for administrative and research use the archival and ephemeral material of the archives. They may also answer basic reference questions that do not involve policy decisions and may assist in the planning and preparation of exhibits among other duties.

e. Student help. Student workers may be employed in a variety of tasks in the archives. At a minimum, they may transport accessions to the archives. If adequate supervision is provided, students should be assigned tasks commensurate with their abilities, including processing nonsensitive accessions.

f. Volunteers. If adequate supervision is provided, volunteers may be used as receptionists, typists, processors, and in planning and mounting exhibits.

C. Justification for Staff Increases

Staff needs should be reviewed in the light of the following:

1. Number of reference requests and/or daily registrations.
2. Volume and nature of accessions.
3. Number of requests from campus departments for records management assistance (records inventory, analysis, and scheduling).
4. Volume of unprocessed holdings.
5. Additional assignments.

V. FACILITIES AND EQUIPMENT

Although the space requirements and facilities will vary with the size of the institution and the development of the archives program, the following facilities and equipment are minimal for the proper functioning of the archives:

A. Facilities

1. General considerations for archives facilities:

a. The archives should be located in a fire-resistant or fireproof building and equipped with fire extinguishers.

b. Temperature and humidity conditions should be maintained as constant as possible. Since most archives store many different types of material together, each with different optimum storage conditions, it will be impossible to provide ideal conditions for all material.
Suggested ranges:
Temperature: 60 - 70 F. (16 - 21 C.)
Relative Humidity: 40%-50%
Fluctuations within the suggested ranges should be minimized.

c. All archives areas should be provided with locks; access to keys to these locks should be strictly limited.

d. The archives should be equipped with a heat and smoke detector system and preferably a water detector system.

e. The archives should be protected by a security alarm system.

f. If there are windows in the archives, they should be covered with ultraviolet screening and heavily curtained.

g. If fluorescent lighting is used in the archives it should be covered with ultraviolet filter screens, particularly in display areas and areas in which archival material is stored on open shelves.

h. The archives should be located in an area with convenient access to a loading dock.

i. The archives should be located in an area with convenient access to running water.

2. Consideration for a reading room for researchers where access and use may be supervised and restricted:

a. The reading room should be easily accessible to the stacks.

b. The reading room should accommodate several users.

c. The reading room should be well lighted and furnished with appropriate furniture. This furniture should not provide the opportunity for the concealment of archival material.

d. The reading room should also contain guides to the collection; a desk and chair for supervisory personnel; an area for checking book bags, briefcases, and coats; and an area for registering users.

3. Considerations for other area requirements:

a. Archives require a stack area where access can be limited to archives personnel. The size of the stack area will be determined by the present size of the holdings and the volume of annual accessions.

b. An area must be provided for the processing of unorganized collections. This area should be physically separated from the reading area and preferably from the stack area. A regular office may often serve this function. It should be provided with shelving, a large flat table, chair, and enough space to accommodate the staff and supplies used in processing.

B. Equipment

1. Shelving should be provided for present holdings plus five years projected accessions.

2. Preferably, the shelving should be metal with adjustable metal shelves of adequate width and load-bearing capacity.

3. Special storage equipment for oversize items such as large photographs, maps, and blueprints should be provided, as well as appropriate filing cabinets as needed.

4. Acid-free covered document cases.

5. Acid-free file folders, both legal and letter size.

6. Records storage or transfer cartons.

7. Catalog cards.

8. Typewriters.

9. Equipment for transporting containers.

10. Clerical supplies and equipment.

VI. SUPPORTING SERVICES

The following supporting services or equipment are required for proper functioning of archives:

A. A dry-process copying machine or easy access to copying facilities that accept archival quality paper. If possible, archival material should not be left at a central copying facility.

B. Easy access to microfilm and microfiche readers. If the volume of microfilm use is high, the archives should be provided with its own reader.

C. Easy access to audiovisual equipment.

D. Access to photo and sound duplicating facilities.

E. Access to microfilming and processing facilities or services.

F. Access to preservation facilities or services, especially fumigation and document repair.

G. Access to facilities is necessary for the research use of any nonprint material.

VII. RECORDS MANAGEMENT

The archives should play a key role in the development and implementation of a campus records management program. The following recommendations outline procedures for archives involved in records management.

A. A records management/archives policy and program should insure:

1. Improvement in the quality of records by evaluating and controlling creation of records, forms, and filing systems.

2. Improvement in the flow of paper and records currently in use in the organization.

3. Improvement in the control of and access to needed information.

4. Compliance with federal and state statutes if they govern the disposition of the university records.

5. Identification and protection of those records series which are vital to the continuance of the institution.

6. Preservation of materials essential to understanding the organization's purposes and operations or having other permanent value.

7. Elimination of noncurrent records not needed for the continuing operation of the organization.

B. Development, implementation, and operation of the campus records management policy and program is the responsibility of:

1. The archivist and the designated records manager (where one exists), with division and coordination of responsibilities as delineated below.

2. On campuses where no designated records manager exists, the archivist may serve as the records manager.

C. The records management/archives policy should provide for the following procedures:

1. Creation of forms, records, and microforms should be evaluated and approved by a designated officer.

a. On campuses where no designated forms control officer exists, the archivist or records manager may serve as forms control officer.

b. The archivist should be consulted on a regular basis regarding creation of records and control of forms.

2. Formal advising on:

a. The control and maintenance of university records.

b. The designation of material as public record as defined by state and federal statutes, if applicable.

3. Inventorying, scheduling, and orderly disposition of all university records as described in D-F below.

D. Inventorying includes the identification, description, and information gathering for each records series, which will serve as the basis for a records retention schedule.

1. The archivist or the records manager may inventory the records of any office or department of the university.

a. At the department's or office's request, or

b. At the initiation of the archivist or records manager and in cooperation with the department or administrative office.

2. All completed inventories should be reported to the archivist and the records manager, and a list of completed inventories should be maintained in both offices.

3. A list should be developed by the archivist and records manager to set priorities for future inventories to accommodate departments equitably and sufficiently protect important university records.

E. Establishing records retention schedules and submitting records disposition authorizations for review by appropriate university or state bodies. Records retention schedules are forms that specify for each record series the time period, the format, and the location in which the records are to be retained. Public institutions may fall within the guidelines of their state's public records board or commission. Therefore, the records retention and disposition schedules for those institutions should have the approval of that body.

1. Following the inventory of an office's or department's records, a meeting should be called to discuss the proper retention periods for the records inventories. The meeting should include the records manager, the archivist, the office or department head or a designated representative.

2. A retention schedule should be prepared by the office performing the inventory and copies sent for approval to the archivist, the records manager, the office or department head, and the legal counsel for the university. The archivist has the responsibility and authority to designate those records which shall be retained permanently in the archives.

3. The archivist or records manager may recommend to the campus administration the establishment of a representative body to review records retention schedules and recommend records policy and procedural statements. This body should include, but not be limited to: legal counsel, a business office representative, the archivist, and the records manager. If this body is established, approval of retention schedules would require approval by all members of this review body.

4. Copies of the approved retention schedule should be filed in the offices of the records manager, the archivist, and in the office of origin.

5. The records manager should prepare from the approved retention schedule a records disposition authorization and submit it to the appropriate agencies for approval. The records manager and the university archivist must review, approve, and sign disposal authorizations before submission.

6. Review or revision of existing and approved retention schedules may be initiated by the archivist, the records manager, the office of origin; or at the direction of the public records board. Revision of the schedule should follow the same procedures as the initial schedule.

F. Additional responsibilities of the records manager.

1. Microfilming records as required by approved retention schedules.

2. Destroying records as required by approved retention schedules.

3. Retaining inactive records in the records center as required by approved retention schedules, if such a facility for inactive records storage exists or is created.

4. Maintaining control of and providing reference service for records stored in the records center.

5. Acting in an advisory capacity on records-related problems.

6. Compiling and distribution an archives-records management manual to all offices within the institution.

G. Additional responsibilities of the archivist regarding records management.

1. Transferring materials to the archives according to approved retention schedules.

2. Preserving a security copy of microfilm produced by any vital records program.

3. Acting in an advisory capacity on records-related problems, especially by interpreting and communicating archival requirements to those involved in the generation and maintenance of records.

Appendix 3

Resolution on Theses and Dissertations*

SAA College and University Archives Committee

WHEREAS, masters' theses and doctoral dissertations constitute a series of records of the graduate college or division of an institution of higher education and serve as the final reports of research conducted at the institution, by students of the institution, under the direction of the faculty of the institution; and,

WHEREAS, theses and dissertations are the evidence of the scholarship of an institution, its faculty and students,

THEREFORE, BE IT RESOLVED by the College and University Archives Committee of the Society of American Archivists that theses and dissertations accepted as fulfillment of part of the requirements for graduate degrees of a college or university constitute records of enduring

---

*Society of American Archivists, College and University Archives Committee, 30 September 1975.

value, and that appropriate steps be taken by each institution to preserve and make available its theses and dissertations.

Appropriate steps include:

1. Keeping a record copy in a noncirculating collection in the institution's archives or other location that has proper security.

2. Being certain that the record copy is on paper that meets archival standards of permanence and durability.

3. Being certain that the record copy does not contain corrections made by liquid, powder, paste-on, or other impermanent methods. Corrections should be made by clean erasure and retyping. A clean photo- or electrostatic copy is more consistent with the permanent value of the records than an original containing impermanent portions.

4. Providing appropriate finding aids for locating theses and dissertations by author and subject at the minimum, and preferably by principal faculty advisor and title as well.

BE IT FURTHER RESOLVED that a copy of this resolution be placed in the records of the College and University Archives Committee of the Society of American Archivists and that it be included in a policy manual for college and university archivists if and when a manual is completed.

RESOLVED at the annual business meeting of the College and University Archives Committee of the Society of American Archivists at John M. Clayton Hall, University of Delaware, Newark, Delaware, this 30th day of September, 1975.

Appendix 4

Bibliography of Sources

This bibliography guides the reader to works central to archival theory and practice, and it aids in use of this book's notes by providing complete references to works cited more than once in the text.

Beginning with the Spring 1992 issue, *Midwestern Archivist* changed its name to *Archival Issues, the Journal of the Midwest Archives Conference.* Citations herein are to the publication as *Midwestern Archivist.*

Aitchison, Jean, and Alan Gilchrist. *Thesaurus Construction.* 2d ed. London: Association for Information Management, 1986.

Alpert, Daniel. "Performance and Paralysis: The Organizational Context of the American Research University." *Journal of Higher Education* 56 (1985): 241-81.

American Association of Collegiate Registrars and Admissions Offices. *Retention of Records: A Guide for Retention and Disposal of Student Records.* Washington, D. C., 1987.

"American Library Association—Society of American Archivists Joint Statement on Access to Original Research Materials in Libraries, Archives and Manuscript Repositories." *American Archivist* 42 (1979): 536-38; reprinted in Gary M. Peterson and Trudy Huskamp

Peterson. *Archives & Manuscripts: Law.* Chicago: Society of American Archivists, 1985, 98.

Banks, Paul N. *A Selective Bibliography on the Conservation of Research Library Materials.* Chicago: Newberry Library, 1981.

Bartlett, Nancy. "Respect des Fonds: The Origins of the Modern Archival Principle of Provenance." *Primary Sources and Original Works* 1 (1991): 107-15.

Barton, John P., and Johanna G. Wellheiser, eds. *An Ounce of Preservation: A Handbook on Disaster Contingency Planning for Archives, Libraries and Records Centers.* Toronto: Toronto Area Archivists, 1985.

"Basic Glossary for Archivists, Manuscripts Curators, and Records Managers." *American Archivist* 37 (1974): 415-33.

Bauer, G. Philip. "The Appraisal of Current and Recent Records." *National Archives Staff Information Circulars* 13 (1946).

Baum, Willa K. *Transcribing and Editing Oral History.* Nashville, Tenn.: American Association of State and Local History, 1977.

Bellardo, Lewis, and Lynn Lady Bellardo. *A Glossary for Archivists, Manuscript Curators, and Records Managers.* Chicago: Society of American Archivists, 1991.

Benedon, William. *Records Management.* Englewood Cliffs, N.J.: Prentice-Hall, 1969.

Berner, Richard C. *Archival Theory and Practice in the United States: A Historical Analysis.* Seattle: University of Washington Press, 1983.

_____. "Arrangement and Description of Manuscripts." *Drexel Library Quarterly* 11 (January 1975): 34-54.

_____. "Perspectives on the Record Group Concept." *Georgia Archive* 4 (Winter 1976): 48-55.

Boles, Frank. "Exploring the Black Box: The Appraisal of University Administrative Records." *American Archivist* 48 (1985): 121-40.

_____. "Understanding Contemporary Records Selection Processes." *American Archivist* 50 (1987): 356-68.

Boles, Frank, and Julia Marks Young. "The Archival Selection Process: Report of the Boles-Young Appraisal Project." Preliminary draft, 1988.

Booth, Larry, and Jane Booth. "Duplication of Cellulose Nitrate Negatives." *Picturescope* 30 (1982): 12-19.

Bopp, Richard E., and Linda Smith. *Reference and Information Services: An Introduction.* Littleton, Colo.: Libraries Unlimited, 1991.

Borck, Helga. "Preparing Material for Microfilming: A Bibliography." *Microform Review* 14 (1985): 241-43.

Bordin, Ruth B., and Robert M. Warner. *The Modern Manuscript Library.* New York: Scarecrow Press, 1966.

Boyd, Jane, and Don Etherington. *Preparation of Archival Copies of Theses and Dissertations.* Chicago: American Library Association, 1986.

Brichford, Maynard. "Academic Archives: Überlieferungs-bildung." *American Archivist* 43 (1980): 449-60.

_____. *Archives & Manuscripts: Appraisal and Accessioning.* Chicago: Society of American Archivists, 1977.

_____. "Provenance of Provenance in Germanic Areas." *Provenance* 7 (Fall 1989): 54-70.

_____. *Scientific and Technical Documentation.* Urbana, Ill.: University of Illinois, 1969.

_____. "University Archives: Relationships with Faculty." *American Archivist* 34 (1971): 173-81; reprinted in *College and University Archives: Selected Readings.* Chicago: Society of American Archivists, 1979, 31-37.

Brooks, Philip C. "Archival Procedures for Planned Records Retirement." *American Archivist* 11 (1948): 308-15.

_____. *Research in Archives: The Use of Unpublished Primary Sources.* Chicago: University of Chicago Press, 1969.

Burckel, Nicholas C. "Establishing a College Archives: Possibilities and Priorities." *College and Research Libraries* 36 (1975): 384-92; reprinted in *College and University Archives: Selected Readings.* Chicago: Society of American Archivists, 1979, 38-46.

Burckel, Nicholas C., and J. Frank Cook. "Profile of College and University Archives in the United States." *American Archivist* 45 (1982): 410-28.

Casterline, Gail Farr. *Archives & Manuscripts: Exhibits.* Chicago: Society of American Archivists, 1980.

Chen, Ching-chih, and Peter Hernon. *Information Seeking: Assessing and Anticipating User Needs.* New York: Neal-Schuman, 1982.

College and University Archives: Selected Readings. Chicago: Society of American Archivists, 1979.

Conway, Paul. "Facts and Frameworks: An Approach to Studying the Users of Archives." *American Archivist* 49 (1986): 393-407.

_____. "Research in Presidential Libraries." *Midwestern Archivist* 11 (1986): 35-56.

Cook, J. Frank. "American Archivists and the SAA, 1938-1979 : From Arcana Siwash to the C & U PAG." *American Archivist* 51 (1988): 428-39.

Cox, Richard. "Professionalism and Archivists in the United States." *American Archivist* 49 (1986): 229-47.

Cox, Richard J., and Helen W. Samuels. "The Archivist's First Responsibility: A Research Agenda to Improve the Identification and Retention of Records of Enduring Value." *American Archivist* 51 (1988): 28-42.

Cunha, George M. "Mass Deacidification for Libraries: 1989 Update." *Library Technology Reports* 25:1 (January-February 1989).

Davis, Cullom, Kathryn Back, and Kay MacLean. *Oral History: From Tape to Type.* Chicago: American Library Association, 1977.

Dearstyne, Bruce W. "What Is the Use of Archives: A Challenge for the Profession." *American Archivist* 50 (1987): 76-87.

Dollar, Charles M. "Appraising Machine-Readable Records." *American Archivist* 41 (1978): 423-30.

_____. *Electronic Records Management and Archives in International Organizations: A RAMP Study with Guidelines.* Paris: UNESCO, 1986.

Dowler, Lawrence. "The Role of Use in Defining Archival Practice and Principles." *American Archivist* 51 (1988): 78-80.

Duchein, Michel. *Archive Buildings and Equipment.* International Council on Archives ICA Handbook 1. Munich: Verlag Dokumentation, 1977.

Duckett, Kenneth W. *Modern Manuscripts: A Practical*

Manual for Their Management, Care and Use. Nashville,
Tenn.: American Association of State and Local History,
1975.

Duranti, Luciana. "Diplomatics: New Uses for an Old
Science." *Archivaria* 28 (Summer 1989): 7-29.

Ehrenberg, Ralph E. *Archives & Manuscripts: Maps and
Architectural Drawings*. Chicago: Society of American
Archivists, 1982.

Elston, Charles B. "University Student Records: Research
Use, Privacy Rights and the Buckley Law." *Midwestern
Archivist* 1:1 (1976): 16-32; reprinted in *College and
University Archives: Selected Readings*. Chicago: Society
of American Archivists, 1979, 68-79.

Endelman, Judith E. "Looking Backward to Plan for the
Future: Collection Analysis for Manuscript Repositories."
American Archivist 50 (1987): 340-55.

Ericson, Timothy. " 'Preoccupied with Our Own Gardens':
Outreach and Archivists." *Archivaria* 31 (Winter 1990-91):
114-22.

Evans, Max J. "Authority Control: An Alternative to the
Record Group Concept." *American Archivist* 49 (1986):
249-61.

Fleckner, John A. *Archives & Manuscripts: Surveys*. Chicago:
Society of American Archivists, 1977.

Freeman, Elsie T. "Buying Quarter Inch Holes: Public
Support Through Results." *Midwestern Archivist* 10 (1985):
89-97.

_____. "In the Eye of the Beholder: Archives Administration
from the User's Point of View." *American Archivist* 47
(1984): 111-23.

Gardner, Richard D. *Library Collections: Their Origin,
Selection and Development*. New York: McGraw-Hill, 1981.

Geller, Sidney B. *Care and Handling of Computer Storage
Media*. NBS SP 500-101. Washington, D.C.: National
Bureau of Standards, 1983.

Gondos, Victor. *Reader for Archives and Records Center
Buildings*. Chicago: Society of American Archivists, 19ʳ

Gorman, Michael, and Paul W. Winkler, eds. *Anglo-Americɪ
Cataloging Rules*. 2d ed. Chicago: American Library
Association, 1988.

Gracy, David B. *Archives & Manuscripts: Arrangement and Description.* Chicago: Society of American Archivists, 197⁷

Guidelines for College & University Archives. Chicago: Society of American Archivists, 1979.

Gwinn, Nancy W. *Preservation Microfilming: A Guide for Librarians and Archivists.* Chicago: American Library Association, 1987.

Hackman, Larry, and Joan Warnow-Blewett. "The Documentation Strategy Process: A Model and a Case Study." *American Archivist* 50 (1987): 12-47.

Ham, F. Gerald. "Archival Strategies for the Post-Custodial Era." *American Archivist* 44 (1981): 207-16.

Harris, George, and Robert Huffman. "Cataloging of Theses: A Survey." *Cataloging & Classification Quarterly* 5 (Summer 1985): 1-11.

Harrison, Helen P. *The Archival Appraisal of Sound Recordings and Related Materials: A RAMP Study with Guidelines.* Paris: UNESCO, 1987.

Haskell, Thomas J., ed. *The Authority of Experts: Studies in History and Theory.* Bloomington, Ind.: Indiana University Press, 1984.

Hedstrom, Margaret L. *Archives & Manuscripts: Machine-Readable Records.* Chicago: Society of American Archivists, 1984.

Henn, Harry G. *Copyright Law: A Practitioner's Guide.* New York: Practicing Law Institution, 1988.

Henry, Linda J. "Collecting Policies of Special-Subject Repositories." *American Archivist* 43 (1980): 57-63.

Hensen, Steven. *Archives, Personal Papers and Manuscripts: A Cataloging Manual.* 2d ed. Chicago: Society of American Archivists, 1989.

_____. "The Use of Standards in the Application of the AMC Format." *American Archivist* 49 (1986): 31-40.

Holden, Harley. "The Collecting of Faculty Papers." *Harvard Library Bulletin* 19 (1971): 187-93.

Holmes, Oliver W. "Archival Arrangement—Five Different Operations at Five Different Levels." *American Archivist* 27 (1964): 21-42.

Honhart, Frederick L. "The Solicitation, Appraisal, and

Acquisition of Faculty Papers." *College and Research Libraries* 44 (1983): 236-41.

Horn, Andrew H. "The Thesis Problem." *American Archivist* 15 (1952): 321-31.

Information Resources Management Service, General Services Administration. *Electronic Recordkeeping.* Washington, D. C.: Government Printing Office, 1989.

Inventories and Registers: A Handbook of Techniques and Examples. Chicago: Society of American Archivists, 1976.

Janzen, Mary E. "Pruning the Groves of Academe: Appraisal, Arrangement and Description of Faculty Papers." *Georgia Archive* 9:2 (Fall 1981): 31-40.

Jones, Craig. "Film/Videotape Factsheet." *Conservation Administration News* 22 (July 1985): 6, 21.

_____. *16mm Motion Picture Film Maintenance Manual.* Consortium of University Film Centers. Monograph Series 1. Dubuque, Iowa: Kendall/Hunt Publishing Co., 1983.

Joyce, William L. "Archivists and Research Use." *American Archivist* 47 (1984): 124-33.

Kathman, Michael D., and Jane M. Kathman. "Management Problems of Student Workers in Academic Libraries." *College and Research Libraries* 39 (1978): 118-22.

Kesner, Richard M., et al. "Collection Processing as a Team Effort." *American Archivist* 44 (1981): 356-58.

Kula, Sam. *The Archival Appraisal of Moving Images: A RAMP Study with Guidelines.* Paris: UNESCO, 1983.

Kyle, Hedi. *Library Materials Preservation Manual.* Bronxville, N.Y.: Nicholas T. Smith, 1983.

Lancaster, F. W. *Indexing and Abstracting in Theory and Practice.* Champaign, Ill.: University of Illinois Graduate School of Library and Information Science, 1991.

Lathrop, Alan K. "The Provenance and Preservation of Architectural Records." *American Archivist* 43 (1980): 325-38.

Long, Linda J. "Question Negotiation in the Archival Setting: The Use of Interpersonal Communication Techniques in the Reference Interview." *American Archivist* 52 (1989): 40-50.

Lopez, Manuel D. "Dissertations: A Need for New Approaches to Acquisition." *Journal of Academic Librarianship* 14 (1988): 297-301.

Lummis, Trevor. "Structure and Validity in Oral Evidence." *International Journal of Oral History* 2 (1981): 109-20.

MacLeish, A. Bruce. *The Care of Antiques and Historical Collections.* 2d ed. Nashville, Tenn.: American Association of State and Local History, 1985.

Maedke, Wilmer O., Mary F. Robek, and Gerald F. Brown. *Information and Records Management.* 2d ed. Encino, Calif.: Glencoe Publishing, 1981.

Maher, William J. "Contexts for Understanding Professional Certification: Opening Pandora's Box?" *American Archivist* 52 (1988): 408-27.

_____. "The Current State of Academic Archives: A Procrustean Bed for Archival Principles?" *American Archivist* 59 (1989): 342-49.

_____. "Improving Archives-Library Relations: User-Centered Solutions to a Sibling Rivalry." *Journal of Academic Librarianship* 15 (1990): 355-63.

_____. "The Use of User Studies." *Midwestern Archivist* 11 (1986): 15-16.

Marks, Donald D. "AACRAO's Guide for Retention and Disposal of Student Records: A Critical Review." *Midwestern Archivist* 8 (1983): 27-33.

McCarthy, Paul H. "Photofiching: A Catchy New Technique." *Conservation Administration News* 22 (July 1985): 1-2, 18-19.

McCrank, Lawrence J. "The Impact of Automation: Integrating Archival and Bibliographic Systems." In *Archives and Library Administration: Divergent Traditions and Common Concerns.* Ed. Lawrence J. McCrank. New York: Haworth Press, 1986, 74-75, 77-81, 84-86.

McCree, Mary Lynn. "Defining Collections." *Drexel Library Quarterly* 11 (January 1975): 27-33.

McWilliams, Jerry. "Care and Preservation of Sound Recordings." *Conservation Administration News* 23 (October 1985): 4-5, 24.

_____. *Preservation and Restoration of Sound Recordings.*
Nashville, Tenn.: American Association of State and Local
History, 1979.
Melnyk, Andrew. "Student Aids in Our Library." *Illinois
Libraries* 58 (1976): 141-44.
Metcalf, Keyes D. *Planning Academic and Research Library
Buildings.* 2d ed. Eds. Philip D. Leighton and David
C. Weber. Chicago: American Library Association, 1986.
Miller, Jerome K. *Applying the New Copyright Law.* Chicago:
American Library Association, 1979.
Minister of Supply and Services. *Handle With Care: Fragile,
A Guide to the Preservation of Archival Materials.* Ottawa:
Minister of Supply and Services, 1977.
Morrow, Carolyn Clark, and Carole Dyal. *Conservation
Treatment Procedures: Step by Step Procedures for
Maintenance and Repair of Library Materials.* 2d ed.
Littleton, Colo.: Libraries Unlimited, 1986.
Morrow, Carolyn Clark, and Steven B. Schoenly. *A
Conservation Bibliography for Librarians, Archivists, and
Administrators.* Troy, N.Y.: Whitston Publishing Company,
1979.
Mosher, Paul. "Collection Evaluation: Matching Library
Acquisitions to Library Needs." In *Collection Development
in Libraries.* Eds. Robert D. Stueart and George B. Miller.
Published as *Foundations in Library and Information
Science* 10 (Greenwich, Conn.: JAI, 1980): 527-46.
Moss, William. "Oral History: An Appreciation." *American
Archivist* 40 (1977): 429-39.
_____. *Oral History Program Manual.* New York: Praeger,
1974.
Moss, William W., and Peter C. Mazikana. *Archives, Oral
History and Oral Tradition: A RAMP Study with
Guidelines.* Paris: UNESCO, 1986.
Muller, S., J. A. Feith, and R. Fruin. *Manual for the
Arrangement and Description of Archives.* Trans. from the
2d ed. by Arthur H. Leavitt. New York: H. W. Wilson,
1940.
Murray, Toby. "Bibliography on Disasters, Disaster
Preparedness and Disaster Recovery." Oklahoma City:
Oklahoma Department of Libraries, updated annually.

National Archives and Records Administration. _Managing Cartographic, Aerial Photographic, Architectural, and Engineering Records._ Instructional Guide Series. Washington, D. C.: National Archives and Records Administration, 1989.

Noble, David F. "Higher Education as an Industrial Process: What University Archives Reveal about the History of Corporate, Scientific America." _Midwestern Archivist_ 2:2 (1977): 35-53.

Noble, Richard. "Archival Preservation of Motion Pictures." American Association for State and Local History, _Technical Leaflet_ 126, published in _History News_ 35 (April 1980): 23-30.

Parker, Thomas A. _Studies on Integrated Pest Management for Libraries and Archives._ Paris: UNESCO, 1988.

Patterson, Kelly, Carol White, and Martha Whittaker. "Thesis Handling in University Libraries." _Library Resources & Technical Services_ 21 (1977): 274-85.

Pederson, Ann E., ed. _Keeping Archives._ Sydney: Australian Society of Archivists, 1987.

Pederson, Ann E., and Gail Farr Casterline. _Archives & Manuscripts: Public Programs._ Chicago: Society of American Archivists, 1982.

Penn, Ira A., Anne Morddel, Gail Pennix, and Kelvin Smith. _Records Management Handbook._ Aldershot, England: Gower, 1989.

Perkins, David L., ed. _Guidelines for Collection Development._ Chicago: American Library Association, 1979.

Peterson, Gary M., and Trudy Huskamp Peterson. _Archives & Manuscripts: Law._ Chicago: Society of American Archivists, 1985, 28-29.

Posner, Ernst. _American State Archives._ Chicago: University of Chicago Press, 1964.

Potts, David B. "College Archives as Windows on American Society." _American Archivist_ 40 (1977): 43-49; reprinted in _College and University Archives: Selected Readings._ Chicago: Society of American Archivists, 1979, 89-96.

Quinn, Patrick M. "Academic Archivists and Their Current Practice." _Georgia Archive_ 10:2 (Fall 1982): 14-24.

Rapport, Leonard. "No Grandfather Clause: Reappraising Accessioned Records." *American Archivist* 44 (1981): 143-50.

Research Libraries Group. *RLG Preservation Manual.* Stanford, Calif.: Research Libraries Group, 1986.

Ritzenthaler, Mary Lynn, Gerald J. Munoff, and Margery S. Long. *Archives & Manuscripts: Administration of Photographic Collections.* Chicago: Society of American Archivists, 1984.

Rundell, Walter. "Photographs as Historical Evidence: Early Texas Oil." *American Archivist* 41 (1978): 373-91.

Saffady, William. "A University Archives and Records Management Program." *College and Research Libraries* 35 (1974): 204-10; reprinted in *College and University Archives: Selected Readings.* Chicago: Society of American Archivists, 1979, 97-103.

Sahli, Nancy A. "Interpretation and Application of the AMC Format." *American Archivist* 49 (1986): 9-20.

Samuels, Helen. *Varsity Letters: Documenting Modern Colleges and Universities.* Chicago: Society of American Archivists, forthcoming.

_____. "Who Controls the Past." *American Archivist* 49 (1986): 109-24.

Schellenberg, T. R. "The Appraisal of Modern Public Records." National Archives Bulletin 8. Washington, D. C.: National Archives and Records Service, 1956; reprinted in Daniels, Maygene F., and Timothy Walch, eds. *A Modern Archives Reader.* Washington, D. C.: National Archives and Records Service, 1984, 57-70.

_____. *The Management of Archives.* New York: Columbia University Press, 1965.

_____. *Modern Archives: Principles and Techniques.* Chicago: University of Chicago Press, 1956.

Schlereth, Thomas J., ed. *Material Culture Studies in America.* Nashville, Tenn.: American Association of State and Local History, 1982.

Sichel, Beatrice. "Utilizing Student Assistants in Small Libraries." *Journal of Library Administration* 3 (1982): 35-45.

Skemer, Don C., and Geoffrey P. Williams. "Managing the
    Records of Higher Education: The State of Records
    Management in American Colleges and Universities."
    American Archivist 53 (Fall 1990): 532-47.
Steinmetz, Lawrence L. *Managing the Marginal &
    Unsatisfactory Performer.* 2d ed. Reading, Mass.:
    Addison-Wesley, 1985.
Stielow, Frederick J. *Management of Oral History Sound
    Archives.* Westport, Conn.: Greenwood Press, 1986.
Systems Procedures and Exchange Center. *Library
    Publications Programs.* SPEC Kit 145. Washington, D. C.:
    Association of Research Libraries, 1988.
Tagg, John. *Burden of Representation.* Amherst, Mass.:
    University of Massachusetts Press, 1988.
Tatem, Jill, and Jeff Rollinson. *Thesaurus of University
    Terms.* Cleveland, Ohio: Case Western Reserve University,
    1986.
Taylor, Hugh. "Documentary Art and the Role of the
    Archivist." *American Archivist* 42 (1979): 417-28.
Treleven, Dale E. "Oral History, Audio Technology, and the
    TAPE System." *International Journal of Oral History* 2
    (1981): 26-45.
Turnbaugh, Roy C. "Archival Mission and User Studies."
    Midwestern Archivist 11 (1986): 27-29.
_____. "Living with a Guide." *American Archivist* 46 (1983):
    449-52.
U. S. Library of Congress. *Specifications for Microfilming
    Manuscripts.* Washington, D. C.: Library of Congress,
    1980.
Veysey, Laurence R. *The Emergence of the American
    University.* Chicago: University of Chicago Press, 1965.
Weinstein, Robert A., and Larry Booth. *Collection, Use and
    Care of Historical Photographs.* Nashville, Tenn.:
    American Association of State and Local History, 1977.
Welzenbach, Lanora F. *College and University Business
    Administration.* 4th ed. Washington, D. C.: National
    Association of College and University Business Offices,
    1982.
Wolff, Jane. "Faculty Papers and Special-Subject
    Repositories." *American Archivist* 44 (1981): 346-51.

Appendix 5

Model Archival Forms

The forms that are included in this appendix can be conveniently reproduced by the reader for use in archives management.

These forms are blank copies of Figures 3, 5, 6, 9, 10, and 12. Figures 3, 9, and 12 may be enlarged (on a photocopy machine) by 139 percent. Figures 5 and 6 may be reproduced at their current size. Figure 10 may be enlarged by 167 percent. These enlargements will bring the current book size of the form to the standard 8 1/2 x 11 size. The reader is hereby granted permission to make as many copies as desired for personal or institutional use, but not for resale.

The reader may also contact the author, in care of the Society of American Archivists (600 S. Federal, Suite 504, Chicago, IL 60605) to obtain copies of these forms in the standard 8 1/2 x 11 size.

UNIVERSITY ARCHIVES ACCESSION REGISTER

Date Received	Title of Record Series / Collection	Rec. Group Number	Physical Description	Volume	Location	Source and Notes

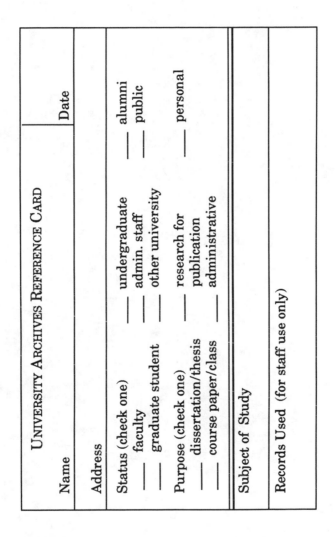

UNIVERSITY ARCHIVES REFERENCE CARD

Name	Date

Address

Status (check one)
___ faculty
___ graduate student
___ undergraduate
___ admin. staff
___ other university
___ alumni
___ public

Purpose (check one)
___ dissertation/thesis
___ course paper/class
___ research for
___ publication
___ administrative
___ personal

Subject of Study

Records Used (for staff use only)

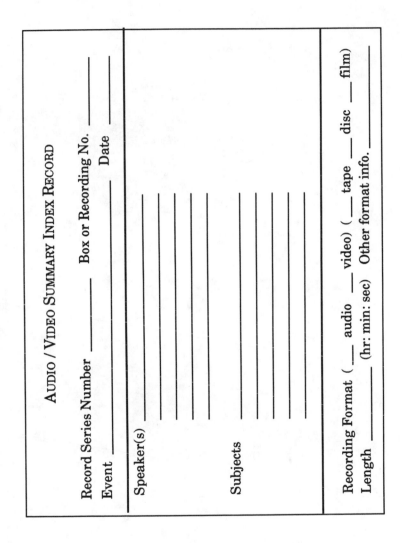

AUDIO / VIDEO SUMMARY INDEX RECORD

Record Series Number _____   Box or Recording No. ____

Event _____   Date ____

Speaker(s) _____
_____
_____
_____

Subjects _____
_____
_____
_____

Recording Format (___ audio ___ video) (___ tape ___ disc ___ film)

Length ____ (hr: min: sec)   Other format info. ____

SUMMARY RECORDS LIST

Department/ Office: _____   Person Completing Inventory: _____   Date: _____   Page ____ of ____

Bldg.	Room	Area	Storage Equipment	Volume	Years	Brief Title

Total Volume: _____   Total Separate Record Series: _____

<table>
<tr><td></td><td>Date   Sheet</td></tr>
<tr><td>UNIVERSITY ARCHIVES
RECORDS INVENTORY WORK SHEET</td><td>Completed by</td></tr>
<tr><td></td><td>Record Series Number</td></tr>
</table>

CONTROL INFORMATION Record Group (college or major administrative unit)	Contact Person and Phone	
Record Sub-Group (department, office or unit)	Location	
Record Series Title (name of file)	Dates of File	

PHYSICAL DESCRIPTION Number & size of files, drawers, or documents	Volume (in cubic feet)	Annual Growth

Physical Condition

CONTENT DESCRIPTION (Indicate: formats and types of material, dates of responsibility of creating office, functions, subjects, duplication, missing or purged material.)

Arrangement

Index, file guides, or relationship to other files

USE:
Number of times retrieved: _____ weekly _____ monthly _____ annually.
Oldest documents used on monthly basis: _____

Legal, accounting or regulatory use, or audits of file? Yes/ No ____ Explain:

RETENTION RECOMMENDATION

UNIVERSITY ARCHIVES **RECORDS DISPOSITION SCHEDULE**	Schedule No. _____ Page of
College or Administrative Unit	APPROVALS: (*sign and date*)
Department	Archivist
Office	
I find and recommend that the records described in this request have no further administrative value and request that authority for their disposal be granted pursuant to the University Records Policy as approved by the Board of Regents. _____ _____ (*head of college, department or office*) (*date*)	Campus

Record Series Number	Description of record series, inclusive dates, annual accumulation, arrangement, and disposition recommendation

Index